Finding Your Way in Science

How you can combine character, compassion, and productivity in your research career

Note for Librarians: a cataloguing record for this book that includes Dewey Classification and US Library of Congress numbers is available from the National Library of Canada. The complete cataloguing record can be obtained from the National Library's online database at: www.nlc-bnc.ca/amicus/index-e.html
ISBN 1-4120-3388-8

TRAFFORD

This book was published on-demand in cooperation with Trafford Publishing.
On-demand publishing is a unique process and service of making a book available for retail sale to the public taking advantage of on-demand manufacturing and Internet marketing. On-demand publishing includes promotions, retail sales, manufacturing, order fulfilment, accounting and collecting royalties on behalf of the author.

Suite 6E, 2333 Government St., Victoria, B.C. V8T 4P4, CANADA

Phone   250-383-6864   Toll-free 1-888-232-4444 (Canada & US)
Fax   250-383-6804   E-mail   sales@trafford.com
Web site www.trafford.com   TRAFFORD PUBLISHING IS A DIVISION OF TRAFFORD HOLDINGS LTD.
Trafford Catalogue #04-1215   www.trafford.com/robots/04-1215.html

10   9   8   7   6   5   4

Other books by Lemuel A. Moyé

Statistical Reasoning in Medicine: The Intuitive P–Value Primer

Difference Equations with Public Health Applications (with Asha S. Kapadia)

Multiple Analyses in Clinical Trials: Fundamentals for Investigators

Probability and Statistical Inference: Applications, Computations, and Solutions (with Asha S. Kapadia and Wen Chan)

Lemuel A. Moyé

Finding Your Way in Science

How you can combine character, compassion, and productivity in your research career

Lemuel A. Moyé
University of Texas
School of Public Health
1200 Herman Pressler – E815
Houston, Texas 77030
USA
Lemuel.A.Moye@uth.tmc.edu

To Dixie and the Bennett Street Boys

Preface

Since I want you to be prepared for this unusual book, it would be best if we could first spend a few minutes together discussing its motivation and themes.

As a young man enrolled in college in the early 1970's, I believed that the combination of 1) an affirmative selection of a career in science, and 2) consistent hard work would be the only requirements for my professional success. These choices were to work like switching an aircraft's controls from manual to autopilot, automatically steering my career around and away from dangerous obstacles. I was wrong. Blind overwork was not part of my the flight plan, but I crashed into it anyway. Neither dissatisfaction, despondency, nor divorce appeared on my career radarscope; nevertheless I rammed into each of these mountains as well. While I have overcome much of the damage from these accidents, I am often reminded of the visionless efforts that haunted my early days as a scientist. I fell into the trap of believing that energy, knowledge and the best of intentions was an adequate substitute for wisdom.

While this is the fifth book that I have written that focuses of science, its emphasis is quite different than my previous works. Those earlier texts were directed to technical discussions involving epidemiologists, physicians, and statisticians who were conducting complicated clinical research. Here, I have taken a different tack, navigating not toward physicians or statisticians but, instead, bearing toward the researcher in general, and the junior researcher in particular.

If you are a graduate student who is near the completion of your training, or are a scientist just starting out in a busy department with both feet firmly set on the bottom rung of your career ladder, then it is your attention that I seek. What initially started as a bright career can be drenched by the interminable rain of uninspiring and exhausting work. At this early point in your career, your daily work may be unsatisfying, your measurable impact small, your activities unfulfilling, and your pay miserly. Frequently overworked, facing both aggressive analysis plans and demanding teaching schedules, it is all too easy for you to become a chronically fatigued, grumbling worker whose daily goal is simply to make some small progress through an ever growing task list. Such young scientists, seeing nothing but technical proficiency before them, begin to withdraw the very best part of themselves from their new career. The result is both professionally and spiritually destructive.

Your experiences right now will shape your future, and it is my goal to help you contour these early experiences in a way that is, first, good for you and then, ultimately, good for us all. Just as today's critical scientific issues are decided by researchers who were once junior scientists, there will be a time when you will play a pivotal role in shaping the impact of science on society. Like tomorrow's sunrise, that time is coming. When your time arrives, you want to meet it squarely, with strength, wisdom, and compassion, and not emptied of your best, like an egg with its yolk sucked out. You want character construction, not character destruction.

A guiding philosophy and approach to the work and development of the scientist is essential to character growth. The occasional and inevitable missteps that have punctuated my early career had their roots not in a mistaken scientific decision, but in a character defect or flaw that I neglected. Pushing this idea a little further, if I had recognized at the time that my focus should have been as much on character development as it was on productivity, then I would have more quickly identified those early mistakes as opportunities for maturation.

I have examined many textbooks that researchers read and write, and have not found a careful discussion of the role of character and personality development for the scientist. Nevertheless, it seems that personality growth is essential to the healthy development of a research career, so I decided to write about it here.

One final note. An important segment of the junior scientist population is comprised of women. Therefore, in the examples offered in this book, I have tried to alternate between examples using men and examples using women. While this is the most illustrative and the least exclusionary approach, it does require some mental alacrity on the reader's part as gender changes from example to example.

Lemuel A. Moyé
University of Texas
School of Public Health
August, 2004

Acknowledgments

I have had the opportunity, privilege, and pleasure to work with many junior investigators. Their kinetic questions have energized me, and their intellectual challenges have provided critical illumination as I have walked my own career path. Both their and my trajectories has been altered in the course of our interactions.

Many have contributed to the content of the book by either inspiring it, or by taking time from their schedules to comment upon and criticize its early drafts. Dr. Craig Hanis and Dr. Susan Day provided important advice about the utility of subcontracts for the junior scientist. Heather Lyons, Dr. Sarah Baraniuk, Dr. Wendy Nembhart, and Dr. Sharon Johnatty were especially helpful in their suggestions. More importantly, they were artful in their tact, convincing me to include important material that I initially did not consider discussing. If the text is instructive and serves you well, then these hard-working young scientists have earned and should get a full measure of the credit. Any problems, misstatements, or inaccuracies in the text's content are mine and mine alone.

Also, I am long overdue in acknowledging Jerry Abramson, Ph.D. and Viola Mae Young, Ph.D. who were the first two practicing scientists I had ever met and come to know. Even though they have long since retired from the Baltimore Cancer Research Institute where I, as an undergraduate, first met them in 1973, the tone of scientific rigor and compassion that they created in their laboratories still vibrates within me.

Finally, my dearest thanks go to Dixie, my wife, on whose personality, character, love, and common sense I have come to rely, and to Flora and Bella Ardon, whose continued emotional and spiritual growth reveals anew to me each day that, through God, all things are possible.

Lemuel A. Moyé, M.D., Ph.D.
University of Texas
School of Public Health
Houston, Texas, USA
August, 2004

Table of Contents

Introduction

Research in science has evolved, growing in breath and complexity. In genetics, agriculture, epidemiology, avionics, mathematics, biology, astronomy, economics, and medicine, the story in the same; research today is more complicated than it have ever been before. In the older paradigm that was in operation for hundreds of years, research efforts were crippled by the absence of technology, but propelled by competent, disciplined thought. Time was readily available for research design and personal development.

Today, technological demands eagerly consume our time as we take advantage of an ever expanding world of opportunity. If you permit it, your day is easily consumed with productive activities, e.g. electronic literature searches using a high speed internet connection at the airport, followed by an airborne grant-writing session as you travel to yet one more meeting. Researchers used to have to wait in line to use a computer. Now, computers stand ready to word process, calculate, and even simulate experiments at our behest. The computational and dissemination systems of science can now accept more work product than we can produce. The faster we work, the faster the production of analyses, the quicker the generation of papers and products, the more rapid the pace of progress. In the old paradigm, travel and technological capacity were the rate limiting step. Now — we are.

This new dynamic places a greater premium on scientific productivity, yet isn't there is more to a career than productivity? The principles, judgment, conduct, ethic, and temperament of researchers must develop simultaneously with their work product if these scientists are to develop into mature professionals. Although junior scientists have fine educational backgrounds, they frequently do not yet have the poise, vision, or coping skills that they need to identify and sustain the optimum productivity level in their careers. A philosophical approach that would help them achieve this balance would serve as an important foundation. However, junior scientists typically give little consideration to the development of a set of guiding principles. Often neglected, these researchers are left to stumble to this equipoise on their own. Unfortunately, many talented young scientists never find their balance, and can be confused, disoriented, and ultimately discouraged by their undirected search.

Finding Your Way In Science lays out for the scientist the principles that can produce and sustain the character growth that guides the development of the scientific professional.

The central thesis of *Finding Your Way in Science* is that the relentless pursuit of productivity is not a worthy career goal for the junior scientist. While productivity is and will be a fundamental attribute of the professional, there are other core themes that must be allowed to develop, appear, and exert their influences as well. The presence of self-control and patience, of moral excellence and compassion, of discipline and flexibility are as critical to the development of the junior scientist as is the acquisition of technical skills. The presence of these traits engenders collegiality, persuasive strength, responsibility, administrative diligence, influence, and vision, i.e. the qualities of charitable leadership.

Chapter One focuses on the need for the scientist to take stock of herself, carefully measuring her strengths and weaknesses. This chapter articulates the theme that is the foundation of the book; productivity, so highly emphasized in academia, in private industry and in government, is not the only star by which the scientist should steer. Chapter One delineates the dimensions of the scientist's character that must also be expanded in addition to the natural extension of knowledge that takes place at this time in her career. A broad overview of the role of the scientist's self-respect, ethics, sense of charity, and collegiality is provided. Concentrating on developing the strengths, skills, and outlook of a mature, professional scientist will not only amplify your productive efforts, but will also buffer and protect you as you face the unseen challenges that lie ahead. The specific scientific advances that your work produces will, in all likelihood, be overshadowed and surpassed by the future advances of others. However, the principles for which you stand as both a scientist and as an individual can resonate indefinitely.

Chapter Two discusses the philosophy of data interpretation in research that is based on a sample from a much larger population. The role of the "surprise result" and the importance of result confirmation are provided in clear, non-mathematical language for the scientist. It is important for the scientist to recognize that they are not explorers or "searchers" but "*re*searchers", and that their primary contribution is to provide confirmed scientific results that can be extended to larger populations.

The important of diligent administration is discussed in Chapter Three. This is a topic that many scientists shun because of its non-scientific nature and absence of direct scientific productivity. However, without the development of skill in this area, the scientist runs the risk of inefficiency in his efforts as he struggles to identify and obtain the critical resources that he needs for his projects. The importance of mastering the logistics that researchers require to carry out their scientific developments is emphasized. Three focal points are identified that will help the scientist in his first role as principal investigator.

Chapter Four discusses the role of the scientist in collaborative projects. Being the junior member of a research team is a fine opportunity to gain the experience and intuition under the tutelage of senior colleagues. Practical advice is provided for communicating with scientists in others fields whose technical language you do not understand, and who may not understand the language of your specialty. Concrete guidance is provided on the role of proper work product documentation; use of email and the development of mature scientific judgment is discussed. Special emphasis is provided on the approaches that one can use when communicating with and educating investigators more senior than you. Junior investigators are advised to master the new scientific knowledge base, and then to be quick to take advantage of the mastery. However, these strategies work best it they are set of a solid bedrock of self-value that is independent of the approval of others.

Important instruction in Chapter Five is provided to the scientist on making presentations before audiences. A body of knowledge is offered to help place the scientist at ease in presenting results to both small and large audiences. Presentation anxiety ("stage fright") is a real concern for the scientist, and its causes, followed by a prescription for its elimination, is offered. The investigator is reminded that the biggest cause of collapse in a presentation is not the intensity of the interchange with the audience but the presenter's own fear of failure. Guidance for preparation and delivery of the presentation is given. Specific suggestions for responding during a post-presentation question and answer session are provided.

Chapter Six is devoted to ethical concerns. Examples of ethical failings of scientists in the past are provided and illuminated so that the investigator can determine if the seeds of this unethical behavior reside in herself. Specific corrective steps are recommended to the junior investigator whose superior is abusive or flagrantly unethical. Guidance on recognizing the unethical investigator, how to have discussions with that investigator, and how to foster an environment of high ethical scientific conduct is presented.

The discussion in Chapter Seven is specifically for the junior scientist who works in academia. This traditional environment is rapidly changing, and the time-tested concepts of academic freedom must now go hand in hand with the newer idea of academic accountability. The definition of productivity within the modern academic setting is provided, and the three metrics of teaching, research, and community service are motivated. Since so much of the academician's progress is measured by publications, advice is provided for developing a smooth, positive trajectory for being productive in this arena without being consumed with productivity. The concepts of promotion and tenure are discussed. The importance of determining a long term plan, and the need for developing a good and sustaining personal work-lifestyle is motivated. As in other fields, productivity alone is insufficient for career development within the university environment. Character development is essential in this setting as well.

Leadership spirit and capability is locked away in the heart of every devoted scientist, and Chapter Eight discusses ways in which the scientist can discover and develop her leadership ability. The importance of 1) taking authority, but not providing too much direction to skilled subordinates, and 2) leading not as an exercise of authority but from a force of honesty and righteousness are just two of the several strategies for successful team leadership that are provided in this chapter. Junior investigators are exposed to the concept that many scientists who disappoint their own expectations do so because they will not accept, at the controversial moment, responsibility for an immediate decision that they are called upon to make. While investigators can fear rashness, they must also fear irresolution. Concluding comments are provided in Chapter Nine.

Each of the topics in this book is discussed with the goal of not just imparting tactical advice to the investigator, but to support the general theme that the investigator must develop his professional character in parallel with his productivity record. Like the apples of gold in settings of silver, good character and productivity must go together to develop strong scientists.

The audience for this book is broad in scope. It is written at a level for all advanced graduate students, post doctoral researchers, and scientists. It is applicable to all scientific fields, and to researchers in industry, government, and academic institutions.

Chapter 1
Nurturing the Investigator

.... in reality the easy part is writing the grant proposal. The truly hard part is conducting the study! Most people are not prepared for the difficulties of hiring/firing and managing staff, managing budgets, balancing grant management, teaching, administrative and other responsibilities...There is a whole other side that scientists are not prepared for...

A frustrated junior scientist, 2003

1.1 A Wounded Madness

The handshake, phone call, letter or email finalizing your first post-graduate job is a seminal moment for you as a scientist. While many of the professional challenges and obstacles that will cross your career path are not yet in view, you may nevertheless be buoyed by a natural sense of optimism. After all, didn't your combination of intellect, computational skill, and promise guide and sustain you through graduate school? Wasn't one of the points of graduate school to deliver you here, to this moment, for this new job? Certainly, those natural abilities that guided your path thus far will not fail you now. Past success should promote future victories, right?

For some among us, the arrival of the new job's confirmation is greeted with dread. Perhaps while you are accepting the congratulations of the CEO, the project manager, the principle investigator, or the department chair, you cannot free yourself of the angst that this new experience will be a bad one. You fear that a combination of circumstances beyond your control lies in wait and will befall you. You know that you will do your best, but just like the cowboy rider who grips the rope on the bull's neck as tightly as possible, you fear that, once the gate opens and the rides starts, the early calm will be followed by a few quick bucks and a hard fall.

At the beginning of their careers, scientists like yourself are rarely prepared for what awaits them. You are entering a profession that simultaneously requires careful planning and frenetic activity, that demands both deliberative thought and incisive action, and that rewards the quick and audacious choice of the right solution, rapidly leaving those behind who cannot stay current. While the product of these labors are often professionally, emotionally, and spiritually satisfying, this good labor is often produced in a cauldron of tumult and upheaval, a wounded madness that can disorient, confuse, and dishearten you.

1.1.1 The Requirement of New Skills

"Scientists are people of very dissimilar temperament doing very different things in very different ways. Among scientists are collectors, classifiers, and compulsive tidiers-up, many are detectives and many are explorers. There are poet-scientists and philosopher-scientists, and even a few mystics." [1].

Whether you are a statistician working in a clinical trial, an epidemiologist in a government surveillance group, a biologist in a reputable laboratory, a behaviorist in a research project, or a new assistant professor in a university, the dizzying pace of activity can be overwhelming.

As a new scientist, you rapidly learn that you are in great demand. While you are commonly expected to develop your own new project *de novo*, you are perhaps more likely to be asked to provide important technical, computational, or intellectual support to other projects. The principal investigators on these projects require computational competence, clarity of thought, and at least passable communication skills from you. Quickly, and through no great effort of your own, you can easily find yourself on two or three projects within the first few short weeks of your new job. Since each of these projects has a set of production goals (e.g., grant applications, interim reports, abstracts, and manuscripts), you will swiftly find yourself immersed in activity.

If you are part of a teaching center (e.g. a medical school, school of public health, graduate school, or other college or university program) you will also have instructional obligations. The fact that there is a shortage of teaching scientists quickly translates into heavy teaching loads for all such faculty, from which junior faculty find no protection. If you are lucky, there will be a short probationary period during which you will be permitted to strengthen your didactic skills under the aegis of a senior instructor. However, whether you are lucky or not, you will soon be responsible for teaching at least one course on your own. Specifically, you will be creating lectures, grading assignments, and evaluating examinations. In addition, you will have to develop the capability of providing constructive time for your students who need your help and support (a talent that you may have silently excoriated your own professors for not having). Additionally, you must navigate the sometimes treacherous waters of local politics.

Acquiring these new skills requires that you master new technology. Computing continues to become more pervasive and is now easily accessible to workers at all levels. As main frame machines shrank to minicomputers, and minicomputers shrank to desktop workstations, and workstations shrank to notebooks, and notebooks to personal digital assistants (PDA's), we now find ourselves working in an atmosphere of ubiquitous calculation — we can compute anywhere. In fact, if you a quantitative scientist, and your career is affirmatively based in computing and electronics, you may find that you are expected to have the greatest adeptness with these new tools since they are, after all "part of your specialty".[*]

These computing tools allow you to work on a manuscript in an airport, then spend a significant proportion of the subsequent flying time working on an analysis for a research project. You can develop and re-develop a slide presentation up to the time you stand up, connect your notebook computer or palmtop into the projector and actually give the lecture.

Hand in hand with omnipresent computation comes connectivity. We can reach out and be reached electronically. Instant messaging makes us instantly accessible. The use of email that can incorporate attachments makes it possible for you to write a grant and interact with your colleagues while you are in a hotel room far from your office. Students can reach you via email and electronic blackboards; co-investigators can locate you through your cell phone. The ability to work anywhere threatens to reduce our existence to working everywhere.

All of this activity underlies and supports a pervasive theme of modern science; you, as a scientist, are blessed with 1) productive opportunities and 2) new and modern tools to support your productivity. There are always new projects to take part in, and new ideas to generate. Your marching orders are to wield these tools in order to produce, to present, to proselytize, to publish, and to promulgate.

1.2 Survival vs. Prosperity

You can, in all likelihood, easily accomplish any one of the skills of teaching, scholarship, research productivity, administrative competence, or computational mastery. The difficult source of frustration is that you must develop skills to deal with them simultaneously. You need to gain useful abilities with each in real time, and at the same time.

---

[*]This discussion sets aside the additional, consistently required efforts on your part to keep up with software upgrades, hardware maintenance, and securing your work from viruses, worms, Trojan horses, spyware, and "pop-ups" that plague computer use and the internet in the early 21st century.

1.2.1 Why Did You Do This?

It is useful to begin with two acknowledgments. The first is that you are uncommonly intelligent. Nothing about the current frenzy of activities that characterizes your early research career has or will ever change that. Secondly, you need more than uncommon intelligence to master these simultaneous challenges. Basically, you need to upgrade your coping skills.

Recall your motivations for entering the difficult and challenging field that you have chosen. Since, by and large, scientists do not wind up in the upper financial crust of our society, financial motivation was, in all likelihood, not your prime motivator. The fact is, many of your non-scientific peers, who are not as smart as you, will nevertheless have careers that are more lucrative than yours.

Why are you in science, if you did not enter if for the money? One reason is commonly that you want to make a difference; to impact the lives of populations for the better. It is important to recognize that your unique combination of scientific precision, talent of perception, facility with numbers, and sense of charity holds the great potential of making a profound difference in other peoples lives. Unlike an investment banker, you cannot, with a few well considered keystrokes, earn $17,000 in a single morning. However, your work can beneficially impact a populations of thousands, tens of thousands, or millions of people; the pecuniary manager can not come close to exerting this influence.

For example, a single, well designed, and well executed research effort can change the paradigm of health care for a critical need.* Consider the work of James Lind[2] who, over six days during 1747 on the HMS Salisbury, completed work that saved the lives of thousands of sailors who undoubtedly would have fallen victim to the ravishes of scurvy. The link between fine research and beneficial population effects has been the central theme in most research for over 2000 years.

Scientists are well poised to make this caliber of contribution. You are involved in the design, execution, and analysis of research

---

*The CARE, HOPE and ALLHAT clinical trials are fine examples of such clinical studies that have produced wide ranging beneficial effects on the treatment of ischemic heart disease.

efforts whose effects can be seen in people of all economic strata, creeds and colors. If you are a junior educator, than you will provide the training that others need to carry out the analysis and interpretation of these research efforts. Through an intricate combination of altruism, perception, intelligence and strength, you have chosen to affect people and change lives. You have decided to sacrifice a career of excess financial riches for another that affects entire populations. For this, these populations are waiting for and relying on your judgment, compassion, productivity, and vision.

1.2.2 Inadequacy of the Survival Mentality

However lofty this mission statement is, your feet are still stuck in the muck of establishing new coping skills. Let your first steps be to lift yourself out of the survival mentality.

The definition of survival is simply the state of being alive. Since as a junior scientist you have too much to do, it is easy to set your sights on "just surviving" i.e., completing as many of the necessary and required tasks that lay before you. It may seem that all of your skills are devoted to the simple idea of "getting through" and completing your task list. Just surviving can seem like quite an accomplishment given the chaotic days that a junior scientist experiences.

That is precisely the problem with the survival mentality. Surviving implies that all of your talents and energies are expended on simply "getting through". If all of your resources are committed to just "making it until the end of the day", then you have no other resources, or energy to support others. The survival instinct sometimes turns into a self-centered justification for committing all of your resources to your own existence and forward progress. This is a poor start on the path of service for the good of others.

Survivalism is a minimalist goal that you as a scientist must resolutely resist. Replace it with the notion of prosperity. Prosperity contains survival but is simultaneously much greater. It is about development, growth, and strength. Prosperity is being comfortable (at peace) with where you are, rather than restlessly and ceaselessly agitating for what you don't have. The prosperous person has resources not just for themselves, but can provide support, time, and encouragement for others.

The suggestion that scientists can be intellectually prosperous does not equate prosperity with bovine satisfaction. Prosperity for you as a scientist means that, having worked patiently and diligently in assembling a good career trajectory for the future, you are comfortable with your current location on that trajectory now, knowing that your condition will improve as time and your consistent efforts move you forward on that path to your ultimate goal. Prosperity is not an automatic consequence or benefit that accrues to all talented individuals.

Replacing the agitating passion generated by superheated days with the peace of prosperity pays immediate dividends to you. First, you are free to deviate from your daily task list without guilt, because you understand that you will find the time and resources to handle whatever unexpected issues arise. A prosperous scientist or faculty member can think above the day's task list. It is a fact of life that sometimes the best occurrence of the day comes as a surprise. Disappointment does not arrive on a schedule either.

Expect and anticipate that your day will be both more rewarding, and more challenging than what your list of daily scheduled activities suggests. Also, understand that you will have the strength and insight that you need to meet those challenges, even if you cannot find those characteristics in yourself at the moment. Rest, assured that the strengths that you will require will be within easy reach when you need them.

One problem that junior scientists have in developing this perspective is that they are too busy immersing themselves in the logistical, scientific, and didactic activities of the day to devote any time to these deeper considerations. Because they have come to expect that every day will be shredded by the daily task-tornado, junior scientists quickly lose hold of the idea that they will ever find time to develop a governing mental attitude. The trap is in falsely believing that your entire career will be characterized by the disorganized and confused state that typifies your early days.

Consider a family that, after a long time of careful consideration and planning, decides to move to and live in a new city. After the move, everything is different. They find an apartment, but are disoriented. Not knowing their way around, the are commonly lost. They can't locate good stores. Buying groceries and pharmaceuticals in these new neighborhoods is a little disorienting. Finding a decent car repair shop is positively unnerving. Their attempts to make new arrangements for healthcare become an absolute nightmare. For this family, the move initially appears to be a giant step backwards.

What would you think of that family if they chose to give up on the new city, that appeared so full of promise before they first arrived? Wouldn't we criticize them, saying that they did not give their new home a chance? Just as this family would be wrong to stigmatize their future at this new home by their unpleasant and disorienting experience for their first six months, so you have to be patient with yourself and others as you work out the circumstances, procedures and lifestyle of a new career environment.

What helps this family to stick it out in the new city is their sense that over time, the lifestyle challenges that were so daunting initially will settle down. In fact, the family will take steps to insist that activities settle down. This is what you must do as well. Begin to thoughtfully consider and develop a long term goal and keep fixed on it. That will direct you to engage in some activities that provide no short-term return but instead will pay a good and satisfying long-term dividend.

1.3 Taking Stock of Yourself

Before you can proceed with gaining some new career coping skills, it pays to be still for a time and enter into a balanced self-appraisal of your own strengths and weaknesses. What do you genuinely enjoy about your work? Which tasks do you recognize as necessary but nevertheless shun? Take the time to take stock of yourself and your motivations. Understanding your motivations is critical because they are the fuel that drive your productivity efforts. Ignoring your motivations while you strive for productivity is like being so enamored with a new car that you furiously drive it, giving no thought to gas or required maintenance. Eventually, your vehicle will stop, perhaps leaving you stranded.

Self appraisal and self respect are critical to your character development. Self respect is your recognition with approval that you have innate value. Self respect is not the respect of your accomplishments; it is the respect of the person who produced those accomplishments, regardless of their weaknesses. There is no clearer gardless of their weaknesses. There is no clearer demonstration of this self-respect than the action of deliberately taking your concentration off of your daily productivity/task list and refocusing that attention onto your own self-development. In this evaluation, you will discover some of your weaknesses. The identification of your weaknesses is a first, affirmative step toward making these weaknesses your strengths.

There are many natural athletes with innate talents who fail. The skilled, mature and successful athletes are the ones who learned that the sure path to failure is to wholly rely on those talents. They have instead adopted the philosophy that success requires both their talents and their ability to convert their weaknesses into strengths. Thus, the basketball player who is a superb right handed dribbler learns to become even more adept at handling the ball with his left hand. The baseball star who is a skilled hitter must also develop superior base running skills. Developing these new skills is very difficult, and requires the athlete to work as hard as the unskilled player. This can be humiliating, putting the natural athlete in an uncomfortable position with which he is unaccustomed. However, converting weaknesses to strengths expands the dimension of their performance. A baseball pitcher who can only throw an overwhelming fastball can be a formidable adversary. However, if he can throw only the fastball, then the opposition gets use to his talent, adapts to it, and eventually defeats him. However, by mastering the curve ball, the pitcher converts himself from being a good pitcher into a masterful one.

In order to succeed, you have to confront the weaknesses that you fear and convert them to strengths. Get used to doing what you don't feel like doing in order to be the scientist that you want to become.

1.3.1 What is West Virginia?

As you take stock of yourself and review your development, you will inevitably turn to your most recent experience. That may be at a previous job, or in graduate school. For you, as for everyone, a candid self appraisal will reveal both triumphs and failures. Examine both, but avoid the easy path of assuming that past victories alone determine your career future. Past failure can be a wonderful trainer, although it certainly does not feel wonderful at the time. Defeats commonly lay the foundation for future victories. Alternatively, previous victories can set the stage for future failure.

Consider the curious story of West Virginia. While the entire state of Virginia moved with the other twelve colonies to become an original member of the new United States of America, the birth of West Virginia was violent and disruptive. At the inception of the Civil War in 1861, many states plunged into internal turmoil as they considered seceding from the Union. The secession of Virginia, while actively supported by many of its citizens, was resisted by a collection of the state's western counties. Since the North saw political and tactical advantage in gaining control of western Virginia, and the South saw equally clear advantage in retaining all of Virginia for its cause, both sides sent armed forces to the western sectors of this state in order to seize these counties. By doing so they hoped to gain control of the local political apparatus and, subsequently, claim that part of the state for their cause.

These armies were commanded by the finest promising soldiers of each side.[3] The Union forces were skillfully controlled by a rising young officer. This officer demonstrated a good strategic sense of the importance of the overall struggle. He developed a unity of command that permitted him to coordinate the military operations in all areas. His reluctance to convert a small victory into a larger battle won him praise, and he was received by laudatory audiences in Washington DC at the conclusion of his victorious campaign. The Union victory in West Virginia that led to the emergence of West Virginia as a free state was a notable Federal triumph in 1861.

On the other hand, the defeat of the confederates left their commander's reputation at a low ebb. His offensive plans were too complex, and his thinking had been overly focused on small details and not on a grand strategy. In addition, he was not able to broker peace between argumentative officers. He had failed to assert himself as a leader of generals.

The fates of the commanding generals of either side were the reverse of what one might anticipate. George B. McClellan, the triumphant Union general, was widely acclaimed as the young Napoleon that the North needed. Flush with his victory in West Virginia, he was rapidly promoted, and immediately returned to his strategy of training capable armies but holding them back from the battle. He understandably hoped that this strategy that had produced a victory in West Virginia would yield additional fruit. Instead his tendency that served him well in West Virginia contributed to future spectacular defeats and political intrigues. Less than two years after his victories in West Virginia, he was removed from command by a thoroughly exasperated President Abraham Lincoln.

The defeated Confederate general was to have a different fate. He carefully examined his loss in West Virginia, choosing to be instructed by his poor reactions to the difficulties that beset him there. Remembering how an army that is trained for combat can be demoralized when the order to advance never comes, he developed an aggressive, fighting instinct. Examining the failure of his offensives led him to become an excellent defensive strategist. Finally his affection for his soldiers and his willingness to intercede between querulous officers produced in him the combination of compassion and fighting spirit that made him one of the most beloved generals in US history — Robert E. Lee.

The early experience for both men was a formative one. Lee learned the right lessons from his defeat to strengthen him, and McClelland learned the wrong lessons from his victory that ultimately weakened him. In your self assessment, it is sometimes useful to remember that in the seeds of your recent victory lies your next defeat, and from the thorns of a recent failure can bloom the flowers of success.

1.4 Productivity and Professional Development

A television commercial that was popular a generation ago asked the smoking audience if they were "smoking more, but enjoying it less". We might consider an adaptation of that commercial that would be directed to scientists, asking them if they are "working more but enjoying it less". Productivity is critical, but the time has come to ask "Is productivity the only critical component of the professional scientist?"

1.4.1 Old vs. New Paradigms

While the evolution and the availability of technology have been undeniably beneficial, we have to be sure that we do not give up the best of
ourselves in using it. I was a college student in the early 1970's, and the
fact that I did not have instant, repeated access to a computer afforded
me the time to think.* Since the analysis would be time consuming and
expensive, I was forced to justify the computing time and expense.
Once I decided to carry out this analysis, I commonly had to physically
stand and wait in line for about ½ hour with both students and senior
scientists to use the single university computer. This provided even
more down time, affording me the opportunity to think about and
sometimes discuss my problem with others. The disadvantage of this
older paradigm was that it was slow and inefficient, but the advantage
was that it had built in time for daily discussion and reflection with
others who were both more junior and more senior than me.

This old productivity paradigm has been replaced. In the old
paradigm, the rate limiting step was technology and the availability of
resources. It did not make sense to plan to travel to many meetings if
air costs were prohibitive. It would have been foolhardy to try to publish a peer reviewed manuscript every month if there were only a small
number of journals that were in your field. If only one or two statistical
analyses could be carried out each day, then each of these analyses had
to be planned carefully, with more time going into the analysis' plan
than into its execution. Now, many of these technology and resource
obstacles have been removed.

Computers now work faster than we can in creating work for
them. The scientific technology-dissemination system can now accept

---

*Then, students did not have their own computers. Instead, we all shared time
on a single university "mainfraim computer" that met the administrative and
research computing needs of the campus. Computer time was alloted for the
entire class as a whole—not for individuals. For example, each class section
(composed of approximately twenty students), would receive thirty minutes of
computing time for the entire class for the whole semester. If the computer time
was "hogged" by a small number of students, thereby consuiming the class'
time before the semester's end, the class could not complete the curriculum.
Thus, the class' computer time consumption was closely monitored by the professor.

more work product than we can produce. The faster we work, the faster the production of analyses, the quicker the development of papers and products, the more rapid the pace of progress. In the old paradigm, travel and computing capacity were the rate limiting step. Now — we are.

This new paradigm creates in the junior scientist the restless feeling that, if she is not busy, then she is missing the opportunity to be busy. The uneasy sense that we have about this new philosophy is well justified. If you were to work 24 hours a day, seven days a week, week after week, month after month, sacrificing both you and your family in the process, you would still miss opportunities to read, theorize, compute, and write. You cannot exhaust the system — you can only exhaust yourself.

1.4.2 Traitors and Heroes

Unfettered productivity, pursued for its own sake can be destructive. An illuminating example of this is an examination of the typical contrast between two contemporaneous figures in U.S. history. Benedict Arnold and George Washington.

Admittedly, neither of these men have any scientific record of note. Almost everyone knows that George Washington is revered for his role in the birth of the United States. He has cities, streets, monuments that commemorate him, and appears on US currency. On the other hand, no city and no monument exists for Benedict Arnold – only a small and unremarkable grave in England. He is the archetype traitor.

Yet this turn of events is hardly what would have been predicted when both men served during the fury that was the Revolutionary War. In the early years of that struggle, General Arnold performed spectacularly. In the first part of the war, Benedict Arnold was in fact the only winning general the colonial army had. He won spectacular victories in upper New England, and he almost seized an important Canadian city for the colonies. In addition, he organized and supervised a fresh water navy that served well on the Great Lakes. These were remarkable achievements for an army officer.

Arnold's accomplishments stand in stark contrast to those of George Washington. While Benedict Arnold continued his record of positive accomplishment defending the new nation in the early years of the war, the campaigns of George Washington were mired in mismanagement and defeat. After Washington withdrew from Massachusetts, he transferred his army to the middle Atlantic states. Here, his strategic blunder led to the route of his army on Long Island to a British general not known for aggressive fighting. Moving west, Washington lost in rapid succession Brooklyn, Manhattan, and Harlem, ceding New York City to the British for the remainder of the war. After two astonishing victories at Trenton and Princeton in 1776-77 (that surprised even him), Washington quickly lost several additional battles in New Jersey. From here, he moved to Pennsylvania where he promptly lost Philadelphia.

This string of defeats was almost unprecedented for a commander-in-chief. During this difficult period, Washington was personally lambasted while Arnold was held up as a fine example of an American officer. Arnold had a good strategic sense, could keep the tactics of a fluid battle clearly in his mind, and was personally courageous when he himself was under fire. It was Benedict Arnold's two victories at Saratoga, New York, during which he was badly wounded that finally convinced the French to enter the war on the side of the colonies, an entry that slowly turned the tide of the war to the favor of the colonists.[*]

Yet Benedict Arnold, productive general that he was, became the quintessential traitor while George Washington, the hapless and nonproductive commander-in-chief became, and remains a national hero. The explanation for these events is that, while here were differences in productivity, there were stronger differences in character.

---

[*] During this frenetic period of negotiation, the British tried to end the war by offering favorable terms to the colonies, but news of the French treaty of support quickly undermined any conciliatory British offers.

As both Washington and Arnold progressed through the war, they each were compelled to react to two influences for which their backgrounds had not prepared them. The first was unearned praise and adulation. The second was unearned, unremitting criticism and hatred. Benedict Arnold, in spite of all of his battlefield productivity, never learned to buffer himself from severe criticism for his small errors, despite his good reputation among many. Subsequently, the personal dislike of him by a small number of influential men denied him promotions that Arnold believed he deserved. His anger at these denials and other perceived slights allowed Arnold to be captured by intense resentment, and then hatred of those whose cause he championed so well. Losing himself in this agitated state, he fell into the traitorous scheming for which he is solely remembered.

George Washington, on the other hand, despite his desperate battlefield record, was able to develop a character that protected him from being warped by painful criticism. The fact that the country and the army stood by Washington is a tribute to how they appreciated his character. As Morrison stated "In no other revolution has a loser of so many battles been supported to the point where he could win."[4]. Rising to become president, his character continued to grow, buffering him from losing himself in the almost hysterical adoration that surrounded him.

Therefore, while a difference between these two men was productivity, the difference that mattered was the difference in their characters. One was able to grow. The other was not.

There is no doubt that productivity is important. One cannot have career development and advancement without a solid productivity track record, a track record that requires consistent, patient, hard work. However, while productivity is an important component, it is not the only important component of your career development. Productivity is necessary, but not sufficient.

While productivity is a high priority, there is a priority that is higher and takes precedence — your character development. Your goal should not be productivity for the sake of productivity, but a balanced plan for professional growth and maturity and includes productivity with other central contributors to your career and development. The remainder of this chapter identifies these other core areas.

1.5 Get Some Rest

Since I do not know you personally, and am not acquainted with the unique combinations of character traits, skills, and talents that you bring to your new career, I can say nothing about the extent to which you may have to adjust if you accept the advisory comments that comprise this chapter. However, there is one thing that you will need of which I am sure. Regardless of your education, knowledge, training, or skill, you will need to be well rested to bring these talents you have to bear on the problems at hand.

One of the most perniciously destructive influences that can ruin your experience as a scientist is chronic overwork. Just like acid burns and corrode your clothes, overwork eats through and ultimately shreds your ability to do anything effectively. Weariness will make you short tempered, ill humored, and sick. Fatigue separates you from the best use of the combination of talents and abilities with which you have been gifted. Important memories hover just out of your reach. You cannot apply the very best of yourself when you are tired. Regardless of the degree of control that you have over your own nervous faculties, you must get rest. *

A surprising aspect to the fatigue issue is that, given that we all can easily and readily acknowledge the harm produced by overwork, we nevertheless do not ensure that we get enough rest. Perhaps the resilience of youth protect you against your self-inflicted, intensive time schedules that denies your body the rest that it needs. However, even

---

* Two examples of men who were known for their capacity to work for long, sleepless periods are Richard Nixon, former President of the United States, and James Longstreet, civil war general. Each was renowned for his ability to control his own nervous energy and work for days without sleep. However, other qualities necessary for good leaders were missing.

among the strongest, the need for rest becomes acute. A useful maneuver that will successfully combat this approach is to actively build sleep and rest into your schedule. Just as you insist that there be time in your schedule to teach your class, or to go to important management meetings, be equally diligent about insisting on getting the rest that you need. Invest the same energy into taking care of yourself as you do with the development of your product or the design of your experiment. Look at your calendar planning, not with the view to crowd out these rest periods, but to protect them. In times of stress, you will need to lengthen them.

The unpredictable changes in your calendar may require a flexible approach to sleep. If naps work, take advantage of them. If you need to find someplace quiet, then find some place quiet. If you have a challenging three days before you, insist on getting more sleep both before and after the stressful period. Whatever your pattern of sleep is, do not neglect it. Additionally, fight for the time that it takes to exercise and to eat properly.

Of course, an obvious argument against the thesis that we need sleep and rest is that these activities take time that we don't have. However, this contention ignores the fact that the productivity gained by working hard and not sleeping is commonly overturned by a collection of mistakes that more easily occur when we work without rest. Incorrect reasoning more easily penetrates the fatigued mind, and produces a thought process that, while attractive when we are tired, reveals its foolhardiness in the bright light of a day following a restful night.

After sleep, restoration and distraction are critical for your development. Plan to take time to get away from work on a regular, not irregular basis. Days away from your daily work efforts give you the space to gain a new perspective about your activities, as well as to support and sustain your personal growth. Remember that time away from work means not just being physically separated from your work activities, but electronically separated as well; while away, skip reading your business email, don't work on reports or manuscripts and avoid "taking advantage of downtime" to work. Downtime, in order to be effective and provide the break that you need, needs to "be down" and "stay down", and not let you "catch up" while you are away. The new insight that is the result of a restful and unhurried extended weekend is often better than the pedestrian-paced advances that you might have made if you continued to work through a fatigue-hazed weekend.

Finally, remember that, while working hard is an enviable endeavor, being consumed by work is sad, and can have tragic consequences.

1.6 Long Term Vision

A central question that you should address as an investigator is perhaps one of the most difficult, but one of the most clarifying. As a scientist, you understand the importance of having a long-term scientific goal. Before you carry out an experiment, or energetically move forward on a project, you must know how this activity fits within your field. What is the long-term goal? What productive work will the research generate? To what new findings will the work contribute?

Just as it is important to have a larger perspective on your scientific work, it is critical that you develop a long-term vision for yourself. Specifically, what do you want to be doing twenty years from now? Take some time to consider the activities that you want to fill your schedule with in 20 years. Do you hope to spend a lot of time traveling? Do you want to be a writer in your field? Would you like to spend time making presentations? Do you see yourself ultimately developing new technology? Will you own a company? The process of producing a long-term vision, gauging your talents, evaluating your weaknesses, sifting and separating hope from reality, can be remarkably revealing. If you have a family, than what do your loved ones think and expect of you? Decisions about family will often influence, and are influenced by, the long-term goals of you and your partner.

If, after much thoughtful consideration, including conversations with your family, your mentors, and your close friends, you develop a vision, then let it capture your focus. A long term vision illuminates the path that you should walk. Keeping your long-term goal close at hand gives you a new, good metric, allowing you to measure the role that your current activities play in meeting that goal. Furthermore, the development of a distant goal worthy of your pursuit can simplify many short-term decisions that may be confronting you. Decisions about job opportunities, project options, and working group participation can all be simplified in the presence of a long term strategy. Without a long-term goal, you are at risk of having your career caught up in the random eddies of opportunity, distraction, and the vicissitudes of life. Together these forces can sweep you up and deposit you on a shore that you may not like, but from which there is no real return.

Regularly, during a time of rest, reexamine your long-term goal. Remember that this goal's development and refinement is a serious enterprise, requiring the best of your talents and contemplative skills.* Invest time in developing your own internal compass.

1.7 Develop Perseverance

The very fact that you are a scientist attests to your doggedness. You know how to work against obstacles until the obstacle gives way. This successful effort required that you force and fight your way through classes, exams, papers, reports, theses, and dissertations. Whether you were born with this trait, or you had no choice but to develop it as you progressed through school, you have very likely learned to plow through and/or over intellectual and logistical obstructions as you worked toward your academic degrees. However, as useful as this skill has been for you, it may need your additional attention.

What is the difference between stubbornness and perseverance? The stubborn individual and the perseverant worker have similar traits. They both work hard, and neither is easily diverted by small distractions. Yet of the two, qualities, perseverance is preferred. The persevering individual receives our praise, while the stubborn worker receives only our pity. Both work hard to get somewhere, but the perseverant has the better compass.

As a child on a spring day, I commonly had to wait in the parked family car while my parents completed an errand. Frequently, a housefly would enter the car through an open window, and, not recognizing its surroundings, would try to exit. However, commonly it would spend minutes trying to fly through the same closed window. It knew its attempts to escape were failing, but time after time it would knock itself against that closed window until it exhausted itself and died. This is quintessential stubbornness—visionless effort.

---

* If you cannot decide where you want to be and what you want to be doing, then perhaps you reverse the insight, and ask what do you want to avoid.

The obstreperous worker continues to fight to break through an obstacle that, for reasons that are not clear, continues to block his path. Like the non-comprehending fly, the fact that he cannot understand why his stubborn efforts are failing produce not illumination, but continued, unsuccessful attempts.

Perseverance, however, implies the combination of direction and vision. While an obstacle may have to be overcome, the perseverant is able to pause to see if this particular obstruction has to be overcome at this particular time. If so, she will persist. The perseverant worker will take the time to step back, to thoughtfully consider the problem. Sometimes repeated effort in the same direction is required. However, perhaps redirected effort in another direction is needed. For the stubborn, overcoming obstacles is the key to success. For the persevering, the key to success is continued progress toward a long term goal that has been carefully considered and deemed worthy of consistent, diligent, but not obsessive effort.

Avoid wasting your times on fruitless battles. Don't splinter your effort into activities for multiple goals, none of which places you where thoughtful consideration suggests that you should be. Recognize that there is a time for some activities to be prosecuted in earnest, and a time for that energy to be redirected.

In 2002 I was challenged to lead a computer programming team in the development of a database that would serve as the repository of data for a collection of research activities. These activities were designed to assess the effect of new therapies in their ability to reduce brain injury. Specifically, these treatments were tailored to reduce the damaging effects of blood clots in the brain, commonly known as a strokes.

Our group traditionally used paper forms to collect data. However, in this circumstance, we decided to develop an online internet application that allowed remote data entry with simultaneous "real time" quality control. In this new scheme, there would be a web application that would control the data collection and provide quality assurance. In addition, we would have a computer that would serve as the repository for a modern, remotely accessible database. When this scheme was complete, data entry could proceed at the patient's hospital. This remotely entered data would then be transmitted to our server that would control the data entry and quality control. After the data passed this inspection, it would be automatically transmitted to a second computer that would store the data and be available for report generation. Each of these systems would be guarded by a protective mechanism that used state of the art security measures.

This was a fine objective, but the technology for these systems was very new. The programmer who had accepted responsibility for organizing the data from this project knew very little about these new techniques. We therefore decided to work on this project together. We would have to start from scratch to learn the technology and then build ourselves up to the assembly of an application that we could hopefully deploy.

These were steps out onto *terra incognita*. Like many new and complicated projects, our first efforts were halting and full of aching frustration. We expended a small fortune of our own money on books, and spent many hours at work and at our respective homes on developing the programming skills that we needed. It took approximately one month of painful work to produce the first elementary web page. Slowly, ideas and concepts became clearer to us, and, several months later, we had a tight, functional application that the investigators could use remotely, and that was safe and secure.

The two of us had moved from absolute novices to programmers who were confident in showcasing our work, and we were now able to utilize this technology for new research efforts in different fields. For me personally, this had been a particularly exhilarating experience. I had demonstrated to myself that twenty years spent in research, teaching, and statistical writing had dimmed neither my enthusiasm for, nor my aptitude in, computer programming.

However during a brief break between projects, I found myself plagued by some nagging concerns. I had spent eight months, and approximately 1000 hours working on this project. While this work had not been carried out to the exclusion of my other responsibilities, the press of other professional obligations, including grant involvement and administrative activities was undeniably real. In addition, my coprogrammer, who, like me, started out in this project untrained in these new fields, was now, almost nine months later, able to make fine progress working independently. While at first, we relied on each other, she was now able to proceed without my help. In fact, she had now surpassed my skills, and was preparing to share her expertise with other programmers who needed to learn this new technology.

This combination of realizations led me to the conclusion that it was time for a change in my path. Since I could justify my continued deep investment in programming with the new projects coming up, it would have been easy for me to stubbornly argue that I should continue to play a central role in the programming for these activities. However, it was time for me to move on. My season of programming was fun, but was now over. I would not have recognized this if I hadn't chosen to stop for a period of time for self evaluation.

1.8 Expand Your Knowledge Base

Our careers may start out as general, relatively unfocused careers, but they rapidly narrow, becoming tightly concentrated on an area of sub-specialty. This is, of course, unavoidable as each scientific field discovers new information that its workers must master. However, sub-specialization is not really adequate justification to know nothing else about the advances in our fields, or other fields of science. Tight focus is fine, but tight focus all of the time can produce limited perspectives.[*] After all, even though we believe our work is critical (why would we do it if we didn't?) the fact is that, by and large, the rest of the world does not understand it, and is, by and large, getting along without this comprehension. If this is how your critical work is viewed, then maybe you are ignoring the critical work of other workers in other fields. Why not take the time to learn something about there contributions? There are many activities in other fields that are worthy of your understanding and careful consideration.

Developing a different knowledge base offers several specific advantages. Your examination of other material provides a useful and timely distraction. By applying the analytic skills that you commonly use in your own area of expertise to understand the developments in

---

[*] A humorous adage in medicine is that the physician-specialist, over time, learns more and more about less and less until she knows everything about nothing. The generalist learns less and less about more and more until he know nothing about everything.

another area, you are actually taking the time to sharpen your skills. The fact that you have to regain your focus when you return to your own work requires effort, but with that effort commonly comes a slightly different perspective on the issue in your own field on which you are working.

Your exploration of other fields does not have to be limited to science. It could be the law, art, or history, astronomy or another field of endeavor. There are hard workers in these fields as well. These workers develop good products, and commonly write for people like yourself who wish to familiarize themselves with what these other areas have to offer. A serious examination of this work stretches your outlook, broadens your appreciation, and can commonly help you to find the character extension that you sometimes need to have in order to understand a point of view other than your own.

An important observation is that, when you are stuck on a problem, the solution may not be to work harder on it, but to take your mind off of it. A useful and informative strategy is to speak to some of your colleagues and peers about what they are doing. You might be quite surprised to find that they have a problem that you can help them with. Spending 1-2 hours with a peer will in all likelihood produce no real setbacks for your work, but can produce a tangible benefit for your colleague, both in the measurable advancement of their own work, and also the immeasurable impact that your unfettered generosity has had.

1.9 Moral Excellence

Moral excellence in science is not a passive, inactive, or static state. The challenges provided by science, the private sector, investors, academic promotion, the promises of grants, the offer of a financial reward, the willingness to testify in a courtroom offer important, unpredictable, dynamic, and unceasing challenges to you as you gain experience in your field. You will have to examine each of these possibilities with great consideration. This will mean laying them out next to your moral compass, determining the direction in which they will take you. Make sure that your compass is itself well-calibrated. Test it by challenging it – be alert for the opportunity to be ethical, while being vigilant for the development of any seeds of unethical conduct developing in your own actions. Ethics requires attention and consideration. Ethical conduct is not the passive passenger sleeping comfortably in the back-seat while you drive to your career destination — ethics is the driver. Make sure that you know where it is going.[*]

1.10 Family Development

This is self evident, but as a junior scientist years ago, I heard very little conversation about this important topic from colleagues. Although its complex and personal nature confounds any real attempt to provide specific guidance, we can nevertheless make a general observations. Regardless of culture, creed, or religion, the importance of family is central. Avoid the trap of letting dedication to your family be replaced by dedication to your career. Commit important effort to your career, but devote your life to your family.

Strong family relationships require your continued time commitment, and you, no doubt, already know that you will need to balance responsibilities at home with the demands of work and career. Let your default position be that you will resolve these conflicts in favor of your family. Use this competition for your time as an opportunity to reassert the central role of your family in your life.

As an example, one area that my family has had difficulty with is the separation produced by my travel. Therefore, the night before I leave has become an especially close time for us. We are sure to have a good meal together, and spend the rest of the evening visiting. The difficulty that this presents for my work is that I commonly have unfinished job obligations that must be addressed in order to complete the final preparations for my trip. Try as I might, I never seem to be able to complete this work during the day, and so I bring it home. Thus, the desire to spend time working collides with the need for me to enjoy my family. I have struggled, trying different ways to resolve this over the years, and have finally settled on the following. Since my family is more important than my work, I choose to spend the time with them. The next morning, I will wake up early, say at 3:30AM to complete the unfinished work for the trip. I regain the rest I lost by sleeping on the plane later that day. It has taken me many trips to work this out, but this appears to work best for us.

---

[*] This is the topic of Chapter 6.

1.11 Collegiality

There is no great pride, and no real accomplishment in getting along with people and coworkers who you enjoy. The major obstacle for many of us is the lack of motivation to work closely with people that we do not like. In all probability, you will work with people who are difficult for you to like. Scientists can be strongly opinionated, and sometimes we can get distracted from the benevolent spirit that is the source of their zeal by some small manifestation of that enthusiastic that is objectionable to us. Your colleague may be opinionated in a way that offends you. It is also possible that you believe that he just doesn't like you, and that therefore all you are doing is returning the sentiment.

A sad reality is that people that we commonly do not like are commonly misunderstood. Resentment, hard feelings, and hostility among scientists all too easily take root in the ground left barren by lack of understanding. Spend some effort in trying to understand someone before you give yourself over to active dislike.

1.11.1 "Educate-able"

I have noticed that I have a bad habit when I buy a new music compact disc (CD) from a favorite artist. Almost invariably I don't enjoy the CD as much as I hoped that I would. This is because the music on the new CD did not meet my initial expectation; because those expectations were not met, I react badly to the unanticipated music. However, if I am patient and willing to give the new music another chance, listening to the it several times over a few days, I often find that "the music grows on me". In fact, several of the selections become my new favorites. The problem was that I simply could not appreciate the new music with an old and closed mind. I needed to open up and be willing to accept something new. By overturning the resistance in my own mind, I remade myself. It is not so much that the music "grows on me" as much as it is that I have "grown on it".

Scientists to whom I first reacted badly have, over the years become my valued friends. These scientists are still as different from me now as they were when I first met them, but they have become my friends anyway. They have grown on me, and I have grown on them.

At this point in your career, you have completed over fifteen years in school (and for many of you, several more years than that). You are highly trained and have earned the chance to have an impact on society. However despite the different training and talents that scientists have, there is one trait that is necessary for you to maintain — you must always be "educatable". This is not research "educatability", because we each already know that we will as scientists always be learning new science and new technology. Developing collegial relationships is based on a different style of educatability.

By educatable, we mean the ability to continue to be influenced by, and learn from colleagues in a way that shapes your own behavior. Their training is different, their command of your language is different, their customs are different. They are an unknown to you, and you must replace your vacuum of intuition and understanding about them with new knowledge that you never anticipated that you would have to gain. Their perspective can affect your career, and perhaps, more importantly, your interactions with them can change each of your lives.

As scientists, our only saving grace is that we are "educatable".

1.11.2 Be A Colleague to Make a Colleague

We all want the support of good colleagues. We want to profit from their wise advice, receive their help when we ask for it, rely on their support when our own actions are not enough to solve our professional problems. Ultimately, we would like to be surrounded by a web of good colleagues that can function like a social/professional network for us, on whose strength we can draw. While it is good for scientists to desire this web, it first requires that we must be part of that web. Just as we desire collegial support, we have to recognize that we must provide support for other scientists.

Following the adage "to make a colleague, you must be a colleague" can produce a wonderfully rich working environment. In fact, you can be the spark that helps to start and generate this environment. However, be forewarned that this requires openness, a spirit of generosity, and unselfishness as you bend over backwards to help others with whom you work. Genuine empathy coupled with your thoughtful consideration as a fellow scientist to help a colleague through a difficult period can take time from your own work. Your own progress on a report, or forward motion on an experiment may slow for a time. Perhaps your productivity falters for a few days or so.

It is both instructive and satisfying to see that this temporary reduction in your productivity does you no lasting harm, because your diligent research efforts that you apply at all other times will sustain and can support the temporary decrease in your productivity now. Remember that your long term goal is not isolated productivity; avoid a behavior pattern that places product output above all other considerations. Productivity is an important component, but only one important component of professional development. Since productivity is not the only essential ingredient, it occasionally must be set aside for a time so that other core constituents of your character can appear and exert their different influences. One of these components is the compassion that you draw on to help a colleague. The more strained the atmosphere, the more that compassion makes sense.

1.11.3 Gentle Communicator

Emotional considerations count for much in our interpersonal communications. While we are scientists, it is important to remember that we are simply people who convey scientific information. The fact that we are scientists does not free us of the responsibility of treating each other with respect and decency. Perhaps, the observation that much of the information that we convey to each other is so devoid of emotion means that we must take greater care in delivering the message so that our intent is not misunderstood.

Keep in mind that what you mean to transmit when speaking may not be what is received by the listener. This is a common source of misunderstanding. Your own assessment of the degree to which you convey your intent should be an important component of your self assessment. For example, I have learned that I tend to under-convey the emotional impression that I hope to leave with other scientists. When I am attempting to be courteous, I do not come across as being courteous and kind; instead I come across as simply being "OK". Even though, in my own mind, I believe I am being courteous, that is not the countenance that is perceived by others. On the other hand, if I speak or carry myself in a manner that leads me to believe that I am being "overly courteous", then I am seen not as being too courteous or obsequious, but instead are seen as being pleasantly courteous and friendly. I don't quite understand this, but having recognized this about myself, I try to take advantage of it.

Conversations are so easily facilitated by a simple and honest apology for any misunderstanding. We all know the fortunately rare and rarely fortunate scientist who believe that standing on principle gives him or her the right to be rude and offensive. Whenever it enters your mind to apologize, hold onto and act on that thought rather than dismiss it. Do not resist apologizing. A sincere apology goes a long way to smooth what may be a rough conversation. It doesn't mean that you have to give way on a matter of conviction. Apologizing simply reveals that you have the strength to recognize that you might have caused offense while standing your ground.

Consider apologizing when you believe that you have done nothing wrong and therefore an apology is not warranted. For example, you may have merely attempted to criticize a small technical detail of an otherwise fine report, but the authors perceive your words as a personal criticism of themselves. This is not your fault, and you did not mean to convey any insult, but they nevertheless take it personally. Work on developing an intuition of how others perceive you, striving to adjust your speech and tone so that you communicate is what you intend to convey. Purge any bellicosity from your speaking patterns.[*]

Having worked to ensure that you have the best, honest and benevolent intention in speaking, now work to ensure that the same well-meaning intent is clearly conveyed in an easily understood way. If it is not, then be quick to apologize for the misunderstanding and try again. I have learned that if I cannot as a scientist speak this way, then it is best if I keep my teeth together and say nothing.

1.12 Manage your Anger

During your development as a scientist, you will become angry and you will arouse anger in others. This anger is readily apparent in discussions at professional meetings, in which the sharp exchanges between

---

[*] This is discussed in depth in Chapter Four.

scientists can be tinged with bitterness. Rarely is the motivation for the anger clearly in view, but its presence is undeniably palpable. When anger is present, it gets in your way. Rarely at scientific meetings has the scientific exchange been enhanced by anger. It is more common that the scientist who is attempting to get his point across through his anger has more difficulty enunciating the point clearly. And, sadly, the scientific point he is making is commonly overshadowed by the reaction of the fellow scientists to the anger. Most of the conversation after the exchange is about the anger and not about the scientific points of the debate.

Another occasion for anger to arise is in a group of scientists who are working under tremendous time pressure. With a deadline looming, or an additional work load added, there may not be enough time for you to accomplish the desired task. Frustration and anger can quickly rise up in this circumstance. This anger can ruin your relationships with your colleagues.

Before we discuss what to do about anger, let's first distinguish anger from the energy that comes from a healthy debate or a challenge. Both can excite you. However the productive energy that is generated in you from facing a challenge can animate you, spurring you on to a new line of thought, and causing you to re-evaluate your own scientific theories objectively. On the other hand, anger taps into the belligerent ideas of attack and defense. Facing a challenge helps to polish your ideas, theories, and concepts. Anger, like lye, dissolves them. A good challenge produces productive energy. Anger produces energy that is ultimately self-destructive.

What can you as a scientist do to manage your anger? One way to accomplish this is to predict it. The simple recognition that a situation in which you will be involved may produce anger can be defense enough against its occurrence. Anger commonly presents itself as a reaction to a surprise. If the surprise can be anticipated, then we can block the angry reaction.

Secondly, don't be compelled to respond to a harsh word angrily. Those scientists who have the reputation of losing their self-control, lashing out angrily in response to criticism, essentially give over their self control to others. Their critics can easily control them by speaking softly or harshly depending on their desire. Responding in kind does nothing but bring out the worst in you, and diminish you in the eyes of others who are observing the exchange.

As a scientist, the best reaction to harsh verbal and public criticism directed to you is a kind word. A humorous reaction, uttered kindly, is another healthy response. While this caliber of reply disarms and disorients your critics, elevating you in the eyes of observant others, it is also a reply that is good for you. By resisting your adversary's attempt to place a seed of self destructive anger in you, you have looked after your own well-being in a difficult setting.

Finally, if these tactics do not work, then recognize that the anger you feel is getting in your way and release it. If exercise works, then exercise.[*] Try to do nothing constructive until you have purged yourself of this difficult emotion. Vented anger very rarely produces anything of lasting value. Like poison, it is best to expel it as rapidly as possible.

1.13 Conclusions

Technology and modern advances have produced an environment whose resources you cannot drain. The evolution of computing ability, telecommunications, and advances in instrumentation have evolved simultaneously, and this correlation of forces has generated an environment that easily absorbs your productive efforts. Whether you work on three projects simultaneously, or generate one published manuscript a month, the system will not be exhausted by you; if you let it, the system will exhaust you.

Since all of your efforts can be absorbed by the system resources, and it is therefore possible for you to spend all of your time being productive (i.e. carrying out experiments, executing statistical analyses, writing reports, giving presentations at meetings) you have to ask whether there aren't some other activities in which you should be involved. Should you be productive all of the time just because you *can* be productive all of the time? The answer advocated in this chapter is no. While productivity is an important necessity for your career, it is

---

[*] For me it is a long drive or a hard workout on a punching bag (which never punches back). I feel terrible when I start, and relieved when finished.

not the only critical component. This chapter advocates that you should choose professional development and maturity as your career goal.

Investing all of your effort in productivity, to the exclusion of character growth, will fail you. Incorporating productivity into professional development means that you supplement productivity with maturity. A good first step to make is to take stock of yourself. Professional maturity requires that you be balanced, and that you develop both diligence and the ability to sensitively assess priorities calmly and unhurriedly during the daily cacophony of your calendar.

Carry out a self-appraisal, and then develop a long-term vision first for yourself, and then for your work. Critical to this self evaluation is the need for rest. While there are records of remarkable workers who were able to endure prolonged periods of productive activity without respite, most of us cannot emulate them. Insist on building adequate time for rest into your calendar.

Keeping in mind that rest is not so much about lazy relaxation as it is about restoration, use these restful periods to restore yourself physically, emotionally, spiritually, and psychologically. Measure yourself in every way that reflects your good background, with every cultural metric that you hold valuable. Find your weak points and devote energy to strengthening them. Be sure that you have learned the right lessons from your past training and experiences, but also take the steps to assure yourself that you have not learned the right lessons to well.

Collegiality is central in professional development. Deliberately choosing to turn your face away from your own productivity (and your own needs) in order to come to the aid of a colleague not only helps a coworker who is in some distress, but is good for you. Setting aside the fact that your stature increases as a result of your generous action, placing your own needs voluntarily aside produces its own reward.

Focusing on developing the strengths, skills, and outlook of a mature, professional scientist will not only amplify your consistent productive efforts, but will also buffer and protect you as you face the unseen challenges that lie ahead. The specific scientific advances that your work produces will, in all likelihood, be overshadowed and surpassed by the future advances of others. However, the principles for which you stand as both a scientist and as an individual can resonate indefinitely.

References

1.   Medawar, P. B. (1967). *The Art of the Soluble*, London: Methuen,
2.   Gehan, E.A., Lemak N.A. (1994). *Statistical in Medical Research: Developments in Clinical Trials.* New York. Plenum Publishing Company.
3.   Newell C.R. (1996). *Lee vs. McClellan: The First Campaign. Washington D.C.* Regnery Publishing Inc.
4.   Morrison S.E. (1972). *The Oxford History of the American People. Volume 1.* London. New American Library, p 328.

Chapter 2
Investigators and Research Principles

2.1 The Heart of a Researcher

Learning is the intellectual core of a researcher. Many other worthy fields focus on applying knowledge to a profitable end, e.g. marketing, banking, insurance, travel, regulation, and manufacturing. It is true that each of these areas applies an aspect of research to their efforts. However, what differentiates their primary motivation from that of the researcher is that, in these other applied fields, new knowledge is sought only as a means to an end. To a researcher, the knowledge itself is the end.

A first and crucial finding that a scientist should make is one about herself. Embedded in the researcher is the natural, intrinsic drive to ask and answer questions about their surroundings. Sometimes the question that we are driven to address may be one that other researchers have asked, but whose answer does not satisfy us. Other times, the question may had not been articulated before, as in Albert Einstein's question to himself "What would it be like to ride a light beam traveling at the speed of light?" Despite the disparities and wide differences in our specializations in science, this drive is what we share and what sets us apart from non-researchers.

While there are many awards in science, no accolade provided by others can displace the scientist's reward of having her research question answered. Unbeknownst to their employers, many researchers would pay, rather than be paid, to pursue their own investigations.

2.2 Confirmatory vs. Exploratory Analyses

From ancient Roman scholars and Indian Sharmans to current day nano-technologists and nuclear engineers, learned men and women seek an understanding of their world.1 There are many different tools to address scientific questions in our highly specialized fields, and many of them require specific and intricate instrumentation. However, each of these fields is linked by common principles of scientific investigation. In each culture, in each laboratory, and in each clinic, comprehension is first and foremost based on an honest representation of the facts as best as they can be observed.

2.2.1 Hypothesis Driven Investigation

The basis of the scientific method is hypothesis testing. The researcher formulates a hypothesis, then conducts an experiment that she believes will put this hypothesis to the test. If the experiment is methodologically sound, and is executed according to its plan*, then the experiment will be a true test of that hypothesis. This process, although time consuming, is the most reliable way to gain new knowledge and insight.

2.2.2 Discovery

This deliberative procedure of hypothesis testing stands in contradistinction to another learning process known as "discovery" or "explora-

---

* This plan is often called a protocol.

tion". The discovery process commonly illuminates a surprise result, and such findings can have important implications. The arrival of Christopher Columbus at the island of San Salvador in 1492 heralded the unanticipated "discovery" of the New World. Madam Curie "discovered" radiation. These individuals did not anticipate and were not looking for their discoveries. They stumbled over them precisely because these discoveries were not in their view.

Discovery is an important process, and, as the examples of the previous paragraph have demonstrated, can lead to new knowledge that reshapes our world. However, a "discovery" by itself must be confirmed before it can be accepted as a trustworthy illumination of a scientific issue. Eccentricities of the discovery process e.g. faulty instrumentation, sample-to-sample variability, and outright mistakes in measurements can each mislead the honest researcher and his audience. Yet it is important to include this unplanned, haphazard but nevertheless revealing discovery tool into the scientific thought process.

This integration can be achieved by allowing the result of the exploration to become the central *a priori* hypothesis for a new experiment that seeks to verify the discovery. For example, while it is true that Columbus discovered the New World, he had to return three additional times before he was given credit for his observation. Columbus was essentially forced to prove that he could find the New World when he was actually looking for it. On the other hand, an important and new discovery for the treatment of patients with congestive heart failure[2] had to be reversed when a confirmatory finding could not repeat the original, spectacular surprise result[3].

Given that claims of discovery can commonly misdirect us, it is important for us to distinguish between an evaluation that uses a research effort to confirm a prospectively stated hypothesis, i.e., a confirmatory analysis (truly "*re*-searching") from the identification of a finding for which the research effort was not specifically designed to reliably detect ("searching"). This latter category, into which "discoveries" and other surprise results fall, we will term "hypothesis generating analyses" or "exploratory analyses". While hypothesis generating analyses can provide important new insight into our understanding, their analyses and interpretation must be handled differently than the results of confirmatory analyses. This is a topic to which we will return later in this chapter.

2.3 Good Experimental Design and Execution

The growth and development of mathematical, statistical, and computational analysis in the late 20th century has contributed immensely to our ability to conduct complicated research evaluations. However, the use of these quantitative tools cannot guarantee good research design. Furthermore, the most advanced mathematics and statistics are of limited utility when the research was designed and executed poorly. A solid statistical analysis may be necessary, but it is not sufficient for a good research product.

The importance of good research design and execution has been recognized for generations, and one of the earliest and most cogent articulations of these principles emerged from the early agricultural research literature. An incisive contribution to research methodology was made by Arthur Young in 1763. After inheriting and laboring on a farm, Young published three volumes entitled *Agriculture* [4]. In it, he described ideas that we now clearly recognize as essential to good experimental methodology.

Each of Young's volumes begins with examples of how some authors slant the presented data to support their favored conclusion; an investigator's biased view can alter a research effort's conduct and its interpretation. In addition, Young recognized the perils associated with extending conclusions to an inappropriately broad set of circumstances. He warned that his own conclusions about the influences on crop development and growth could not be trusted to apply to a different farm with different soil and land management practices. By carefully noting that his results were limited, he stressed the pitfalls of what we now call extrapolation.

Young also stated that experiments must be comparative, and he insisted that, when comparing a new method and a standard method, both must be present in the experiment.* He recognized that, even in

---

* This was an important, early admonition against the use of historical controls.

comparative experiments, many factors other then the intervention being tested (e.g. soil fertility, drainage, and insects) contributed to increasing or decreasing crop yields in each of the experimental plots. In addition, because the sum effect of these influences could affect the plot yield in different ways and directions, the results of a single experiment in one year could not be completely trusted. Young therefore deduced that replication would be valuable in producing accurate estimates of an intervention's effect on crop yield. Finally, Young stressed careful measurements of the endpoint of the research. These important principles of 1) clarity of observation, and 2) the ability to attribute an effect to a research intervention apply to present day research execution.

Eighty-six years later, James Johnson followed with the book *"Experimental Agriculture"*(1849), which was a treatise devoted to practical advice on experimental design [5]. A major contribution of Johnson was the emphasis he gave to the primacy of good experimental execution, and his writings are remarkably prescient for today's turbulent scientific environment. Johnson noted that a badly conceived or badly executed experiment was more than a mere waste of time and money – like a bad compass, bad research provided misdirection. He stated that the incorporation of a poor experiment's misleading results into standard textbooks will lead to the premature termination of what would have been promising lines of research. This is because these new avenues of research would appear to be a waste of effort in the face of findings that, unknown to the research community, were spurious. In addition, as other farmers attempted to use these false research results, the crop yields would be lower than predicted, with a resultant waste of resources and money. This perspective on the pervasive implications of poorly conducted research resonate from the 19th to the 21st century.

It is important to note that the afore mentioned issues, while containing mathematics, are not entirely mathematical. Good research efforts require careful observation, clarity of thought, a clear view of the research question, a well designed and well executed experiment, and honesty. Without these integral components, the research effort will ultimately fail. Statistical analyses, so pervasive in research, cannot transform a poorly conceived and/or badly designed research effort into an acceptable one.

2.4 The Compromise of Sample-based Research

Researchers want to apply their results as widely as possible and, of course, one way to do this is to study every person (or animal) in the population. However, this is clearly impossible. A researcher who is studying the relationship between cellular phone use habits of automobile drivers and traffic accidents would, if he could, study all drivers to observe 1) whether they use cell phones, 2) whether the drivers are involved in accidents, and 3) whether their use of cell phones was directly or indirectly related to the accident's occurrence. This thorough investigation would provide the definitive answer to the research question "does cell phone usage cause or contribute to automobile accidents"?

While desirable from an intellectual perspective, this investigative procedure is quite impossible because of the unsolvable financial and logistical issues.* Thus, in full recognition of the limitations of studying everyone, the researcher instead compromises by selecting a sample of drivers. This sampling process provides something that the researcher needs, but, because it is a compromise, sampling also requires that the investigator give up something of value.

What the sampling process provides for the researcher is executability. While he is not in the position to study millions of subjects, he can pay for, obtain informed consent from, and manage 1000 drivers in a study. The researcher can now carry out the effort because, through the sampling process, the scientist now has a scope of investigation that he can engage in and thoroughly evaluate. However, the investigator gives up something of great value in this compromise — certainty.

Specifically, studying a small sample drawn from a large population leaves most of the population unstudied. If the scientist were to study the entire population, the answer to his scientific question

---

* Even if he could solve the intractable financial and logistical problems, many if not most drivers might choose not to be studied.

would be assured. How then can his answer be assured when most of the population of interest remains unstudied in his evaluation?

The simple and honest response is that there is no guarantee that his sample-based answer is accurate. There are practices and procedures that the investigator can follow in order to make if very likely that the sample will reflect the population from which it was drawn. However, the ability to generalize the results from a sample to a population are very limited.

2.4.1 Dealing with Sampling Error

Sampling error is the observation that different samples, when selected from a single population, can provide different answers to the same question. How this occurs is easily seen. When drawing a sample of individuals from a population, we observe that each sample, drawn from the same population, contains different individuals. These individuals have different life experiences, and produce different data. While the data can be similar across some samples, other samples will reveal marked differences. This sample-to-sample variability is called sampling error.

Consider the plight of two researchers who are equally diligent and equally capable. Each obtains different samples from the same population. Each researcher wishes to use their sample to answer the same question, and each obtains a different result. Each scientist believes that the result from their sample is generalizable to the population. However, clearly they both cannot be correct since there is only one answer that governs the population. Which scientist is right?

The principal use of statistics in research is to address the sampling error issue. Statistics deals with this important phenomenon. The nonmathematical comprehension of this process is critical for the scientist who is interested in reaching useful conclusions about the population from which their research sample was drawn.

2.4.2 Simple Random Sampling

A researcher has many selection schemes that she might implement when choosing a sample from a population. The selection criteria are arbitrary and must be carefully considered, because the consequences of their choice can be profound. It is helpful at this point to remember that, in the end, we want the sample to contain, reflect, and therefore reveal relationships that exist in the population. The sample is the researcher's view of the population. If that view is blurred, bent, or otherwise distorted, the researcher will have difficulty discerning what the "population-truth" is from her sample-based observations. The researcher must therefore choose the sample in the manner that allows the sample to be most reflective of the population.

The clearest view of the population is provided if the sample is selected randomly in a manner that is known as simple random selection. The simple random selection mechanism is that collection of procedures which assures that each subject in the population has the same, constant probability of being selected for the sample. This produces a sample that "appears like" the population. A sample that is selected using this mechanism is commonly known as a random sample.

This simple random sampling approach is the best way to ensure that the selected sample represents the population at large, and that the findings in the sample can be generalized to the population from which the sample was obtained. Whenever random sampling does not take place, generalizations from the sample to the population at large are often impossible.*

Some research is quite amenable to the application of the simple random sampling selection mechanism. An example would be the astronomer who wishes to obtain information from a sample of visible stars in the sky. In this case, the researcher can construct a very efficient sampling algorithm that chooses stars randomly from visible star fields. Therefore, the astronomer could more easily generalize results from the findings in his sample to the population of visible stars.†
Alternatively, in medical research involving the treatment and observation of patients, it can be very difficult to use a random patient selection mechanism to select the sample. In human studies, subjects

---

* It is also true that this level of randomization creates in the sample the property of statistical independence, which allows for the multiplication of probabilities so useful in the construction of both parameter estimators and test statistics for hypothesis testing.

† No generalization is permissible to the invisible stars because invisible stars never had the opportunity to be selected for the sample.

mechanism to select the sample. In human studies, subjects have the right to refuse participation in the study after being selected randomly. The influence of these individual decisions, in concert with the presence of other patient inclusion and exclusion criteria, can disable the random selection mechanism. Thus this physician-researcher would have difficulty with any generalization because the inclusion and exclusion criteria necessary to make the study ethical can alter the sample so that it no longer represents the population.

2.4.3 Generalizations to Populations

The arguments presented in the previous section have properly motivated researchers to select their samples randomly whenever possible. However, there are two important complications that must be considered in collecting a random sample. The first is that all samples, including random samples, contain sampling error. This sampling error was created when the sample was obtained from the larger population. Thus, the sample will contain 1) information not created by sampling error and therefore representative of the population, and 2) "information" that is created by sampling error and due entirely to the freak of chance. We must have a reliable way to distinguish between the two.

Secondly, samples provide generalizable answers only to the questions that the sample was designed to answer. The sample will contain a wealth of data. Some of this data is directly responsive to the question that the research was designed to answer. Other data is commonly collected because it is of interest. However, this additional data, while useful in raising new questions, is not likely to be informative about the population from which the sample was selected.

This latter statement restricting a random sample's ability to generalize to the population is not a contradiction. We are not saying that random samples, obtained for their generalizability, are in fact, not generalizable. We are saying that a sample that was designed to illuminate one issue, in general does not illuminate others. Selecting a random sample means that some, but not all, results in that sample are generalizable.

Consider, for example, a scientist interested in collecting and analyzing the annual salaries of all junior scientists who have been employed at their first post graduate job for three years or less. She is interested in identifying whether the average salary of these junior researchers is less than, or greater than $75,000 per year.

In this hypothetical study, she computes that she will need a 1% sample from the population of junior researchers who have held their position for three years or less. She sends all selected scientists a questionnaire, and is able to construct an answer to the salary question that they all answer. However, suppose in her query, she also asked questions about ethnicity and gender. The analysis of the sample data reveals that of those who responded to the gender question, 40% are women and 60% are men. Carrying our further analyses, she finds that the mean salary of women is statistically greater than that of men. As this latter finding is the most provocative of her results, she focuses her conclusions on this surprising discovery. Was she wrong to do this?

To evaluate this situation, we observe that the data in this example contain three analyses. The first is the assessment of the overall mean annual salary. The second is the evaluation of the gender composition of her sample. The third and most provocative result is the finding of higher salaries for female junior researchers. Of these three findings, the first is the most reliable. The additional findings cannot be assumed to be representative and should be interpreted as crude and preliminary findings, requiring that a subsequent study be designed to answer these questions.

In order to understand this conclusion, let us first concede the obvious. The researcher wishes to generalize the findings from her sample to the population at large. Specifically, she wishes to make a statement about the salaries of the junior scientist population when 99% of them have never been queried. Ninety-nine out of one hundred junior scientists have not taken part in the survey, not had their data collected and tabulated, and not had information about their salaries added to this research effort; yet the researcher wishes to draw conclusions about them. Describing people when you do not have data from them is a potentially hazardous, certainly delicate, and can only be attempted after very careful consideration.

Methodology must govern when generalization is acceptable. In this particular example, the sample was designed with the overall salary analysis in mind. It was constructed to be representative of the population and to have a sufficient number of members in order to be

able to identify the mean junior faculty salary with precision. Specifically, the sample was obtained in order to reflect the annual salaries of
junior faculty as a whole, focusing on the proximity of these salaries to
$75,000. The sample is therefore most representative of the location of
the mean salary. It must be pointed out that, even though the sample is
representative of these salaries, it might nevertheless lead to the wrong
conclusion about the amount of money earned on an annual basis by
junior faculty. Despite her best efforts, the population might have produced a sample for the researcher that, just through the play of chance
and the random aggregation of subjects within a sample, misleads her
about the location of the population mean. The magnitude of these
types of sampling errors (known as type I and type II errors) are what a
good statistical analysis will identify.

However, what can be said about the gender proportion analysis? There is no doubt that the sample identified 40% of junior faculty
as women. Since the sample was obtained randomly, does the random
selection mechanism permit this finding to be worthy of consideration
as "population truth" also? No. The sample was identified and chosen
to be representative of faculty salary, leading to its accurate and precise
estimate. However, estimating the proportion of men and women with
the comparable precision of the salary estimate requires a different
sample size. Thus, although her random sample provides accurate and
precise estimates of the mean salary, the same sample does not, in general, provide precise and accurate estimates of gender.

A second complication with the gender assessment is that,
while every subject in the sample contributed information about their
annual salary (a requirement, since the goal of the sample was to obtain
salary data), not every junior faculty member that was selected for inclusion in the sample supplied their gender. Thus, missing data about
gender further distorts the estimates of the gender proportions in the
population. Effectively, the missing data keeps the researcher from
knowing the gender proportions in her sample, blunting her ability to
estimate what they are in the population.

Thus, simple random samples are only representative of the
aspect of the population that they were explicitly and overtly designed
to measure. Seeing a population through a sample is like viewing a
complicated and intricately detailed landscape through glasses. It is

impossible to grind the glass lens so that every object in the landscape can be viewed with the same sharp detail. If the lens is ground to view near objects, then the important features of the distant objects are distorted. On the other hand, if the lens is ground for the clear depiction of distant objects, then near objects are blurred beyond recognition. For our scientist in this example, her research lens was ground to provide a clear view of the overall mean salary of junior faculty. Her view of gender proportions using this same "research lens" is unclear and therefore unreliable.

The problem that complicates the researcher's ability to reliably estimate gender proportions also obfuscates her attempts to draw conclusions from the comparisons of the mean salaries of men and women junior researchers. For example, she will observe that there were some subjects in her sample that responded to her query about salaries, but not about gender. What should the researcher do about this data? The missing gender information is critical in this gender-salary analysis, but can be difficult if not impossible to collect when the research enters its analysis phase. If the researcher had planned to do this analysis (i.e., the research lens was ground to focus on gender during the design phase of the survey) she would have taken steps* to ensure that all essential data were captured.

So, since the research was not designed to evaluate gender, the 1) lack of statistical precision and 2) missing data combine to render the analysis of gender unreliable. However, in addition, there is yet one more difficulty with the gender-salary analysis, a difficulty that is both subtle and lethal.

2.4.4 Untrustworthy Estimators

Let's alter this hypothetical example of the salary sample survey in order to illustrate a more perverse difficulty with the gender-salary analysis. Recall that this evaluation carried out by our researcher identified that the salaries of women junior faculty were larger than the salaries of junior faculty who were men. We already understand that the

---

* Such steps include insisting in the instructions that salary and gender be answered completely, and returning to the subjects with incomplete data in order to obtain the missing information.

impact of missing gender data can skew our analysis. The presence of this missing data means that we cannot even be sure what has happened in our sample, much less try to extend the sample result to the population.

Let's now assume that there is no missing gender data in the sample. Thus, the gender-salary analysis includes data from everyone in the sample. However, even though the sample database is complete, this gender-salary analysis is still likely to be misleading. The sample results are, in all likelihood, not representative of the population.[*]

The unreliability of this sample-based result is rooted in the way in which the scientist's attention was drawn to the gender-salary relationship. Unlike with the overall salary evaluation, that was designed *a priori*, the gender-salary analysis was unplanned. Rather than planning at the study's inception to go in looking for it, the relationship was discovered in the sample. The investigator was drawn to this finding by carrying out several non-pre-specified evaluations, thereby discovering what the sample revealed about gender and salary. Thus, the data, rather than the investigator, chose this new focus. When the data determine the analysis, our commonly used statistical estimators (i.e. means, standard deviations, confidence intervals, and p-values) do not function reliably since they were never designed to apply to this scenario. The formulas for these quantities are no longer accurate. They were designed to handle one source of variability (sampling error). However, in this circumstance, there are two sources; 1) sampling error, and 2) the random selection of the analysis.

This issue requires additional elaboration, because its recognition has important consequences for the interpretation of many research efforts. We pointed out earlier that the careful selection of a sample to address the scientific question of interest does not prevent random sampling error from generating the sample's answers. In order to measure the role of sampling error accurately, the investigator turns to the

---

[*] Also, although we may wish to rely on type I and type II error to provide some assurance that sampling error has not led us to the wrong conclusion about the population, that reliance fails here, for reasons that will be provided shortly.

mathematical procedures supplied by statistics. This quantitative field has provided the computations that convert the sample's information (the data) into the best estimates of effect size (e.g., means and standard deviations). Researchers rely on the accuracy of these estimators to inform them about the population from which the sample was drawn.

It is important to note that these estimators do not remove sampling error. Instead, they channel this sampling error into both effect size estimates (e.g., means) and the variability of these estimates (e.g., standard deviations). If the researcher is also interested in inference (i.e., statistical hypothesis testing), then statistical procedures will channel sampling error into p-values[*] and power[†]. Thus, when used correctly, statistical methodology will appropriately recognize and transmit sampling error into familiar quantities that researchers can interpret.

Unfortunately, these estimators are corrupted when there is a source of random variability beyond that produced by sampling error. In the case of our investigator, the second source of variability is produced by the random analysis selection.

Recall that, in this example, the scientific question that was planned during the design phase of the study was whether the overall mean salary was \$75,000. However this question has been supplanted by the question of the equality of salaries between men and women junior faculty. This replacement was suggested to the investigator by the data. Specifically, this means that the researcher would not have selected this question if the data did not suggest that the salaries of men and women were different. The sample data produced an answer to a question that the researcher had not asked, inducing the researcher to ask the question in a *post hoc* fashion.

---

[*] A p-value is the probability that that there is no effect in the population, but the population has produced a sample in which there is an effect due to chance alone. Thus, the p-value is a measure of sampling error.

[†] Power in this example is the likelihood that there is an important gender-salary relationship in the population, but the population has produced a sample in which, strictly due to chance alone, no gender-salary relationship is observed.

However the sample data is full of sampling error. Other samples obtained from the same population would provide not just a different answer to the gender-salary relationship question, but, in addition, would supply other "answers" to questions that had not been asked. Since the data are random, and the data are proposing the research analyses, then the analyses themselves are random. This is the random research paradigm.

Statistical estimators do not perform well in this environment, losing their optimal properties. Operating like blind guides, they mislead us about what we would see in the population based on our observations in the sample. Therefore, since we do not have good estimators of the effect of interest in the population, the best that we can say is that these *post hoc* findings are exploratory and must be confirmed.

2.4.5 The Valid Rendered Invalid

We can quickly show in an example that our commonly used estimators are misleading in the random analysis or random research paradigm. An arboreal scientist wishes to estimate the height of tree saplings planted two years ago. He collects a sample of n saplings and measures their heights $x_1, x_2, x_3, \ldots, x_n$. As an estimate of the average tree height in the population of two year old saplings, he simply uses the sample

mean, $\bar{x} = \dfrac{\sum_{i=1}^{n} x_i}{n}$. This is the natural estimator that is most commonly

and appropriately used to estimate the population mean. What is the motivation for this estimate? First, we select the variable that we want to measure. In this case, we let x_i be the height of the ith tree. The height of the ith tree follows a normal distribution. This permits us to write the

probability "density" function of X as $f_X(x_i) = \left(2\pi\sigma^{-2}\right)^{-1} e^{-\frac{1}{2\sigma^2}(x_i - \mu)^2}$.

Next, we acknowledge that we observe a sample of n tree heights. The fact that the measurements are independent of one another allows us to multiply the normal distributions together to create a likelihood func-

tion $L\left(x_1, x_2, \ldots x_n\right)$, where $L\left(x_1, x_2, \ldots x_n\right) = \left(2\pi\sigma^{-2}\right)^{-n} e^{-\frac{1}{2\sigma^2}\sum_{i=1}^{n}(x_i - \mu)^2}$.

Taking a derivative to find the maximum of this function reveals that

$\sum_{i=1}^{n} x_i - n\hat{\mu} = 0$, or $\hat{\mu} = \sum_{i=1}^{n} x_i \Big/ n$. Additional work demonstrates that this arithmetic average is not just a good estimate of the mean, but is in fact the best, unbiased estimate of the population mean [6].

Note however, that, in this brief mathematical development, the only variability that was permitted was variability among the sapling heights. The methodology on which the mathematics depended was 1) fix the variable you want to measure using a process external to the data, and 2) observe a sample of n of these measurements from a normal distribution. Once the scientist said that he would measure height, the sampling error that is generated is based on the sample-to-sample differences in heights, heights that follow a normal distribution.

However, now suppose that the investigator saw something unusual about the girth of the trees. Based on what the data revealed to him, he now wishes to use the estimator $\overline{Y}_n = \sum_{i=1}^{n} y_i \Big/ n$ to measure mean girth where y_i, $i = 1, 2, 3, \ldots, n$ are the girths of the saplings. However, the sampling process is different. In this case, the data suggested to the investigator that it may be worthwhile to estimate sampling girth. Thus, the sampling process is now 1) let the data select the girth variable, and 2) observe a sample of n tree sapling girths from the normal distribution. This leads to a different, and much more complicated estimate of the sample mean, since sampling error must be taken into account for the variable selection. Attempting to implement the usual sample mean in this circumstance is using an estimator that has non-optimal properties. The new, random methodology has rendered the arithmetic mean invalid, and untrustworthy. This is the hallmark of random research.

2.4.6 Exploratory vs. Confirmatory Analyses

In the setting of random research, the usual sample estimators are undermined because the assumption on which their accuracy is based is false. The estimators are designed to be accurate when there is only one source of variability, a situation that occurs when there is a fixed analysis plan and only one source of variability. In the preceding circumstance, there are two sources of variability 1) the random sample's selection of the analysis and 2) the sample-to-sample variability of the data. These two sources of variability wreck the ability of our commonly used estimators to provide reliable estimates of the true population measures. This is the trait of exploratory estimators.

A graphic example of a dysfunctional estimator would be as follows. Assume that a young parent discovers that his child is sick. An emergency visit to the pediatrician reveals that the child has an acute illness, but one that can be easily treated with the prompt use of a prescription medicine. The parent with the child and prescription go to the pharmacist. The pharmacist, after reviewing the prescription, tells the parent that the required medication is a combination of three compounds that can be quickly mixed and administered. After a brief time, the pharmacist returns with the preparation. Anxious to follow the doctor's orders, the parent prepares to give the child the first teaspoon of medication right there in the pharmacy. However, just when the teaspoon is placed on the child's lips, the pharmacist rushes out, telling the parent that, although the liquid that the parent is preparing to give the child contains the right constituents, the proportions of those compounds are wrong because the device he used to mix them is broken.

The exploratory estimator, like the defective medication mixture, is a distorted and unusable concoction that should be avoided. Most parents would steel themselves and withdraw the teaspoon containing the defective medication. Just as the bad medicine cannot be given, the researcher must exert discipline and avoid hasty interpretation of the exploratory estimator. It is the fortunately rare (and perhaps, rarely fortunate) parent who would insist on giving the defective compound to their child in the face of this news.

Continuing, now that the parent recognizes that the compound is faulty, are their any steps that he can take to remedy the preparation at hand. Should it be diluted? If so, then by how much? Should additional compounds be added? If so, then in what quantities should they be added? Since the precise defect in the compound's formulation cannot be identified, the parent only knows that the medication is defective, and that he cannot correct it. All he can do is ask the pharmacist to dispose of what he has in hand, and then start the process again, this time using the required compounds in the right proportions.

Similarly, an exploratory estimator cannot be repaired. We only know that a critical assumption in the estimator's construction has been violated. Since we cannot rehabilitate the estimator, we can only ask that a study be carried out that does not violate the estimator's assumptions. Specifically, this means that the study is 1) designed to answer the prospectively asked question, and 2) the study is executed and its data analyzed as described in the protocol (concordant execution). In this paradigm, the estimators are trustworthy measures of population effects.

2.4.7 Untrustworthy Estimators in Medicine

As an example of the inaccuracy of estimators that are based on exploratory analyses, consider some recent work in the study of congestive heart failure (CHF). CHF occurs when the heart, becomes damaged over time, producing weakness in the heart muscle. This weakness means that the heart is no longer able to pump blood effectively, and blood backs up or "congests" in other organs. Left untreated, the heart failure will worsen, eventually killing the patient. There are many medications used to treat heart failure. One class of them is angiotensin converting enzyme inhibitor (ACE-i). This medication is effective in the treatment of CHF, and its use has increased dramatically since the 1980s. Unfortunately, many ACE-i treated patients experience undesirable side effects of this therapy; among the worst of these is kidney failure.

As a response to this undesirable side effect profile, angiotensin II type I receptor blockers were developed. It was hoped that this newer class of agents would be safer than the original ACE-i treatment while continuing to confer a survival benefit for patients with CHF. In order to compare the relative safety of angiotensin II type i receptor blockers to that of ACE-i therapy, the Evaluation of Losartan in the Elderly Study (ELITE) was undertaken[7]. This was an expensive clinical study that was designed to compare the effectiveness of the angiotensin II type I receptor blocker losartan to the ACE-i captopril.

The primary analysis goal of this research was to compare the ability of these two drugs to preserve kidney function.

This study recruited 722 patients and followed them in for 48 weeks. At the conclusion of ELITE, the investigators determined that the kidney function was equally preserved by the two medications. However, the investigators discovered that 17 deaths occurred in the losartan group and 32 deaths in the captopril group, a result that produced a p-value of 0.035. These finding received the principle emphasis in the discussion section of the manuscript. Although the need to repeat the trial was mentioned in the abstract, the balance of the discussion focused on the reduced mortality rate of losartan. According to the authors, "This study demonstrated that losartan reduced mortality compared with captopril; whether the apparent mortality advantage for losartan over captopril holds true for other ACE inhibitors requires further study." Others even went so far as to attempt to explain the mechanism for the reduction in sudden death observed in ELITE 1 [8], [9].

To the investigators' credit, ELITE II [10] was executed to confirm the superiority of losartan over captopril in improving survival in patients with heart failure. The primary endpoint in ELITE II was total mortality, an endpoint that required 3152 patients. This was almost five times the number of patients recruited for the ELITE I study. These patients were followed for 18 months, almost twice as long as the duration of follow-up in ELITE I. At the conclusion of ELITE II, the cumulative all-cause mortality rate was not significantly different between the losartan and captopril groups. The investigators conceded "More likely, the superiority of losartan to captopril in reducing mortality, mainly due to decreasing sudden cardiac death, seen in ELITE should be taken as a chance finding."

Although the finding in ELITE I may have been due to chance alone, the principle difficulty presented by the first study was that the statistical estimators commonly used to measure the mortality effect were inaccurate when applied to this surprise finding. Specifically, the ELITE I investigators reacted to the unanticipated mortality benefit by moving the focus of their study from the prospectively declared kidney function analysis to the new mortality trend seen in the data. This decision was generated by the finding in the sample. However, since the sample was random (selected as one of millions of possible samples from patients with CHF), the selection mechanism for the analysis is random (since other samples would have produced other unanticipated findings). In this random analysis setting, the usual statistical estimators provided misleading information about the population effect from the observed findings in the sample. This is the hallmark of the random protocol. By letting the data decide the analysis, the analysis, and the experiment, becomes random, and the resulting statistical estimators become untrustworthy.

2.4.8 Strip Mining the Dataset

Exploratory analyses are often not prospectively announced. Since the analyses are chosen by the data, the estimates of effects derived from these evaluations can produce false and misleading results. However, exploratory analyses can still retain the semblance of structure and clear direction. Data dredging, on the other hand, is the examination of all possible relationships in a database for significance[11].

If confirmatory analyses can be described as the process by which a selected, well planned, circumscribed treasure site is excavated for a jewel that all reliable evidence suggests is present, then data dredging represents the complete and methodical strip mining of the data-site. This process churns up the information landscape, searching for any pattern at all in the data and proclaiming that the association leeched from the sample is present in the population. Data dredging is rarely announced *a priori*. Conclusions from data dredging are often incorrectly interpreted, as though every association that is observed in the sample reflects a true association in the population. As Dr. Miles declares, "If you torture your data long enough, they will tell you whatever you want to hear" [11].

The problem with such an exhaustive examination is that the dataset contains many red herrings and false leads that are due entirely to the random aggregation of events and are therefore not reflective of a true finding in the population. Such findings are misleading and can misdirect the scientific community. These spurious relationships appear because only a small number of subjects were chosen for the sample, and the pattern exists only for those subjects. If a larger number of subjects were selected, the pattern would disappear. The difficulty is that one cannot be certain when a pattern appearing in the sample is a true reflection of a pattern appearing in the population. We must keep in mind that a dataset's value is limited to the degree to which it accurately reflects the findings in the population, and that the scope of this reflection is limited. While data dredging can tell us much about the sample, it can be remarkably unrevealing about the population.

2.4.9 Subgroup Analyses

Subgroup analysis refers to the examination of the findings of a research effort's endpoint(s) for only one of the many subsets of the entire study cohort. There are many different subgroups of subjects in a research effort. In subgroup analyses, the effect being evaluated in the research effort is evaluated within different strata (e.g. gender, or income level). Since subgroup analyses are commonly not declared prospectively, and are identified often because they appear to display interesting relationships in the data, they are appropriately viewed as exploratory.

The best advice to the researcher when examining the subgroup analyses of others is "look, but don't touch". In carrying out subgroup analyses, the researcher must be aware that, unless they are planned very precisely[12, 13], they too represent exploratory analyses.

2.4.10 Analyzing the Entire Population

It is important for the researcher to differentiate between confirmatory vs. exploratory analyses. The essential difference between confirmatory analyses and exploratory analyses is timing and planning. Confirmatory analyses are planned prospectively in order to ensure that the appropriate data are precisely collected, and that bias-reducing protective mechanism are in place. Type I error bounds for confirmatory analysis plans are provided and are set before the data are collected. A statistical power analysis is completed to ensure relationships that are identified between variables in the population are very likely to be embedded in the sample. Having the analysis plan in place before the data are collected ensures that the findings in the data (that contains sampling error) do not influence the analysis plan. Exploratory analyses arise commonly from observations that are made based on the data. Since the data choose the analyses, and the data are random, the analyses become random. In this setting, the statistical estimators are untrustworthy, and the results based on these analyses cannot be generalized to the population.

However, when the sample equals the population, the situation is quite different, and the concern for random research vanishes. Recall that the root of the difficulty in random research is how to handle sampling error. This necessity is removed immediately if the researcher can study every subject in the population; in this case there is no sampling error. In fact, there is no "estimation" since the population parameters are directly measured.

As an example [14], consider a laboratory researcher interested in characterizing the measure of abnormal glucose metabolism in diabetic patients who are admitted to a community hospital during July and August 2003. There are two possible candidates for the research endpoint — glycosylated hemoglobin (HbA1c) or fasting blood glucose levels. In this circumstance, there is no requirement for choosing only one prospectively. Here, the sample is the population, and the issues of sample extension and generalizing results are not germane. The investigator chooses and studies every member of her population. She does not estimate parameters; she simply measures them. There is no need for standard errors, and no need for inference testing, because sampling error was not involved in the selection of the subjects. There is freedom in choosing (and re-choosing) the endpoint here.

However, this endpoint selection liberty gained by studying the entire population is counterbalanced by the generalizability restriction — the results of this two-month evaluation apply only to this hospital and only for the time frame during which the measurements were made. They cannot be applied to other community hospitals, and should not be applied to the same hospital for different time frames.

The distinction between analyzing a sample and analyzing a population is critical. In population research, every result applies to the population (since the entire population was included in the analysis), but there can be no attempt to generalize beyond the population. In sample-based research, only a small number of analyses are reliable, but these analyses can be extended to a much larger population from which the sample was obtained.

2.5 The Utility of Exploratory Analyses

At this point, the reader will have realized that the use of exploratory analyses is prevalent in research. In fact, we are surrounded by evaluations that are based on exploratory analyses. Such analyses include, but are not limited to 1) changes in the analysis of an endpoint measure that was selected *a priori*, 2) the selection of a new endpoint based on an observation in the data, and 3) an analysis in a subgroup of the data. Whenever the execution of a research effort is altered due to an unanticipated finding in the data, the research becomes discordant (i.e. its execution is no longer governed by the prospectively written protocol) and the analyses are exploratory.

However, we must also concede that researchers cannot be expected to identify at the outset of a research effort the totality of the analyses that they will want to carry out at the study's conclusion. While scientists will certainly want to have a prospectively asked question that motivates the generation of the sample, the logistical efficiency of the research effort will suggest that they should collect as much relevant information as possible from their sample for "additional analyses". In addition, when it is time to publish the results, the scientists will have to affirmatively reply to journal reviewers and editors who may like to see additional analyses carried out. A researcher unwilling to execute these additional, unplanned analyses may be accused of hiding data.

Thus, the research efforts will be combinations of confirmatory and exploratory analyses. The sequence of events is typically that an interesting exploratory analysis is followed by a confirmatory one, the latter being used to confirm the former. This confirmatory analysis should not represent an attempt to slavishly reproduce the findings of exploratory analysis, as in the following humorous example:

> The chef at a hotel in Switzerland lost a finger in a meat cutting machine and, after a little hopping around, submitted a claim to his insurance company. The company, suspecting negligence, sent out one of its men to have a look for

himself. He tried the machine out and lost a finger. The chef's claim was approved.*

Exploratory analyses are commonly useful because they provide the first data-based view of the future. Thus, despite their limitations, exploratory analyses will continue to play an important role in research efforts. However, they should be reported at a level and tenor consistent with the inaccuracy of the estimators on which they are based.

On the other hand, the confirmatory work to reproduce the exploratory analysis should be designed to evoke and elaborate in detail the result of the exploratory analysis so that information about the mechanism that produced the exploratory relationship becomes clearer. The confirmatory analysis will, in all likelihood, require a different number of subjects, perhaps a more precise measure of the endpoint, and a different analysis than that presented in the exploratory study.

2.6 The Process of Analysis Triage

It has been commonly argued that investigators should choose a small number of endpoints to analyze in a research effort, putting all of their effort into measuring these endpoint accurately. However, the relative affordability of statistical analyses suggest that investigators, once they have the data in hand, carry out all of the analyses they believe are relevant. As we stated in the previous section, practice tells us that we cannot prospectively identify all of the analyses that we will want to carry out; some *post hoc* evaluations will be necessary.

The researcher must retain control on the scope of the research analyses. However, it is critical to understand that analysis control does not mean analysis reduction. Analysis control means the deliberate, prospective selection of that small number of analyses on which the benefit of the research intervention will be judged from among the many analyses that the investigators will execute. Thus, control here does not mean reducing the number of endpoint evaluations and end-

---

* Candidate story for the Darwin award, 2003.

point hypotheses tests to be executed. However, control does require that the investigators prospectively decide on the few analyses that will permit generalizations to the population at large.

The best advice that can be given to the researcher is to divide or triage their analyses during the design phase of the study. This triage process first requires that the investigator decide which analyses will be confirmatory and which will be exploratory. The confirmatory analyses will be those evaluations on which the research will have its primary assessment made. These analyses must be prospectively declared.[*] The non-prospectively declared findings are described as exploratory.

When the results of the research are described, the findings will be divided into two sections. The first, receiving the greatest prominence, will be the confirmatory findings. After these have been presented in detail, the *post hoc* analyses should be appear in a following section that is clearly denoted as exploratory. This process will make it clear to the reader which analyses can be generalized to the population at large, and which will require additional work.

2.7 The Pros and Cons of P-values

Scientists engaged in sample-based research have, at one point or another, had to come to grips with the rigidity of *p*-values. This tool has a long and complicated history.

The idea of the *p*-value and significance testing is based on the work of the agricultural statistician Ronald Fisher. As he worked through the design and analyses of agrarian experiments in the 1920s, he concluded that one must consider the likelihood that findings from the research sample were just due to sample-to- sample variability. He further stated that, if there was a greater than five percent chance that a population that had no positive findings produced a sample with positive findings, the positive findings in the sample should be discarded since the likelihood that they were due to the random, meaningless aggregation of events was too great[15,16].

---

[*] In clinical research, these confirmatory analyses are commonly divided into primary analyses and secondary analyses according to well defined rules. For example see Chapter four of Moyé LA. *Multiple Analyses in Clinical Trials: Fundamentals for Investigators* (2003). New York. Springer.

It was this latter concept that was completely absorbed by some scientific circles, particularly the medical research community. The pre-eminence of the 0.05 level is all the more astonishing since this threshold set by Fisher was completely arbitrary, with no buttressing theory identifying this level as an appropriate threshold for any of the non-agrarian, scientific discipline. There is no deep, mathematical theory that points to 0.05 as the optimum type I error level—only tradition.

The complex motivations for the wholesale embrace of hypothesis testing and p-values have been discussed by Goodman [17,18]. Unfortunately, many researchers have substituted the 0.05 criterion for their own thoughtful, critical review of a research effort, and this replacement has led to uninformed research interpretation. For example, in some studies, highly statistically significant effects (i.e., results associated with small p-values) have been produced by small, inconsequential effect sizes. In other research efforts, small p-values themselves were rendered meaningless when the assumptions on which they had been computed were violated. Additionally, there is the observation that statistical significance may not indicate true scientific, biologic, clinical, or economic significance. These problems have been noted in the literature [19, 20, 21, 22, 23]. Poole [24] pointed out that the mechanical, reflexive acceptance of p-values at the 0.05 level is the nonscientific, easy way out of critical and necessary scientific discussions.

The reduction of a complex research endeavor's result to a single p-value is perhaps at the root of the inappropriate role of significance testing. This condensation effort may be due to the fact that the p-value is itself constructed from several constituents. Sample size, effect size, and effect size variability are important components of the p-value and are directly incorporated into the p-value's formulation. However, in reality, what is produced is not a balanced measure of these important contributory components, but only a measure of the role of sampling error as a possible explanation for the results observed in the research sample. Thus, p-values are deficient reflections of the results of a research effort, and must be supplemented with additional information (sample size, effect size, and effect size precision) in order for the study to receive a fair and balanced interpretation.

The measures of research effort concordance[*], sample size, effect size, and effect size precision are all important perspectives that the investigator must jointly consider with the *p*-value when interpreting a research endeavor's results.

2.8 Multiple Testing Issues

By multiple analyses, we mean the collection of statistical hypothesis tests that are executed at the conclusion of a research effort. The term "collection" is deliberately broad, encompassing all of the evaluations that investigators understandably feel compelled to conduct during the analysis phase of the research.

The combination of 1) the well-motivated concerns for complete use of the database, 2) the generation of mechanistic evidence to understand the true nature of the relationship that is being studied, and 3) the need thoroughly examine the results are all motivations for the use of multiple analyses in research. Since each of these analyses involves a statistical hypothesis test, and each hypothesis test produces a *p*-value, a relevant question is "How should this collection of *p*-values be interpreted"?

Specialists have argued in articles [25] and editorials [26] that these *p*-values should be ignored. Some have contended that they should be interpreted as though the value of 0.05 is the cutoff point for statistical significance, regardless of how many *p*-values have been produced by the study.[†] Others believe that investigators should be able to analyze all of the data, and then choose the results they want to disseminate [27], [28], [29].

The discussion earlier in this chapter forces us to reject the results of the investigator who, after inspecting the magnitudes of each of the *p*-values, makes an after-the-fact, or *post hoc* choice, from among them. This "wait and see what analysis is positive" approach violates the underlying critical assumption of the *p*-value construction (i.e., that

---

[*] Concordance is the desirable property of research that derives from the tight match between the research execution and the plans for its execution as stated in the research protocol.

[†] This interpretative procedure is termed "nominal significance testing" or "marginal significance".

the data with its embedded sampling error should not choose the analysis), and must itself be rejected. However, this rejection requires us to have a clear plan to deal with the multiple testing issue.

2.8.1 Familywise Error Rates

Keeping track of the likelihood that we make at least one type I error in the K hypothesis tests that have been carried out is a useful approach to the multiple testing issue. This measure of the overall type I error rate has previously been termed the familywise (type I) error probability (or error level). It is commonly abbreviated as FWER [30], [31] and will be designated as ξ.

There is a critical difference between the standard type I error level for a single endpoint and ξ. The type I error probability for a single, individual analysis focuses on the occurrence of a misleading positive result for one and only one evaluation. This is the single test (or test-specific) error level. Alternatively, the familywise error level focuses on the occurrence of at least one type I error in the entire collection of analyses. Thus, ξ incorporates the test-specific type I error levels for each of the analyses taken one at a time, and in addition, includes the combinations of type I errors.

2.8.2 The Bonferroni Procedure

One of the most important, easily used methods to accomplish this prospective control over type I error rate using FWER is the Bonferroni procedure [32]. This procedure is briefly developed here.

Assume in a research effort that there are K analyses, each analysis consisting of a hypothesis test. Assume also that each hypothesis test is to be carried out with a prospectively defined type I error probability of α; this is the test-specific type I error level or the test-specific α level. We will also make the simplifying assumption that the result of each of the hypothesis tests is independent of the others. This last assumption allows us to multiply type I error rates for the statistical hypothesis tests when we consider their possible joint results.

Our goal in this evaluation is to easily compute the familywise type I error level, ξ. This is simply the probability that there is a least one type I error among each of the K statistical hypothesis tests. In probability theory, the occurrence of at least one event is defined as the *union* of events.

An exact computation for the familywise type I error rate is readily available. Let α be the test-specific alpha error probability for each of K tests. We need to find the probability that there is not a single type I error among these K statistical hypothesis tests. Under our assumption of independence, this probability is simply the product of the probabilities that there is no type I error for each of the K statistical tests. Write

$$\left(1-\alpha\right)\left(1-\alpha\right)\left(1-\alpha\right)...\left(1-\alpha\right) = \prod_{j=1}^{K}\left(1-\alpha\right). \qquad (2.1)$$

Therefore ξ, the probability of the occurrence of at least one type I error, is one minus the probability of no type I error among any of the K tests, or

$$\xi = 1 - \prod_{j=1}^{K}\left(1-\alpha\right) = 1 - \left(1-\alpha\right)^{K}. \qquad (2.2)$$

From equation (2.2), we see that identifying the value of ξ requires some computation. Bonferroni simplified this using Boole's inequality that states that the probability of the occurrence of at least one of a collection of events is less than or equal to the sum of the probabilities of these events. This is all that we need to know to write

$$\xi = P[at\ least\ one\ type\ I\ error] \leq \sum_{i=1}^{K}\alpha_{i}. \qquad (2.3)$$

If each of the test-specific type I error levels is the same value α, (2.3) reduces to

$$\xi \leq K\alpha. \qquad (2.4)$$

Equation (2.4) of course can be rewritten as

$$\alpha \leq \frac{\xi}{K}, \qquad (2.5)$$

expressing the fact that a reasonable approximation for the α level for each of K hypothesis test can be computed by dividing the familywise error level by the number of statistical hypothesis tests to be carried out. We will now explore the possibilities provided by unequal α rate allocation.

2.8.3 Differential Alpha Allocation

As an illustration of the Bonferroni procedure, consider a research effort in which the investigators choose 5 of 15 prospectively defined endpoints as primary analyses (for convenience we number these primary analyses as 1 to 5). From equation (2.5) that each of these endpoints will be assessed will have a test specific alpha error of $\xi/K = 0.05/5 = 0.01$. Thus, the test-specific α level rates will be $\alpha_1 = \alpha_2 = \alpha_3 = \alpha_4 = \alpha_5 = 0.01$. Since the sample size of a research effort increases as the type I error level decreases (assuming everything else about the comparison, e.g., event rates, type II error levels, etc., remains constant), then the sample size required to be able to carry out the statistical hypothesis test for an α error rate of 0.01 may be prohibitively high for the investigators. The specter of inappropriately small test-specific α error rate thresholds remains even after the investigators reduce the number of endpoints for which statistical hypothesis tests will be carried out.

As an alternative [33], we might consider applying different weights to the type I error levels. Looking at the example in the previous paragraph, consider the possibility of $\alpha_1 = 0.03$, $\alpha_2 = 0.01$, and $\alpha_3 = \alpha_4 = \alpha_5 = 0.0033$. In this situation, there are three separate α levels. Since $\alpha_1 + \alpha_2 + \alpha_3 + \alpha_4 + \alpha_5 = 0.0499$ which is less than 0.05, this test-specific α allocation conserves the familywise error level. Once we designate different α level thresholds for each endpoint, we introduce a new distinction between the trial's confirmatory, primary analyses. The specific differential allocation of α introduced in this paragraph permits a greater risk of a type I error for primary endpoint 1, less risk of a type

I error for primary endpoint 2, and even a smaller type I error level for primary endpoints 3 to 5.[*]

This is a useful procedure but its implementation begs the question of how to choose the weights for the test-specific α error levels. Formal mathematical arguments to optimize the choice of the test-specific α error levels should be shunned in favor of developing the researchers' *a priori* intuitions for the choice of these weights. This intuition should be built upon (1) understanding the research question, (2) the relative persuasive power of the endpoints to convince the scientific community of the effect of the intervention, and (3) the need to keep the sample size of the study small enough for the study to be executable.

Alternative approaches to the multiple testing issue include sequentially rejective procedures [34, 35, 36, 37], and *p*-value resampling [38, 39, 40]. These are automated calculations by which computer algorithms calculate the *p*-value threshold of significance. However, it is the author's view that the investigators are the ones who should choose the appropriate type I error level for each of the hypothesis tests that will be used to control the familywise error rate.

2.9 Sample Size Computations

Good research efforts, regardless of their size, are characterized by careful planning, controlled execution, and disciplined analysis. An important component of the design of a clinical trial is the sample size calculation. The sample size computation is the mathematical formulation that determines how many subjects the study should recruit. It is based on the area of application, the magnitude of the finding of interest, and background data concerning the variables to be measured.

The mathematics of sample size computations are well described in the literature [i.e., 41, 42, 43, 44, 45]. It can be said that the sample size computation is the forge upon which the research effort is hammered. Since the sample size computation requires 1) a clear set of assumptions about the primary scientific question to be addressed by

---

[*] Some of the more complicated consequences of this approach are discussed in Chapter four of Moyé LA. *Multiple Analyses in Clinical Trials: Fundamentals for Investigators* (2003). New York. Springer.

the study, 2) the expected experience of the control group, 3) the change anticipated to be induced by the research intervention or exposure, and 4) concerns about type I and type II errors, clearly both the investigators and quantitative methodologists must be involved in the estimation of these entities.

However, the sample size computation, although composed only of mathematics, must also reflect the administrative and financial settings in which the study will be executed. These important logistical considerations that are not explicitly included in the arithmetic of the sample size calculation must nevertheless receive primary attention. For example, the availability of subjects may be an issue. Alternatively, in the case where a new intervention has been developed at great cost, its accessibility may be the factor that limits the size of the research effort.

These latter, nonmathematical considerations must be factored into the final sample size determination in order for the experiment to be executable. They are blended into the plans for the research in general, and the sample size in particular, through several mechanisms during the design phase of the study. Among these mechanisms are (1) re-examination and alteration of the population from which the research sample will be recruited, (2) re-formulation of the primary analysis of the study, and (3) changing the anticipated duration of the study if the study involves following subjects over time. Each of these maneuvers is acceptable when considered and finalized during the design phase of the study.

For this appropriate mixture of statistics, expertise from the field of application, and administrative considerations to occur, the dialogue between all involved parties should be frank, honest, and collegial. The resulting robust research design with its recomputed sample size will be consistent with scientific, logistical, and financial considerations, making the study both scientifically rigorous and executable.

2.10 Conclusions

The investigator must develop two different skill sets to carry out illuminating research. The first is the talent of discernment. The researcher must be a careful observer. Always interested in identifying a new and sometimes useful relationship, the researcher is served by a natural drive to be a curious and on the lookout. This is a skill that can be fun to develop and satisfying to carry out. However, when developed in isolation, this skill will produce very little of lasting value.

In order to be truly illuminating, the skill of asking the right question must be matched by the ability to obtain the correct answer. This second skill depends on very different talents than the first. While the first skill of observation requires innovative vision, the second requires steadfastness, and where the first skill requires imagination, the second requires discipline and patient effort. The best investigators have devoted time and patient energy to sharpening both of these characteristics.

In sample-based research, the investigation's results must be viewed through the prism of methodology. Tantalizing results produced by bad methodology are relatively meaningless and, in all likelihood are impossible to be reproduced. This is because clearly defined principles must be followed in order to accurately estimate what happens to subjects in a large population from observations on only a few of its members. These principles require that the data generated should not produce the question that the data are then used to address. While there are important logistical reasons for prospectively asking the research question before the data are collected, the principle reason is to anchor the research question, protecting it from the influence of sample error in the data.

Some researchers may believe that this restriction places unnecessarily restraints on them; that they are being asked to view the research results "from the prison" rather than "through the prism" of methodology. However, there are a wealth of design tools that are available to researchers, providing some of the keys to release (or at least loosen) their shackles. A first principle in this process is that no team of investigators should be denied or discouraged from analyzing any component of the dataset that they desire. The unique combination of inquisitiveness, insight, and intuition that investigators possess should be encouraged, not repressed. However, it is best that, once these large number of analyses are selected, that they be divided into those that are prospectively planned, and, those that are selected based on findings in the data.

The major advantages of prospectively planned analyses are that the estimates of effect size, confidence intervals, and standard errors are trustworthy. Non-prospectively planned, exploratory results can be carried out and reported, but they must be clearly labeled as exploratory. Because, these exploratory analyses are essentially chosen by the data (i.e., the investigator was not obligated to report the result of the analysis, but chose to report it because of the magnitude and direction of the finding), the commonly used statistical estimators are corrupted and frequently provide misleading results.

The second level of triage during the design phase of a study is carried out among the prospectively planned analyses, dividing them into primary analyses or secondary analyses. Primary analyses are those analyses on which the conclusions of the study will rest. Each of the primary analyses will have a prospectively set type I error level attached to it in such a way that the familywise error does not exceed the community accepted level (traditionally 0.05). This is consistent with the statement that a small number of key questions should be addressed, accompanied by careful consideration of the necessity and extent of adjustment for multiple comparisons [46].

Several tools are available to investigators as they allocate type I error rates among the primary analyses of their clinical trial. Among the first is the unequal allocation of type I error levels. The Bonferroni procedure provides equal allocation of the α error among the several primary analyses. This typically produces type I error levels that are too small for some of the analyses, in turn generating a sample size that is beyond the attainable. Investigators can allocate type I error selectively among the different primary analyses. The only rules that they are obligated to follow are that the allocation be made prospectively and that the type I error levels be made to conserve the familywise error level ξ.

Finally, the concordant research effort's results must be based on the joint consideration of the effect size estimate and that estimate's precision, magnitude of the confidence interval width, the p-value (and, when appropriate, the power). Once we are convinced that the findings of a well designed and well executed research effort are not due to random chance, we can then use our interpretative skills to determine whether the study findings are truly pearls of great price.

References

1   Kapadia A,, Chan W, Moyé L. (2004). Mathematical Statistics with Applications. New York. Marcel Dekker.

2. Pitt B, Segal, R., Martinez, F.A. et al. on behalf of the ELITE Study Investigators (1997). Randomized trial of losartan versus captopril in patients over 65 with heart failure. *Lancet* 349:747–52.

3. Packer, M., O'Connor, C.M., Ghali, J.K., et al for the Prospective Randomized Amlodipine Survival Evaluation Study Group (1996). Effect of amlodipine on morbidity and mortality in severe chronic heart failure. *New England Journal of Medicine*.**335**:1107–14.

4. Young, A. (1771). *A Course of Experimental Agriculture*. Dublin, Exshaw et al.

5. Owen D.B 1976. *On the History of Probability and Statistics*. New York and Basal Marcel Dekker, Inc.

6. Bickel P.J., Doksum K.A. (1977). *Mathematical Statistics: Basic Ideas and Selected Topics.* San Francisco: Holden-Day 312-332.

7. Pitt, B, Segal, R., Martinez, F.A. et al. on behalf of the ELITE Study Investigators (1997). Randomized trial of losartan versus captopril in patients over 65 with heart failure. *Lancet* **349**:747–52.

8. Jensen, B.V., Nielsen, S.L. (1997). Correspondence: Losartan versus captopril in elderly patients with heart failure. *Lancet* **349**:1473

9. Fournier A., Achard J.M., Fernandez L.A. (1997). Correspondence: Losartan versus captopril in elderly patients with heart failure. *Lancet* **349**:1473.

10. Pitt, B., Poole-Wilson P.A., Segal, R., et. al (2000). Effect of losartan compared with captopril on mortality in patients with symptomatic heart failure randomized trial–The losartan heart failure survival study. ELITE II. *Lancet*.**355**:1582–87.

11. Mills, J.L. (1993). Data torturing. *New England Journal of Medicine*. 329;(16).

12. Yusuf, S, Wittes J., Probstfield, J., Tyroler, H.A. (1991). Analysis and interpretation of treatment effects in subgroups of patients in randomized clinical trials. *Journal of the American Medical Association*. **266**:93–8.

13. Moyé, L.A., Deswal, A. (2001). Trials within trials; confirmatory subgroup analyses in controlled clinical experiments. *Control Clinical Trials.***22**:605–619.
14. Moyé L.A. (2001). The perils of nonprospectively planned research. Part 1: Drawing conlcusions from sample-based research. *American Clinical Laboratory*: April 2001. 34–36.
15. Fisher, R. A. (1926). *Statistical Methods for Research Workers.* Edinburg.Oliver and Boyd.
16. Fisher R. A. (1933). The arrangement of field experiments. *Journal of the Ministry of Agriculture.* 503 - 513.
17. Goodman, S.N. (1999). Toward Evidence–Based Medical Statistics. 1: The p-value fallacy. *Annals of Internal Medicine.* **130**:995–1004.
18. Gigerenzer, G., Swijtink, Z., Porter, T., Dasxton, L., Beatty, J., Kruger, L. (1989). *The Empire of Chance.* Cambridge, Cambridge University Press.
19. Walker, A.M. (1986). Significance tests [sic] represent consensus and standard practice (Letter). *American Journal of Public Health* 76:1033. (See also journal erratum **76**:1087.
20. Fleiss, J.L. (1986). Significance tests have a role in epidemiologic research; reactions to A.M. Walker. (different views) *American Journal of Public Health.***76**:559–560.
21. Fleiss, J.L. (1986). Dr. Fleiss response (Letter) *American Journal of Public Health.* **76**:1033–1034.
22. Walker, A.M. (1986). Reporting the results of epidemiologic studies. *American Journal of Public Health.***76**:556–558.
23. Thompson, W.D. (1987). Statistical criteria in the interpretation of epidemiologic data (different views) *American Journal of Public Health* **77**:191–194.
24. Poole, C. (1987). Beyond the confidence interval. *American Journal of Public Health.* **77**:195–199.
25. Nester, M.R., (1996). An applied statistician's creed. *Applied Statistics.* 45: 4401–410.
26. Rothman, R.J. No adjustments are needed for multiple comparisons. *Epidemiology* **1**:43–46.

27. Fisher, L.D., Moyé, L.A. (1999). Carvedilol and the Food and Drug Administration Approval Process: An Introduction. *Controlled Clinical Trials* **20**:1–15.
28. Fisher, L.D. (1999). Carvedilol and the FDA approval process: the FDA paradigm and reflections upon hypothesis testing. *Controlled Clinical Trials* **20**:16–39.
29. Moyé, L.A. (1999). P–Value Interpretation in Clinical Trials. The Case for Discipline. *Controlled Clinical Trials* **20**:40–49.
30. Hochberg, Y., Tamhane, A.C. (1987). *Multiple Comparison Procedures*, New York , Wiley.
31. Westfall, P.H., Young S.S. (1993). *Resampling Based Multiple Testing: Examples and Methods for P-Value Adjustment.* New York. Wiley.
32. Miller, R.G. (1981) *Simultaneous Statistical Inference,* 2nd ed. New York Springer.
33. Cook, R.J., Farewell, V.T. (1996). Multiplicity consideration in the design and analysis of clinical trials. *Journal of the Royal Statistical Association.* **159**:93–110.
34. Zhang, J., Qwuan, H., Ng, J., Stepanavage, M.E. (1997). Some statistical methods for mulitple endpoints in clinical trials. *Controlled Clinical Trials* **18**: 204–221.
35. Wright, S.P. (1992). Adjusted P–values for simultaneous inference. *Biometrics* **48**:1005–1013.
36. Hommel, G. (1988). A stepwise rejective multiple test procedure based on a modified Bonferroni test. *Biometrika* **75**:383–386.
37. Shaffer, J.P. (1986). Modified sequentially rejective multiple test procedures. *Journal of the American Statistical Association* **81**:826–831.
38. Westfall P.H., Young S.S., Wright S.P. (1993). Adjusting *p*-values for multiplicity. *Biometrics* **49**:941–945.
39. Westfall, P.H., Young, S. *P*-value adjustments for mulitple tests in multivariate binomial models. *Journal of the American Statistical Association* **84**:780–786.
40. Westfall, P.H., Krishnen, A., Young, S.S. (1998). Using prior information to allocate significance levels for multiple endpoints. *Statistics in Medicine* **17**:2107–2119.

41. Lachim J.M. (1981) "Introduction to sample size determinations and power analyses for clinical trials". *Controlled Clinical Trials* **2**: 93-114.
42. Sahai H., Khurshid A. (1996). "Formulae and tables for determination of sample size and power in clinical trials for testing differences in proportions for the two sample design". *Statistics in Medicine* **15**.1-21.
43. Davy S.J., Graham, O.T.(1991). "Sample size estimation for comparing two or more treatment groups in clinical trials". *Statistics in Medicine* **10**: 3-43.
44. Donner A. 1984 ."Approach to sample size estimation in the design of clinical trials - a review".Statistics in Medicine **3**: 199-214.
45. George S.L. and Desue M.M.1974." Planning the size and duration of a clinical trial studying the time to some critical event". Journal of Chronic Disease **27**:15-24.
46. Proschan, M.A, Waclawiw, M.A. (2000). Practical guidelines for multiplicity adjustment in clinical trials. *Controlled Clinical Trials.***21**:527–539.

Chapter 3
The Investigator and Administration

3.1 The Proposition

Devote regular and frequent time to administrative duties. For the first month of employment as a junior scientist, spend 50% of your time working through administrative issues. The next four months, reduce this effort to 25% of your time. Beyond that, reduce the time that you spend in administrative activities to between 10% and 15% of your effort. When you become the principal investigator of a research project, increase your administrative time commitment to between 30% and 40%.

It is my hope that, at the conclusion of this chapter, you will be convinced of the preceding statement's worthiness.

3.2 Administrative Oxygen

The underlying theme of this text is that professional development, not productivity, is the star by which the investigator should steer their career. Therefore, since the unremitting pursuit of productivity is not the only metric that determines the scientist's worth to either themselves or their institution, productivity can temporarily be set aside, replaced by other worthy considerations. Chief among these is administration knowledge and obligation.

There are many administrative activities that must occur in order for us to carry out our research and pursue our careers; we frequently relegate these activities to the background. Our buildings are available for us to use. Our offices are provided, always available, and amply heated and lit. The telephones, faxes, and elevators work. Paychecks get delivered. Support staff get paid in a regular and predictable fashion. However, although we commonly consider such activities as autonomic affairs, their proper execution is not guaranteed. Administration handles all of these for us, yet we are frequently oblivious to these important efforts. In some sense, administration is like oxygen. Whether we acknowledge it or not, whether we like it or not, we need it and therefore take advantage of it.

3.3 Experience vs. Expertise

Before we begin, we have to remove from our consideration one unhelpful notion, i.e., that scientists can work without administrative experience. This is a canard. Every scientist gains administrative experience. The real issue at hand is whether the scientist can gain good, useful and industrious administrative skills rather than dreadful, frustrating and counterproductive practices. For many, experience is simply repeating the same mistakes. Therefore, as a junior investigator, you are not interested in gaining mere experience, but in acquiring expertise. You are interested in learning the right lessons from your past and applying these lessons to future occurrences.

Administrative diligence is commonly the least appreciated but the most useful and rapidly acquired skill that the investigator can acquire. Attention to administration can facilitate your inter-collegial interactions, speed your travel arrangements, allow you to purchase necessary equipment, and help you to obtain teaching assistant support for your class. Administrative attentiveness is the means to these productive ends. In essence, the successful application of administrative efforts allows you to more quickly bring needed resources to bear in order to carry out your work

3.4 Learn Your Administrative Surroundings

As a junior scientist, you will no doubt feel (and sometimes be made to feel) that you have to get to work right away. This commonly means that you will work with a small number of individuals, talking and communicating with them regularly. If your work is technical, then you will in all likelihood be required to focus your attention on small but important methodological details. However, it is very useful and instructive to gain a larger view on your institutional surroundings. Learning how your school, university, corporation, or institute views you and your work product will provide a new and important point of view.

3.4.1 Institutional vs. Personal Perspectives

A common practice that many institutions have is the review of the productivity of each of its scientists. This review can take place locally (e.g. peer review of the caliber and quantity of your professional activities), or regionally. Commonly, reviews for important promotions are considered at a state or national level. These assessments are carried out by proficient scientists who may work at areas and locales both different and distant from yours.

Many junior scientists are surprised when reviews of their work by these distant superiors are negative. The lackluster comments of these evaluations fly in the face of the young scientist's own anticipations. These personal expectations were based on the fact that the junior investigator believed that he had been industrious. Not only did the young scientist work hard, but, in many cases, this hard work held the promise of productivity. For example, these activities for which the researcher received little credit may have hastened the development of a product. Alternatively, the junior scientist's concerted work effort may have actively contributed to the appearance of several journal articles. Nevertheless, the reviewing professionals were not persuaded by this scientific output.

The most likely explanation for the concerns[*] expressed in the evaluation was the sense that the junior scientist's work was not really contributory. The reviewers did not deny the productivity; they simply don't think that the productivity was on track. From the reviewers' perspective, the contributions were not helpful and were not in accord with their goals and expectations for the junior scientist. Even though the junior researcher came to believe in the importance of his work, the institutional perspective on his activities was quite different. The junior scientist may have anticipated this reaction if he had understood his organization's perspective on his own work. However, this understanding was missing, because, like most of his peers, he was just too busy working to seek it out.

As a junior investigator, you may or may not agree with the institution's current priorities, but you certainly have to learn them. Most commonly, this means taking the time to learn about and absorb these goals. If you work for a corporation, then a clear understanding of the agenda of the company and how you fit into that corporate schema can be very instructive. A junior faculty member at a university is best served if she understands the mission statement of the school, and how that mission statement is translated into goals and objectives for faculty activities. Knowing the institution's ideas and plans for your own work can be an illuminating and early guide to the junior scientist as you begin to shape your own research agenda. This knowledge can help you to avoid surprise reactions by distant superiors to the reviews of your work, superiors who are more closely aligned with the institution's ideas and plans than you are. Similarly, understanding institutional goals and objectives can remove misunderstandings of the importance

---

[*] In a small minority of cases, these reviews may have been meant to do damage and be personally disparaging. This is an issue that we will discuss in Chapter 6.

of your own work, misunderstandings that can be lethal to your career advancement.

3.4.2 Focusing on Your Local Environment

Assume that you will work forty hour a week (clearly an underestimate for most of us) for fifty weeks a year over forty years. This reveals that your career will span at least 80,000 hours. Choosing to take only 15-20 of these 80,000 hours to learn what it is that the people who support your department actually do can pay handsome dividends for everyone; dividends that far exceed your relatively small time investment in this matter.

It is a truism that most institutions that hire scientists recognize the support that scientific productivity needs. This support includes editing support, drafting and figure support, photographic support, scheduling support, and support for supply procurement. To this traditional list, we can add information technology support, that includes, but is certainly not limited to, computer hardware support, e-mail support, electronic security, and software support. These echelon units do not exist merely for themselves. They are provided for the purpose of assisting you. Specifically, their raison d'être is to support your work. Yet these resources are squandered if you do not know how to use them in the right combinations that will amplify and not suppress your attempts to be productive.

The best way to understand how these units can shore up your work efforts is to appreciate 1) what it is that these support units provide, 2) how their product is offered, and 3) who pays for them. This requires an investment of your time and effort. To be sure, some of this material will be covered in whatever orientation that your institution offers you as a junior scientist. However, sometimes efficiently run orientations can be disorienting because they cover so much relatively unrelated material so quickly. Thus the planned orientation process can be overwhelming and you may not be able to absorb it all.

Therefore, consider the following strategy in order to more properly understand the role of these assistance groups. Several days after the official orientation has concluded, conduct your own unofficial re-orientation. Revisit the departments to learn in some detail what is that they do, and specifically how that work can support your own productivity goals and objectives. Most importantly, be sure to add the names, phone numbers and email address of these support people to your contact list. Take the time to add a note about what it is that these people do.* Understanding what the various departments accomplish and how they interact creates a solid logistical foundation for your work. However, you have to be willing to spend the time to learn who is available, and what it is that they do. Only then will you know who to contact when you need them.

Additionally, this re-orientation not only provides a more complete assessment of the roles of these individuals, but your presence appropriately produces in the support staff a sense of satisfaction. People react positively when they see that the professionals who they support have taken the time to express a genuine interest in both them and their activities.

A critical component of these discussions is to learn how these individuals are financially supported. Remember that their departments, like all institutional divisions, have to justify their work. If you choose to use their services, you should acknowledge their services appropriately. However, it can be unclear as to what is the best way to express this acknowledgement. If you are in the process of applying for grants, then you may have to include a specific monetary amount in the grant. Alternatively, you may be asked to complete a job request that would serve as documentation of your use of this service. The point is, you should acknowledge what resources you use appropriately. The only way to learn to do this is to speak with the people whose services you require.

Occasionally, you may be moved to write a letter to the director of your institution, or to the dean of your school, formally acknowledging the pivotal work of support staff for your product. Certainly, this effort would take some more of your valuable time. However in uncertain economic periods, when support staff are commonly those who lose their positions because they are "unessential", an honestly expressed show of support from a promising scientist can have a bene-

---

* I have found that while I can remember an individual fairly easily, I unfortunately will quickly forget what it is that they do. A brief note embedded in their contact information can refresh my memory at once.

ficial impact far beyond the twenty minutes that it took to compose the letter.

3.4.3 Be Familiar with the Rules

Perhaps there will soon be a day when scientists and their support staff can function in an unfettered and regulation-less environment, but today is not that day. Whether you are working at a private institution, for the government, or in academia you can be sure of two things; 1) there are rules where you work that attempt to set the parameters of interaction and behavior, and 2) the number of those rules is growing.

The reasons for the growth of these rules are multitudinous and beyond the scope of this discourse. The simple message here is that you will need to pay some attention to these rules. You may not be aware of it, but, in all likelihood, part of the agreement or contract that you signed to seal your agreement to work at your institution binds you to follow all of its rules.

Although you certainly have an idea about the caliber of professional conduct, you may not know some important details. Ignorance of these details can get you into some difficulty. What are the rules for computer use? Can you use official institutional stationary for consultative work? Can the institution scan your computer for inappropriate material (and just what is the definition of inappropriate material)? What constitutes correct and incorrect use of email? How should actual and perceived sexual harassment be handled? How should disputes about research ethics be mediated? Your knowledge of the answers to these questions can have a direct and personal impact on you. In a controversial situation that arises involving your activity and conduct, you may have behaved and acted correctly. However, even though your behavior was well motivated, an important metric that the institution will use to measure your behavior is whether you followed the institution's rules. This may be the final arbiter of your performance in a controversial area.

You don't have to memorize the rules; just have them handy. U.S. Supreme Court justices who make complicated and critical legal determinations are of course expected to know the US Constitution. However, they don't memorize it, instead commonly carrying small, inexpensive copies of the US Constitution with them for easy reference.

Since the justices of the highest court in the land don't memorize the highest law of the land, you should not feel compelled to try to memorize your institutional rules. However, like the justices, you should keep a copy of these regulations within easy reach. At some institutions, these rules are in electronic format on an institutional Web site. If so, consider book marking them. If their size is not overwhelming, consider placing a copy of them in your personal computing device. Remember, you don't have to commit them to memory. You simply have to be familiar with them, and know where to find them when you need them.*

3.5 Mentoring Committees

One of the first, constructive administrative acts in which the junior scientist can involve herself is in the creation of a mentoring committee. While the first reaction to this suggestion is commonly a combination of helplessness, indecision, and impatience, the dividends derived from this committee's construction can be profound. Sometimes, this committee can save your career.

A mentoring committee is a small and select group of senior scientists that provide useful instruction to you based on their experiences. They can point out useful activities for you to become involved in, and, just as importantly, help to direct you away from career hazards that you cannot yet see but that they can easily visualize. As a junior scientist, you are constructing your career compass that will point out the direction in which you should move and develop. This compass must be regularly tested, and it is the mentoring committee that can provide this critical calibration on a regular and frequent basis.

While this committee's advice can be formal and is sometimes predictable, the committee's counsel can be most effective and timely when it is based on solid knowledge about you. The more that they can know and understand about your motivations and talents, the better able they are to serve you. The greater your investment in this process, the

---

* Keep in mind that in the dynamic environment that the workplace is, rules can change over time. Therefore, you need to examine them periodically (say, yearly), to make sure that important alterations have not occurred without your knowledge.

greater the benefit that you derive. Therefore, play an active role in the committee discussions.

Take the time to lay a solid foundation for their advice to you. While there are many circumstances in which the hyper-efficient use of time is important, meeting with mentoring committees is not one of them. In order for the committee to provide information that is tailor-made for you, the committee members must know you, understand you, and gain a full and fair appreciation of your strengths and weaknesses. Therefore, avoid meeting with your committee by email or by telephone conversation, instead choosing to visit with them personally. Meet with them on a regular basis, providing your own complete and honest appraisal of your progress and setbacks. In order for them to assist and counsel you, they must know of your defeats as well as your victories The broader and deeper their perspective on you, the better the caliber of advice that they can provide to you.

Keep in mind that you will be most helped by fair, critical appraisal. A mentoring committee that always and only finds good things to say about you may be comforting but not constructive. Seek an honest critique from your committee. Create the cordial environment that permits its members to be comfortable in making a fair and balanced appraisal of you. Of course, remember that while criticism of your professional development is essential, it should also be supportive and not destructive.

Crises in your career, like periodic droughts and floods where you may live, are unavoidable. While you cannot always predict them, you can take some important steps to prepare for their inevitable arrival. Creating a mentoring committee whose members have good institutional standing is an important preparatory step. The right mentoring committee can be instrumental in a crisis. During your time of trouble, you will need the best support that you can find. You may be so overwhelmed by the difficult circumstance that, for a time, you may be unable to rely on your own professional judgment. In this desperate situation, you will need all of the best and instructive advice that you can find. A good, mature, and knowledgeable mentoring committee can be a solid anchor to which you can cling during these tumultuous times. If you have stayed in regular and frequent contact with them throughout your career, they will have come to know and understand you. With the depth of this knowledge in full view, this committee can provide timely and important advice for you in your time of difficulty.

Since the demands that you will place on the mentoring committee will be critical to your career growth and development, give its membership the closest and most careful consideration. Some mentoring committees are automatically assigned by the junior scientist's governing institution to give the researcher a modicum of a support structure. While this can be a good beginning, it is only a beginning. Spend a few months speaking with, and perhaps, most importantly, observing senior scientists where you work. When the committee begins to fall into place in your own mind, approach the prospective members individually, asking them to consider being a member of your committee.

Additionally, you may consider assembling a smaller committee composed of scientists who are not in close physical proximity. This type of committee can be very useful as well, providing information and feedback to you that you cannot receive from counselors who work where you do. The distant, and sometimes non-institutional perspective can provide important pieces that you need in order to complete an objective picture of your career progress.

Finally, keep in mind that, at some point in your career, you will be asked to provide mentoring advice to scientists who are much younger and much less experienced then you. Dwell on your experience as a junior, mentored scientist as you consider your role on their committee. Have the goal of providing as good as, if not better, mentoring advice to them than you received.

3.6 The Genesis of Research Team Leadership

A natural consideration for any junior researcher is reflection on the possibility of their playing a future role in team leadership. While the different components of leadership skills is discussed in detail in Chapter 8, one of the key features of leadership is administrative diligence. Without the ability to successfully administrate a research team, your capacity to be responsive to that team's logistical needs is impaired. As a consequence of this defect, the ability of your team to produce its best science will be blunted because it cannot bring to bear the resources that it needs to create the best scientific product. In this section we will discuss the administrative side of leadership with specific focus on research team management.

While you may get the opportunity to work on the science of the research project regularly, you will have to come to grips with the administration of the grant on a daily basis. This includes, but is not limited to, communications with the agency that funds your grant, discussions with co-investigators who work in distant research centers, talks with your research team, conversations with animal and human protection committees, as well as communications with ancillary study committees, compliance committees, core lab committees, and publication committees. You will also directly and indirectly supervise the work of receptionists, secretaries, information system operators, and computer specialists. In order for your project to function smoothly, these specialists must have confidence in their own abilities and understand their roles in the research project.

As in any activity, there will be important questions and conflicts that arise. In these predictably common and potentially tumultuous circumstances, your colleagues and support teams will look to you to resolve those conflicts, and to keep the research project moving in the right direction. Whether a computer programmer, or a secretary can keep their jobs will depend on your ability to carefully and skillfully manage the financial aspect of the grant.

3.6.1 When in Command.....Command.

Being principal investigator can be a daunting experience that junior investigators shy away from. However, when the opportunity presents itself, you have to seize it, applying the very best of yourself to this new challenge, whatever the consequences. Defeat comes more from the fear of failure than from taking a bold and calculated risk. Consider the following example.

> Chester Nimitz was the commander of the United States Naval Pacific Fleet immediately after the US suffered its major defeat at Pearl Harbor in 1941. After this debacle, Nimitz's major responsibility was to maintain a naval presence in the Pacific Ocean until the United States could recover from its

losses of men and equipment. Sensing that the enemy was moving across the Pacific Ocean toward Hawaii, he chose to face them at Midway Island. Nimitz's strategy of choosing to defend this little known island far from the expected line of enemy attack, instead of placing his remaining forces to protect the Hawaiian Islands, ran contrary to the naval strategy at the time. This idea also led to severe, vocal criticism of him by the governing powers in Washington D.C.

To make matters worse, Nimitz's senior commander, Admiral Halsey, was stricken with a debilitating skin disease, effectively removing Halsey from any role in the anticipated upcoming battle. When Nimitz asked Halsey to name his own replacement for the upcoming confrontation with the enemy, Halsey immediately replied "Ray Spruance"

Ray Spruance was known to Nimitz. A promising younger officer, Spruance had demonstrated his skill at handling smaller ships in battle. However, Spruance had never been in command of a naval task force, and it was unknown whether he would have the character, temperament and faculties to command a large combination of ships of different types in action. When Nimitz, somewhat uncomfortably, wondered aloud about the reaction to this controversial appointment from political leaders who were already critical of Nimitz's decision to defend Midway Island, Halsey calmly replied "Chet, when in command....command."

As a junior investigator, you will most likely have the opportunity to manage a small grant that has a microcosm of these problems. However the management skills that you master in small research activities will serve you well as you progress to the administration of larger projects.

3.7 "Business is Not My Business!"

Before proceeding any further, we need to clearly face one issue. If you are named as the principal investigator on a research activity, be it a grant, or contract, then it is yours (and no one else's) responsibility to

administer that project. In order to be a productive scientist, you must
become a competent administrator.

    This can be a difficult responsibility for junior investigators to
accept. You probably have no formal education or training in business
administration, and most junior scientists have never run a business.
We have spent most of our productive time becoming scientists, not
attending business schools. Commonly, when asked, a junior scientist
will retort that their business is not business, but science.

    Therefore, lacking the knowledge, training, experience, and
expertise to manage a business enterprise, many junior scientists balk at
the prospect of accepting administrative responsibility for a project.
They are unable to learn the important coping skills that they must master in order to successfully run a grant because they cannot purge themselves of the notion that running the grant is not their affair. Because
these researchers think that administration is not their business, they
refuse to open themselves to learning the skills and abilities that they
must master in order to successfully supervise the grant. In the young
researcher's mind, she sees herself as the scientist, not the grant supervisor. The job of administration, so she thinks, is someone else's job,
perhaps anybody else's job, but certainly not her job!

    The problem worsens for these new principal investigators as
they are first approached by, and then pursued by important and unre-
solved administrative matters in which they have no stated interest and
no real concern. These scientists find that their days are increasingly
consumed by increasingly frustrating supervisory difficulties. Because
they are never really handled successfully, these administrative problems rise up like weeds to strangle the scientific content of the grant. It
is no wonder that these junior workers find the entire grant experience a
messy and discomforting business; an affair that should be shunned —
not pursued.

    To some, the reaction of the junior scientist to the specter of
administrative management is like the response of a new and naïve
parent to the newly discovered difficulties of raising a child. Much of
the work is unpredictable, messy, and sometimes painful. However, it
is the rare parent who does not divest themselves of their naiveté about
parenting for the sake of their child. Good parents learn everything that
they can learn, and do anything that they can do, for the sake of their

children. Leaving their preconceived notions behind, they plunge (or are plunged) into the problems of childrearing, using everything they know and can comprehend in order to raise their child right. Their responsibility is not to be perfect, but to simply and in an open-hearted fashion do the best that they can know and learn to do. As a junior investigator, you are better served by this model than by one that is based on thickening the husk that separates you from administrative matters.

3.8 Three Rules for Basic Project Management

We have pointed out the plain truth — administrative support and sustenance are the tracks on which the research train runs. Just as the train will not reach its destination if the tracks are twisted or bent, your research grant cannot proceed unless its administration is smooth and predictable. Specifically, you will not be able to carry out the science of your project, (that was the reason that you applied for an accepted the research role), unless you can get its administration running easily and efficiently. We have also affirmatively stated that the successful execution of the both the administration and the science of the project has been placed squarely, unavoidably, and undeniably on your shoulders.

Completely accepting this onerous responsibility is your first major task as principal investigator. Carrying out the related activities is, however, relatively straightforward. The successful administration of the research project requires your time and your knowledge. Specifically, in order to successfully administer the grant you must

1 – (Take the time to) know the subject matter.
2 – (Take the time to) know your people on the grant.
3 – (Take the time to) effectively communicate.

If you are willing to devote the best of your time and effort to these activities on a regular and frequent basis, project management will, by and large, be straightforward. Your role as an administrator will probably not be (and, perhaps, should not be) effortless. Careful consideration of these three conventions will always be required, but to degrees and variations that are dictated by the dynamics of the research efforts.

However, by providing consistent and patient attention to each of these three tenets, solutions to complicated administrative problems will commonly be readily at hand. We will consider each of these in turn.

3.8.1 Know the Subject Matter

The foundation of the research project is scientific knowledge. On this bedrock was laid the research question that motivated the project. Upon the conclusion of the project, what has been learned is added to the growing repository of scientific information. It should be no surprise that scientific concerns are the basis of administrative decisions.

Essentially, the administration of the research project is the creation and delivery of the right combination of financial, technological, and human resources to allow the scientific work to progress. Administering the grant is analogous to building the tracks on which the research train will ride. Someone must know the direction in which the train is to go, so that the tracks are laid correctly and on the right bearing. A thorough knowledge of the underlying science is required to correctly identify this heading.

Administrative research diligence begins with superior knowledge about the science of the research grant. Whether to hire an additional project coordinator or an additional programmer is based on the scientific needs of the project. Whether an additional receptionist is necessary may depend on whether more investigators are needed for the project, which in turn is based on the project's underlying science. The administrative decisions that are made are decided for the benefit of the project; therefore a complete understanding of the underlying science is critical.

The requirement of this knowledge base mastery by the principal investigator may not be as self-evident as it first appears. Certainly, you as principal investigator, are expected to understand the scientific content of the research that you are directing. However, understanding the technical details of just one component of the grant, leaving the rest of the details to others, with only a broad and general understanding of the science in these other areas is not sufficient. You must be conversant with it all.

Discussions about administration are commonly more about the details of the research project than they are about its overarching theme. As the science becomes more technical, more specialists are necessary to conduct the research. An anticipated and natural consequence of this is the distribution of knowledge base among several scientists. The problem this fragmentation produces is that, when an administrative problem arises, its solution requires different and disparate facts about the project. One person does not know all of the facts, but a combination of people do. Thus, the conversations necessary to solve these problems have to be delayed because either 1) the required scientists with the critical information cannot get together due to interminable schedule conflicts, or 2) the scientists are unable to successfully integrate the required pieces of information that they have because they do not understand (or are not willing to take the time to understand) the administrative problem. Thus, the administrative problem, like a nagging toothache, becomes a chronic issue, growing into a larger and larger distraction from the research effort. However, if the principal investigator takes the lead in mastering the knowledge base of each component, many of these administrative difficulties can be quickly resolved because she has already absorbed the requisite knowledge.

A solid knowledge background is one of the pivotal quantities on which leadership skills are built.[*] Mastery of this material requires a great effort. A research project that contains a collection of clinical, genetic, and quality of life components that will be entered into a central database requires the principal investigator to learn important details of each of these components. The principal investigator should also understand the data entry component. Learning this material is not hard, however, it does takes time.

For example, if you have no computing or programming background, but are the principal investigator of a project that requires these skills for either data base development, data entry, or data analysis, then you should plan to spend several hours over a relatively short period of time discussing data base architecture with the information technologist of the project. Work with her, asking her the same questions repeatedly and in different ways and formats until you understand what it is that she is telling you about the project's development.

---

[*] Chapter 8 is devoted to a full discussion of the development of leadership capabilities.

There are two benefits that come from this effort. First (and obviously), you gain a new understanding of the use of a database for your project. When issues come up in discussions of the project, you will have a new knowledge base from which to draw, as well as the confidence that comes from gaining new critical information about an essential component of your research project. Additionally, you are viewed with new confidence by your research team as you demonstrate your commitment to the project, since this knowledge directly translates into a refined sense of the goal and direction of the project. Finally, you gain the appreciation of the information technologists since you have demonstrated the importance of their commitment to this project by affirmatively choosing to spend time with them, allowing them to explain their work to you. This kind of commitment can pay handsome rewards later in the project when they may be expected to "go the extra mile" and work unanticipated long hours for the good of the study.

In addition to learning the details of the many different scientific areas that are essential to the research project's success, it is important to integrate the scientific and administrative components of the project. There are timelines that must be satisfied for the scientific progress of the study. The arrival of specimens to a core lab must be timely in order to complete one component of the research. Data monitoring meetings must be scheduled and planned. Meetings of animal and human subject committees must be folded into the research execution. Data will be required for these meetings. Therefore, data will have to be collected, data-entered, checked for accuracy, analyzed, understood, and presented. If each of these activities is not carefully considered and planned, they tend to merge into a blurred mass of events that will continually ambush your research schedule. In addition, there is always the unexpected. All that you will know about this is that it most certainly will occur.

The solution to this aspect of the administration is an investment of your time. There is no substitute for the careful and methodological planning of the numerous research-related events that can be scheduled. This preparation requires the junior researcher to develop and improve his ability to correlate and coordinate these many activities. There is no doubt that this careful preparation is time consuming.

However, since this careful forecasting is necessary, devote an important component of your time to it so that your plans are accurate, reasonable and executable.

If you have a portable computing device, affirmatively use it to help you schedule and track these events. After all, if these devices are good for anything, they are good for keeping track of dates and deadlines. In addition, handheld digital recorders are available to log and save spontaneous verbal notes and memos to yourself. If you get an idea or remember and issue but cannot take the time to write it down, use the recorder. Later, play it back and write down the message.

Improve your management skills by actually mapping the timeline of your research in detail. Layout each component and meeting that the research effort will require for the foreseeable future of the research scheme. There is software available that allows you to do this on personal computers. There is even software that will run on a personal desktop assistant. If you are comfortable using electronic devices for these planning activities, this software can be invaluable to your planning.

There are two advantages that you derive from creating this research activity map. The first is that you will have a legible record of the progress of your research with its many deadlines against that you can more objectively gauge the process of your research. Secondly, and more importantly, engaging in this process demonstrates to yourself the limits of your own knowledge of the research project's activities. By developing the map, the information that you do not have but require in order to complete the schema of activities and deadlines becomes clear to you. New questions arise as you review the timing of meetings and the data that you will be required to supply at these meetings. Choke points in the research activity will also become apparent to you as you begin to lay the activities of the research out.

When the map is complete, just don't set it aside. Continually apprise and update it as time and your research project activities advance. Take the time to update your task map as new developments occur. Schedule and vigilantly protect the time you need to review the progress of the research in all of its aspects.

By devoting the time to master the subject matter of your research, you place yourself in a perfect position to efficiently, accurately, and benevolently make decisions about resource availability to keep your research project on track. Examined another way, the maximum size of the research project that you can constructively manage is, to a great extent, determined by the degree to which you can master the contents of the research's subject matter.

3.8.2 Know Your People

In all likelihood, although you, as principal investigator, hold the ultimate responsibility for the grant, you are not its only worker. There will be co-investigators, information specialists (i.e. data entry and or computer programmers), a business administrator, and perhaps a receptionist or secretary. Each of these workers commits some of their time to your research project, and each has skills and abilities that are different from yours. These team members will work hard because of their professional competence even though they may not derive as much credit from the grant as you.

While some workers may already be on the job, it is not uncommon for you to find that you need to hire additional people. This can be intimidating prospect for the junior researcher for two reasons. The first is that, the skills that you are looking for are very likely skills that you do not have. For example, you may be required to hire a computer programmer with skills in modern data base management. With no such skills yourself, how can you satisfactorily test the knowledge base of the individual that you are hiring? Secondly, you may not have ever hired anyone before in your life.

Try to avoid being over-influenced by an impressive CV. Sometimes, important weaknesses in the interviewee's personality or character can hide behind a thick resume. At a period in my career when I owned a Physician's Association. I had the responsibility of hiring physicians. One physician I considered for the job, had the most impressive curriculum vitae that I had ever seen at the time. In addition to training in medicine, this physician was well versed in both the classics and the hard sciences, having attained a Ph.D. in physics. The CV was over 100 pages long. In fact, it was the only CV that I had seen then (or have ever seen) with a table of contents, and an index. This CV was not a resume – it was a publishable autobiography! I hired him, a choice that was based to a large degree on the persuasive power of this impressive document.

Unfortunately, my decision to hire this physician was one of the worst hiring decisions that I ever made. Within a few short weeks of his employment, it became clear that he was unable to manage patients using the appropriate and accepted standards of the community. Ultimately, he had to be removed from his job for incompetence, an action that produced a hail of angry and litigious correspondence from the discharged physician. Judging the book by its cover led to disaster.

Rely on the expertise of others to judge the competence of the individual. If you are not able to assess the skills of the candidate, allow your colleagues who have such experience to interview the candidate and provide an assessment. Sometimes, you may have to borrow the skills of a worker in another project who is in a better position to assess the abilities of the candidate than you are. This requires that you, at the very least, be able to clearly articulate the needs of your research unit.

Secondly, develop the skill to conduct a balanced and fair interview process. Make sure the candidate understands the requirements of the position that is being offered. Have several people interview the candidate. As a useful metric to help you develop your interviewing skills, find someone more senior than you with whom you can jointly conduct the interview. You can learn a great deal from watching the senior person conduct their component of the interview.

During the interview, be sure to give the candidate an opportunity to fully express their goals, their skills, and why they are a good candidate for the job. If you do not have the expertise the job requires, then encourage the interviewee to explain in simple and plain terms what they will do to accomplish the task. If they can explain this clearly, and the approach can be validated by others who have experience in the field, you may have discovered a fine technical person who also is communicative.

Finally, be sure to be patient. A diligent, capable, and fair-minded search commonly does not yield quick results, but does commonly yield good and lasting ones.

Alternatively, the cadre of workers that are already part of the project require your attention as well. This is not just a statement of your support, but an overt demonstration of that consideration, and the clearest demonstration of that support is your time commitment to them. As professionals, they will work hard without it, but administering this grant becomes much easier if they have regular access to you. Working in an atmosphere where everyone contributes for the good of the project is ideal, but that atmosphere has to be created. It is most simply and directly created if you as the principal investigator demonstrate your willingness to commit your time to help with their problems and issues. The most important commitment that you can make to your research team is your time. Choose to build, and not just live in your dream of a good research endeavor.

There are two purposes for this effort on your part. The first, that pays an immediate dividend, is to learn what it is that each of your team members needs in order to carry out their component of the research project. Changes in technology may require new equipment. A computer may need a replacement hard drive, or a new peripheral device. There may be a personal issue that requires not your solution, but your sympathetic ear. Although one might argue that, theoretically, channels already exist to handles these needs, in reality, the utility of those channels are amplified by your attendance. You are perceived as choosing to take the time away from something else "more important" and, instead, spend that time with someone who may not feel they should have access to your time. This effort on your part speaks volumes about your commitment to the project.

Years ago I was responsible for a large grant involving heart disease. On my project team I had a project manager whose job it was to help coordinate the activities of a team of co-investigators located at other sites. Typically, my encounters with this project coordinator were not good. He would frequently confront me with a new problem that I didn't know the project had, demanding an immediate solution. This individual was not a bad person, and actually, he was a very good project coordinator. Unfortunately, our interactions seem to always take place in crises settings — settings that were becoming more intemperate and unhealthy. While I did not wish to avoid the newly discovered problems with the project, I certainly wanted to stay away from these tempestuous encounters.

In an act of desperation, I hit upon the idea of meeting with the project manager on a regular basis, whether we had a new problem or not. He and I began daily ½ hour meetings that, once started, spanned over five years. As we spent regular time together, I provided for him what he needed from me as his investigator — access. From these meetings I learned much about the basic operation of the project. In addition, we both learned each others operational styles. Thus, we developed a joint management operation that served us well. What I was required to bring to this effort was my time.

I must confess that, as I considered instigating these meetings, part of me rebelled against the concept of meetings, That part of me contemptuously complained that here was yet one more piece of my precious time that would be sliced out of my day. Nevertheless, all that was required of me was the time-sacrifice demanded of an investigator. Bluntly, the time was coming out of my days one way or another. It was up to me whether I supplied that time constructively in meetings, or destructively in acrimonious conversation. I preferred to invest this time working together with a colleague rather than against him.

Also, it might be useful to note that the real solution to this dilemma was not the decision to begin these constructive meetings. The actual solution to this problem was my reaction to the discontent of the disruptive confrontations. Essentially, choosing to take the time to consider the problem led to its solution and the resulting meetings. Again, the solution was time commitment.

The coordinated application of attitude, time and knowledge as you get to know your people can strengthen your project is several dimensions. Attitude simply means that you choose to offer the best of yourself to help each member of your team accomplish their tasks. Be open to the concept that revealing your best outlook is as important a contributor to the team-building concept as your time commitment. An investigator who spends time with an individual on his team when he doesn't want to meet with them merely means that he has chosen to take the time to inflict his team member with his discourtesy and bad mindset. It is a peculiar facet of human nature that each of us can sense when the person we are talking to or interacting with does not want to be with us. This is communicated through a medium of emotions that is only partially conveyed with words.

In one project, the junior principal investigator obtained a grant to develop a research team that would work on a project that spanned several years. She assiduously assembled a collection of investigators, nurses, and programmers. The nature of the project was such that these research personnel worked in several cities, and therefore, the only way to conduct business on a regular basis was by conference call. In the beginning of the research project, this principal investigator was communicative and open. Her willingness to admit an error in judgment and to accept the correction of her team members not only generated an atmosphere that was a pleasure to work in, but also created a fertile intellectual environment that produced good scientific fruit. However, over time, the principal investigator's attitude transformed. Before, the principal investigator was pleased to engage in discussions, answer questions, and guide the discussions of his team. Now, she was clipped and sharp in her comments, and seemed eager to bring conversations to a premature end in order to get on with her daily agenda. Her tone became increasingly clinical, cynical, and critical.

Another change in her style was in how she used her information base. This principal investigator had always been completely knowledgeable about the science of the research. In the beginning, she used this fine familiarity to facilitate discussions among the research team. Now, it was used to bluntly reveal the weaknesses of the arguments of her fellow investigators and staff, i.e. as a weapon to browbeat the staff. Her repository of knowledge, although utilized for the research project, was used against her colleagues.

The reaction of the research team was predictable. Growing tired of the blunt and condemnatory comments of the principal investigator, they volunteered less and less during the conference calls. Their silence shouted volumes about the attitude of the investigator. One by one, the team members began to withdraw the very best of their talents, insight, and expertise from the research project. It would not be fair to characterize the staff as embittered; however, just like we learn to avoid exposing our skin to acid spray, they chose to avoid the caustic comments of the principal investigator. Although the research project produced a few manuscripts, its counterproductive atmosphere of unpleasantness led to the project's rapid productivity demise. The more strident the principal investigator became, the less product the research effort generated.

As a junior investigator, recognize that you have and can succumb to personal tendencies that would lead to this disparaging management style. However, let those dark inclinations be consistently overcome by your willingness and capacity to become an affirmative, encouraging and abetting leader. Bringing the best attitude to a research team encourages the team members to bring their enlightened best to your research project.

While there are some workers who have the unique and special personalities that allow them to give themselves fully even though they receive little respect in return, many more workers require at least a modicum of respect and dignity if they are to redouble their efforts on your project in a crisis. It is sometimes helpful to recall that you are never more than a single telephone call or email from humility. The progress of your grant can be jeopardized by unseen difficulties, and, during these times of trouble, every member of your research team will need to pitch it. Specifically, they will need to work harder than they have had to or may expect to for the good of the project. That decision that they make to go the extra mile is made up of both professionalism and good will.

A good way to begin to know your team members is to learn from them their backgrounds and trainings. Get to know what they like about their jobs and those professional activities that they must engage in but don't care for. As time progresses, you will also come to understand their strengths and weaknesses. The respect that you gain from them places you in the unique position of actually helping them to strengthen their weaknesses. This mutual strengthening activity can be the most important contributions that you can make to your colleagues. Not only do they benefit from this calibration and growth, but they strengthen the research project in the long run.

One way or the other, your work with your team will leave an impact on them. Whether you ride them to the ground, or build them up, you will instill something. Sacrifice your time to build and develop your team, then let you and your team build the research project.

3.8.3 Effective Communication

The major purpose of communication is to influence the thinking and therefore the behavior and actions of others. The key to effective communication is to make the person with whom you are conversing at ease. When we are at ease we are open, and by being open, we are most likely to hear and understand the message that is being transmitted to us. Receiving the message in this spirit permits us to understand it, absorb it, and allow it to influence and guide our behavior and activities.

Sometimes the message is a short, but important one, e.g. "you are not doing your job". This is an example of a difficult message for a worker to receive from you as the principal investigator. Therefore, in order to communicate this message effectively, you will have to spend the time to put this person at ease. Only by being at ease can they accept this message and begin to make the adjustments in their behavior or conduct that would allow them to repair their shortcomings. Thus, in communication, most of the actual conversation will be to ensure that the individual is at ease. This does not mean the conversation must be full of platitudes about the weather or sports teams. Instead, these difficult conversations must use the words that convey the true sense of the topic; that sense is that you have the deficient worker's best interest at heart, are willing to spend some of your time working together with him to improve his difficulty, and that you believe, after coming to know the worker that he can overcome his shortcoming.* Since you do not mean to threaten the worker, the non-threatening language that you need to convey your information about his job performance to him should be within your reach.

Having invested the time to learn about your individual research team members, you are now in an excellent position to know the best words to say to them. There are of course various venues of communication. I would recommend that you use the most complete form

---

* Sometimes, even this approach does not work. A young private in the Confederate army during the US Civil War, when caught in an act of insubordination, was told to report to the local military tribunal for a hearing. When he reported as ordered, the disobedient soldier was shocked to learn that the tribunal for that day was not a low ranking officer, but the commanding general of the army himself, General Robert E. Lee. When brought before the general, the teenaged private began to quake with fear at being disciplined by so distinquished a leader. General Lee, recognizing the fear in this young soldier, quietly said "Don't worry son. You will get justice here." The private promptly replied "General, that's exactly what I'm afraid of!"

of communication that is possible. For example, when the choice is between a face-to-face conversation and a telephone discussion, choose the face-to-face conversation. If the choice is between a telephone conversation and an email, choose the telephone conversation. These choices are the most time consuming, but they are also the most expressive. This is because much more information is supplied by being able to read a person than by simply hearing what a person says. While attitudes can be communicated verbally, they are much more quickly telegraphed through face-to-face conversation.

Of course, much of your communication will be by telephone. Effective communication by telephone requires enhanced communication skills. Since the conversationalists will not be able to see you, they must rely on the both the words you use and the sound of your voice to convey your message. Recall the comments from Chapter One when you have conversations on the phone. Keep any edge out of your voice. Try to speak slowly so that everyone can understand what your message is without feeling that you are rushing through it just to have it over with. Use kinder language than you might use in person. Again, because the person cannot see you and they must focus more of their attention on the words that you use, you must choose these words most carefully.

Try to avoid "dashing off an email". I don't always succeed, but whenever possible, I will revert to telephone conversations rather than email. There is no question about the superior efficiency of email; however, in my view, this efficiency is not always an advantage. Short, terse messages that are rapidly conveyed are not the point of communication. The important communication between scientists should be more influential than efficient. When using email, try to make it evocative, i.e. to actually contain the complete and exact sentiment that you wish to express. My rule of thumb is to overwrite an email, being explicit about my sentiments, hoping that, by being more evocative, the sense of my reaction will be clearly communicated.

Recently I had the opportunity to use email to correspond with a colleague about a paper that he was writing for our research team. Since he was away from the office, and I did not have his traveling phone number, I composed the following first email draft:

> Daniel
> Read your paper. Here are my comments
> 1 – introduction should be more focused on the scientific question
> 2 – methods section doesn't mention the exploratory nature of the work
> 3 – results incomplete – please include subgroup analyses

This portrays the true caliber and description of my response to the manuscript draft. However, the press of time drives me to send the first, terse email draft. The problem is that, if Daniel receives the first draft receiving only my stark suggestions, he can only guess at my motivation. The message does not answer the following important questions:

> "Was my intent to be critical"?
> "Did I not like the manuscript"?
> "Do I not believe that Daniel did a good job"?

The answers to these questions are unclear to him because the message was "efficient" but unrevealing about my motivations. Daniel does not know that the press of time limited my comments, because, after all, if I had more to say to him, I believes that I would have taken the time to say more. I therefore try to send the following, different email.

> Daniel,
> How are you?
> You have worked hard on this manuscript and its present draft reflects your consistent and patient efforts. When you get the opportunity, please consider the following
> 1 – The introduction has many fine components. It would be great if it could focus more attention on the scientific question we hoped to address in our study.
> 2 – It might be best if we were clearer about that component of our work was confirmatory, (i.e. actually answered a prospectively asked question), and that was exploratory. What do you think about adding a comment about this in the methods section?

3 – I have read your results section and it is a clear portrayal of much of our work. Can you consider adding a section that discusses subgroup analyses?

Give me a call if you have any questions. Thanks again for taking the lead on drafting a manuscript describing our controversial findings.

The only way to convey my complete reaction to the manuscript is to write a message that more fully and accurately expressed my total reaction. Thus, when I send email messages, I work hard to emulate the second message and not the first. I do this by first writing the stark email message, and then add to it the terms and phrases I believe will convey my full sentiments and reactions.

When communicating with your staff, be sure to have a clear and explicit component of your conversation that focuses on what they need for you to do that would allow them to move forward with their work. As the senior manager of this project, let your team know that an important part of your responsibility is to see to it that you are doing everything that you can do to ensure that their task go as smoothly as possible.

Avoid keeping secrets. Everyone in the grant should have a complete understanding of both the long term goal of the grant, and the short term grant objectives. They should also have the opportunity to comment on these objectives and the ability to suggest alterations in your plan. As long as your team is focused on their common goal, these suggestions will make your trial stronger. When there are problems with the grant's administration, speak about them clearly and openly answering every groups questions. Recall that the focus of attention in these activities is on not just the grant, but on you as principal investigator. How you conduct yourself is critical. .

3.9 Fiscal Management

By and large, the fiscal management of the grant is easy and straightforward, simply requiring the one thing that you believe that you do not have; time, and energy. What makes the grant management so difficult is that by and large, you only give it the attention that it needs in an emergency, so many circumstances seen unmanageable.

3.10 Conclusions

Make no mistake about it — you will spend a good deal of your time carrying out administrative duties. While you have no choice about this, you can nevertheless choose how to spend this time. You can spend it consumed by and attitude of time-selfishness that will stunt the development of your project. Alternatively, you can be governed by a spirit of time-generosity. Being charitable with your time when there are already so many demands on it is difficult for many, and will appear impossible for some. Since administrative diligence requires this generosity, insist on, and encourage the character growth required for you to accomplish it. This character growth begins with the recognition that your innate value as a scientist is not affected by the external circumstances and demands of your day. We will have more to say about this in Chapter 4.

Chapter 4:
The Investigator as Collaborator

The invitation to join a research team can be a stimulating event for a junior faculty member. Whether that investigational team is newly constituted or has a well-established productivity track record, the invitation for you to become a fellow member can be quite gratifying. This chapter focuses on the particular pressures that you as a junior scientist face in these collaborative environments, and, more importantly, how you might prosper through your involvement.

4.1 Source of Esteem

An invitation for you to join a research team composed of established investigators can be gratifying and self-satisfying. However, from this soil of appreciation can grow the thorns of difficulty. If you do not carefully self-monitor and self-calibrate your response, you can be lured into very easily and, quite voluntarily, placing your own sense of self-worth into the hands of your new collaborators. While this decision can be initially gratifying when they hold you in high regard, it will almost surely damage you in the long run.

As a junior scientist, you are particularly vulnerable to the temptation of turning your sense of self-worth over to others. This is understandable since they seem, at this early stage of your vocation, to hold your career advancement in their hands. For example, whether you obtain an increase in salary is a decision decided by others. Your suitability for promotion is based on what others think of you. Whether you win an award for achievement is determined by someone else. Based on these observations, it may appear that a useful calibration of how well you are doing is how you are perceived by others. It is this natural metric that junior scientists commonly bring to their first collaborative effort. This is an important issue of character and confidence that must be faced before any real collaborative effort should be initiated.

The problems with this approach may not be apparent at first. There may be no sign of difficulty associated with turning over your own sense of self-worth when the project is proceeding well and the interactions between you and your colleagues on the research team are smooth. However, when difficult decisions have to be made, and your point of view diverges from those of your more established team members, you may no longer be held in such high regard. Since you disagree with other team members, they may communicate to you that they don't value your opinions quite so highly any more. Perhaps word gets back to you that they do not value you so highly. This can create an important personal problem for you.

The problem associated with putting your self-worth in the hands of others is that, while their approval buoys your sense of self-value, their criticism can sink it. This occurs when you make the mistake of translating these disparaging comments into the belief that, since they do not value you, you should not value yourself. This false sense that you should punish yourself saddles you with one of the worst possible and least deserved castigations – self-rejection. Self-rejection is a first step to intellectual and emotional self-destruction that you must resolutely resist. You can afford to lose many technical arguments that deal with the scientific issues at hand, but you must not lose the fight for your own self-esteem.

Self-esteem is the core belief that you have innate value independent of the opinions that others have of you, and that you are commendable regardless of what the outside world thinks of you. Sustaining self-esteem is critical to your professional development. As you gain experience in your field, you will make may administrative and scientific decisions; decisions that will generate criticism and disapproval. This disapproval can hurt you if you let if affect your self-esteem. Working to separate and shield your sense of self-worth and value from these critical comments insulates and protect you. This separation permits you to listen to criticism, to ponder criticism, and to accept criticism without injuring your core self-value and destroying yourself.

Self-esteem is not the blinding belief that you are always right. It is the conviction that you retain your value even when you are wrong. Thus, self-esteem does not inure, but instead opens you to the comments and criticisms of others.

Working in a research effort without self-esteem can be a painful affair. The unfortunate junior scientist who takes this tack works hard for the approval of others, because that approval is linked to her own self-value. However, her colleagues, being human and imperfect, sometimes provide inaccurate and unreliable feedback to her. In the face of this destructive feedback, this junior investigator may compound this error by diminishing what she thinks of herself.

With her self-esteemed reduced, the junior scientist becomes dysfunctional as a collaborator. Lacking self-confidence, she is no longer able to trust her intuition and insight, and the progress of her scientific work slowly grinds to a halt. When her research team needs her in a crisis, she is unable to exert her influence productively. The self-visualization that she is valueless and can provide nothing of consequence sinks her performance much like a heavy leg-weight sinks a swimmer.

Self-worth is a natural need, and the scientist who links their own self-worth to the opinion of their superiors will do almost anything to get their approbation. Sometimes this weakness is deliberately exploited. A manipulative senior scientist, recognizing how susceptible you are in this sensitive area, can go so far as to attempt to control you. Essentially, they can dangle acceptance before you, enticing you to carry out work or analyses that you know are wrong. Nevertheless, you may chose to carry out this work because its execution will bring approval and, with it, a false sense of self-worth.

A statistician who worked for a private corporation fell into this ruinous problem. He was an accomplished scientist who functioned effectively as a team statistician for a research project. Always anxious to please his bosses and superiors, he computed sample sizes and analyses for many experiments. However, his ability to accurately and rapidly compute was slowly but inexorably overtaken by the undesirable but real urge to keep his bosses happy. Rather than work to persuade his superiors that his approaches to important technical problems were sound and worthy of consideration, he instead prematurely ceased defending his own professional point of view in the face of this bosses' displeasure.*

The ultimate result in this case was tragic. Being unable to sustain his self-value in the face of criticism from his superiors, this promising researcher lost all confidence in himself as a competent scientist. With no self assurance, he no longer trusted the results of his own calculations. Unable to find his own talents within himself, he was reduced to sending every computation that he was asked to execute out to other statisticians, asking that they confirm his analyses. After working for many months in this wretched state, he left the industry altogether.

Before you proceed with your collaborations, first ensure that you can readily identify your source of self-worth. If that source is de-

---

* This was a difficult task to accomplish because, as we will see later, overbearing superiors can, through intimidation, warp the responses of their junior team members.

rived from a well-anchored sense of your value and significance that is independent of external events, then proceed with confidence into your new environment. However, as for most of us, if you are uncertain of your source of self-worth, stop first and repair it. Sever the link between your self-worth and your acceptance by others. Choose instead a solid, internal, and unwavering source for your sense of value. This source should sustain you regardless of the circumstances of your research.

Character growth requires that you develop the stature to respond with stability in a tempestuous intellectual environment. The ballast of an independent sense of self-worth helps you to maintain your balance in the face of these unpredictable interactions.

Recognize that, as you progress and your character developments, your sense of self-worth will come under assault. Anticipate and expect these attacks, turning them to your advantage. View your most challenging times as the days when your sense of self-value is tested. Use these times to observe how well your source of self-worth sustains you. Examine, and either repudiate or repair your source of self-value if it fails you, thereby shaping your character growth and development. Your short term goal is to have your sense of worth independent of external criticism. Ultimately, you want it to be separate and apart from your career trajectory.

Working toward this goal should not encourage inconsiderate actions on your part. While you should always consider what others think, do not let what they express influence your deep seated sense of how you value yourself. Making a mistake should not change your self esteem, and the need for an apology should not diminish it. In fact a secure sense of self-worth will make it easier to hear clearly, consider carefully, and apologize freely and openly because, while you may be under attack, that attack cannot damage your sense of purpose and self esteem.

Finally, learn to completely and unconditionally understand and accept yourself regardless of your surroundings. This will allow you to detach your sense of innate value from the opinions of others. While your coworkers and superiors can and should provide useful, instructive, and critical information to you about your performance, this source of guidance must not be a component of your self-worth. Your appreciation of your own value, when coupled with your complete and unconditional acceptance of yourself is the basis of your ability to successfully and wholeheartedly participate in a collaborative effort.

4.2 Plunge In

Once you have developed and strengthened your source of self-worth, there is nothing left for you to do but to move ahead into your new role as a collaborative researcher.

If you have several competing opportunities for collaborative effort, examine each of these closely and carefully. Take the time to have several detailed conversations with investigators on each of the projects. For each potential project, more than one conversation will in all likelihood be necessary. The first conversation will require you to listen to a broad description of the research effort. This presentation by investigators who are already involved in the study will cover the purpose of the research, the contribution that the project is expected to make to the scientific community, and the opportunity that the research will provide for your own productivity. Your solicited involvement might be portrayed as a "win-win" scenario; you win by having the opportunity to increase your productivity, and the project wins by having you as a research team member.

While it is not quite fair to call this conversation your investigator has with you a "sales pitch", the conversation nevertheless has some of the definable features of a promotional talk. In this preliminary conversation, the research program is often presented in its most favorable perspective. This is not to be unexpected since the experienced researchers are trying to attract you to their project. However you should not dismiss the discussion simply because the project is presented in its most auspicatory light; in fact you will gain a good education about the scope of the project from this early conversation. However, keep in mind that this discussion is not an end, but is instead a preamble to the more important conversations that must follow.

The subsequent conversations about the project are critically important, because it is in these conversations that you learn the role you will play in the project. Specifically, the central topic of these conversations should shift from "What is the research program about" to "Exactly what will be asked of me in this project"? Be persistent in eliciting exactly what you will be doing in this project, to whom you will report, and a general description of the important timelines of the project. An important goal of this conversation should be an understanding of the percent time and effort that you should exert on this project. In your conversation with the researchers, do your best to pin them down on this issue. This critical information is central to your decision to participation in the project.

Junior investigators are understandably sensitive to irritating their prospective new senior researchers with these types of questions, but clear and early responses to these interrogatives can avoid serious and unfortunate misunderstandings. A useful way for you to begin this conversation would be

"Other investigators in other projects have disappointed both their principal investigators, and themselves by making inappropriate assumptions about the time commitment to this project. I would like to avoid making that mistake, and therefore wish to know what is the time commitment that you expect of me?"

You need a frank, realistic and cordial answer to this important question and, many times, this is exactly what you will receive. However, unfortunately there are some senior investigators who do not react well to these types of questions. This latter group of investigators may believe that such questions betray a sense that the new investigator is interested in working on activities outside of the proposed research project at hand. These researchers may think that the junior investigator is too busy thinking about other activities they will be involved in, rather than focusing on the effort that they will devote to the project.

This cadre of senior researchers often labors under the false assumption that junior investigators should be willing to provide their complete and wholehearted support for the senior investigator's project in order to gain the experience and training that comes from this involvement. In this perspective, the junior investigator should be at their seniors' beck and call, expending many hours, evenings, and weekends on the research project, working above and beyond the degree to which the junior scientist is paid. According to the senior investigator, all of this time and effort is justified by the new knowledge and experience the junior investigator obtains.* A difficulty with this approach is that the junior scientist is not compensated in accordance with their work. This apprentice-style training is still prevalent in and perhaps can be justified in a student's education. However, when the training is complete, the junior scientist should receive adequate compensation for their time commitment.

The propensity for some senior scientists to treat junior researchers like students can be the source of difficulty. The best way that you as a junior scientist can deal with this problem is to face it early and openly. Take an honest, collegial, and direct approach in exploring this issue with your senior investigator, explaining your point of view to these senior scientists. Articulate that you have a solid commitment to work on his project, a commitment that you plan to keep. However, you also have a commitment to work on other activities, commitments that you must keep as well. Explain to him that you take each of your commitments seriously, and therefore must ensure that you have adequate time to fulfill them all.

Some junior investigators might balk at this recommendation, and think that they do not have the courage, or worse, think that it is inappropriate to discuss the matter of time commitment so candidly with a senior investigator. However, courage can commonly be found in the realization that the alternative to a direct approach is far worse in the long run. With no such conversation and understanding, you may find that you are required to work increasingly long hours on this project. In the absence of the conversation that would have set the boundaries of your work, the investigator does not understand your need, and fills this void with his own expectations. He mistakenly believes that your commitment to his project is open-ended. This assumption on his part is to your detriment, because it places increasing demands on your time that you cannot meet. Some of the work that you have been asked to do, you cannot accomplish because of time commitments, leaving

---

* A fine example of this philosophy is in medicine. When a young surgeon-in-training dared to complain to the senior physician that the process of staying in the hospital every other night was reducing the young's doctor's educational experience, the older physician exclaimed "We are doing you a disservice by letting you leave the hospital every other night, because by doing so, you are missing half of the patient admissions"!

much of the work the principal investigator asks you to accomplish undone. Ultimately, there might be a frank, candid and blunt conversation between the two of you. As the exasperated junior scientist you require relief from the overwhelming workload. Unfortunately, your request falls onto the ears of an equally exasperated senior scientist who wants to know why you are unwilling to keep your commitment. This extremely unpleasant circumstance is made all the worse by the recognition that the entire affair could have been avoided by a simpler conversation much earlier in your relationship with the team leader. It is better to have a challenging conversation early in the project than a rancid conversation late in your experience in the program.

If your best effort to convey both your sincere commitment to work on his project and your need for an understanding of your limited time availability is greeted with scorn or derision by the project's senior investigator, and you do not have unlimited time to work on the project, then leave. Work on another project that allows you to fulfill your time commitments. Better to separate while you are still on speaking terms than to let your relationship degenerate to an angry and hostile one.

It is possible that you will have several competing opportunities from which you must choose one program in which to work. While a component of your decision process will be made up of considerations of what would be best for you, it is worthwhile to avoid having this style of thought dominate your decision process. Re-familiarize yourself with the goals of your department, and the goals and mission statements of your institution, and ask yourself which project is the best for the department.

Finally, avoid the kind of thought that suggests that your future depends on your choice of product team or research group with which you choose to work. While the program you choose may have some influence on your development, its ability to set your career trajectory is much less than the influence that you yourself exert. It is the combination of your abilities, your capacity to learn, your communication skills and your intuition that have the dominant role in determining your career trajectory, not the project on which you work. Your chosen project's effect on your career is much like the influence of the wind on a high performance jet aircraft as it flies to its destination. The wind may slightly increase or slightly decrease the duration of the flight, but it has no important impact on the plane's arrival at its destination.

In fact, at this state of your character development, you may be better served by a position on an obscure, little noticed but useful project than on a project that has high visibility and a consilient, overbearing production schedule. Choose a project that requires you to work at a level that is greater than your current level of operation but within your reach. Begin to gain a sense of boldness that is coupled with a grasp of the achievable.

Once you have chosen your project, immerse yourself in it. Plunge in. There are many ways to learn about swimming, but only one way to swim, and that involves getting wet. Like the new (and sometimes not so new) swimmer, you will occasionally swallow some water. That's an expected byproduct of the learning process, so don't be deterred by the occasional difficulty. Splash ahead anyway.

4.3 Mastery

The first important step that you can take in your new project is education. Educate yourself with the science of your new collaborative research effort. Since none of us knows everything, ignorance is no vice. However, being comfortable with ignorance is.

This education process begins with the acknowledgement of what you do not know. This can be a sensitive issue for you, because as the junior investigator, you may already feel insecure about your new appearance before investigators who are perhaps all senior to you and have already established cordial relationships with each other. However, if you have worked hard and patiently to develop your self esteem and confidence as outlined earlier, the new obstacle presented by your lack of knowledge is only a temporary impediment to your progress. Since your source of self-worth is from within yourself and not from without, you can quickly gain the knowledge that you need without being crippled by insecurity.

How you conduct yourself during this phase can be critical to the establishment of your position in the research team. As you learn, be sure to admit your missteps easily and readily. Senior scientists recognize the value of a colleague who easily admits mistakes and is self-correcting.

4.3.1 Learn at Your Level

Before your first meeting with your new co-investigators as a new member of the team, you will naturally want to spend some time reviewing the relevant literature about the new topic that is the subject of this research effort. If the topical content is technical and complicated, then there are some important steps that you can take to become acquainted with the new knowledge base.

First, find a book or other source that is at your level and that you can understand without too much difficulty. One of the most frustrating intellectual experiences for anyone is to attempt to learn material that is presented at a level that is just too advanced and difficult for them to understand.

My most disappointing experience in learning a scientific topic at any point in my career was my first effort to learn measure-theoretic probability. This advanced topic required not just a probability prerequisite, but a formal mathematical analysis background as well. I lacked this latter background, and therefore was unable to satisfactorily progress through the subject matter. I would spend three hours in intense study and, at the end of the study period, I would have only three minutes worth of new and useful knowledge to show for the effort. My intense desire to learn the material, coupled with my substantial time commitment could not overcome the shortcomings of my poor background. However, once I recognized that I was missing the necessary mathematical prerequisite, I brought my fruitless efforts to learn this complicated topic to an end. Holding my readings in advanced probability in abeyance, I took the time to identify an analysis text at my level. Once I had covered and absorbed this material, I was able to return to the measure theoretic material, this time making the consistent and steady progress that was my initial goal. More importantly, I had rediscovered my self-confidence during this relearning process. Acquainting yourself with hard material is of course much easier if you start with material that is within your reach. Stretch yourself, but not to the breaking point.

4.3.2 Systematic Reviews

It can be very useful to carry out a systematic review of the efforts that have led to the research project which you have recently joined. This comprehensive review can involve reading many different manuscripts that cover the important information and describe the relevant advances in the research area. Your review of these manuscripts must be efficient and brisk while simultaneously engaging your abilities of discernment and integration.

There are many ways to engage in a systematic review. They involve both readings and discussions. I would recommend that you begin the process by first educating yourself from the literature, before you start a dialogue with others in the field. Identify a universe of literature, proceeding in chronologic order. This is how your more senior colleagues, who have spend a good deal of their time in the field (most likely contributing to the literature base that you are studying) have developed their knowledge. This methodological process also makes it less likely that you will have missed a key step, a mistake that is more likely to happen if you leap right away to summary or review articles.

Your purpose in reading each manuscript is to identify the contribution the research effort has made. Specifically, this general evaluation reduces to three questions that should be answered.

1. What was the purpose of the research?
2. Do the methods used allow the researcher to answer the question?
3. If so, then what is the answer?

The motivation for the research is determined from a careful study of the introductory section of the manuscript. Commonly replete with citations, this section should clearly delineates the research question that was raised by the investigators.

Whether the investigators are able to answer the research question they asked is determined in the methods section. Your review of this section of the manuscript should be careful and thorough. Was the instrumentation sufficient to provide the measures with the precision that the authors require? If laboratory samples are involved were they preserved using the appropriate environmental conditions?

If the research involves subjects, other questions must be adequately addressed in this critical section of the manuscript that describes the methodology used by the authors. Was there an adequate number of subjects? Is the analysis carried our prospectively delineated, leading to trustworthy estimates of effect sizes, standard errors, confidence intervals, and *p*-values, or were the analyses exploratory, requiring an additional, confirmatory study to sustain the findings*.

If the methodology empowers the investigators to answer their prospectively asked question, then proceed to read the results section, fully planning to integrate the main findings of the research into your fund of knowledge. However, if the methods reveal that the findings from the study are exploratory and not generalizable, then save yourself some time and set the manuscript aside. Findings that are intriguing but cannot be extended to the larger population have no real place in your systematic review.

Avoid the temptation to "study count". "Study counting" is the process of simply counting the number of studies that address an issue and deciding if there "are enough" studies to support the result of interest. Some who are involved in study counting argue that there must be more than one study. Others say that the number of "positive" studies must outnumber the number of "negative" studies. Instead, the scientific reasoning process assesses in detail each of the available studies, carefully dissecting the methodology, sifting through the methodology, and carefully considering the conclusions. Study counting represents the wholesale abandonment of the intellectual principles of careful review.

The specific problem with "study counting" is the implicit *ceteris parabus* (all other things being equal) assumption, i.e. that all of the studies that are being included in the count are equal in methodology, equal in the thoroughness of their design, equal in the rigor of their execution, and equal in the discipline of their analyses and interpretation. This fallacious assumption is far from the truth of scientific discovery. Studies have different strengths and different weaknesses. Different investigators with their own non-uniform standards of discipline execute the research efforts. Some studies give precise results, while

---

* These issues were discussed in Chapter Two.

others are rife with imprecision. The panoply of studies is known not for its homogeneity, but for the heterogeneity of designs and interpretations.

We must distinguish between the appearance of an isolated study, i.e. one study whose finding was contrary to a large body of knowledge available in the literature, and the occurrence of a sole study. There is ample evidence that a sole study, when well designed and well executed can be definitive [1]. What determines the robustness of a research conclusion is not the number of studies but the strength and standing of the available studies, however many there are. Science, like the judicial system, does not merely count evidence – it weighs evidence. This is a critical and germane distinction. Study counting turns a blind eye to study heterogeneity.

Another useful approach to the critique of a research effort is as follows. Start with a review of the hypothesis and goals of the research effort. Then, before proceeding with the actual methodology, turn away from the manuscript and begin to construct for yourself how you would address the hypothesis. Assume in your plan that you have unlimited financial resources, unlimited personnel resources, and unlimited subject resources. Think carefully and compose the best research design, i.e., the design that builds the most objective platform from which to view the results. Only after you have assembled this design yourself should you return to read the methodology, the results, and the actual interpretation of the research effort that was executed. Having constructed your own "virtual" state-of-the-art design, you can easily see the differences between your design and the one that was actually executed by the researchers. After identifying these differences, ask yourself whether and how the compromises made by the researchers limit the findings of the research effort. It they pose no limitations when compared to your design, the researchers did a fine job by your standards. If the researchers have substantial limitations, then the analysis and its generalizability may be crippled. The researchers may have had understandable reasons for the limitations, but these limitations can nevertheless undermine the strength of their findings.

Avoid studying review or summary manuscripts until the end of your review of the original literature. Review manuscripts are fine, but they represent another writer's distillation of the literature. While you can be informed by that summary, first allow yourself to draw your own conclusions about what the data in the research efforts mean. Once you have completed your own synthesis and integration, pause and take the opportunity to carefully think through what you have read and develop an opinion about the implications of the literature that you have studied. From each of the manuscripts, intellectually stitch a composite point of view that includes the reliable findings from these studies. Then, after you have completed this mental synthesis, read the review manuscripts of others, focusing on the differences between their findings and the independent distillation that you have created. These differences may reveal weaknesses in your own integration of the literature that you have reviewed thus far, or represent something that the summaries author missed or inappropriately discounted.

4.3.3 The "Dumb Question"

In my experience, one of the single greatest impediments to the junior scientist on a research team is their almost pertinacious reluctance to ask a question that they think is "dumb". After spending time reviewing the background material, the progress of the junior researcher may be blocked because there is a small intellectual impediment. This block can be relieved by an answer to a "dumb question". Yet, the junior investigator is commonly reluctant to ask the question for fear of embarrassment and ridicule. The inability to ask the question reduces the junior investigator's effectiveness, and can lead to even greater embarrassment in the long run. The reluctance to ask "the dumb question" commonly finds its justification in the fear of humiliation and failure, and the presence of this fear reveals a dependency on the opinions of others that should be addressed as a matter of character assessment and growth.

The unwillingness to ask "the dumb question" is an understandable tendency that you as a junior investigator must resolutely overcome. Any impediment to your ability to absorb a new fund of knowledge should be removed at once with the smallest possible hesitation. While I would not suggest that you will ever enjoy asking questions at this seemingly elementary level of inquiry, neither should you be ashamed. As before, your source of self-esteem is critical here. You are new to the research material, and you have set the commendable and achievable goal of mastering the background knowledge base. Take control of your emotion, banish the embarrassment, ask the question, and remove the impediment. Don't be like the person who would rather stumble around blindly in a dark room rather ask the simple question "where is the light switch"?,

Another reason to ask this style of question is that you as a co-investigator must have all the relevant information that you need in order to make a solid contribution to the product. If you are a sub-specialist, you may be required to make a technical contribution to the project. The details of the technology may not be understood by the investigators. Examples of these contributions are mathematics, database and computer technology, biotechnology, and statistics. You must understand important details of their work in order to custom-fit your contribution to the needs of the project. Any misunderstanding on your part about the research program at the beginning of your participation can lead to a misapplication of your contribution.

This weakness may not be visible toward the beginning of the project, but may be quite apparent at the project's end, when it is time to disseminate the project's efforts and results. Whatever the forum of promulgation, be it on-site reviews, presentations, or publication, there will be the necessary and important opportunity for criticism. Your co-investigators, recognizing that an external dissection of the project is about to commence, will ask themselves and each other important questions about the project to make sure that the program is solid and that all of its pieces fit together to form a cohesive whole. Thus at the project's end, you can expect many questions from your senior colleagues as they assure themselves that they understand the nature as well as many of the specifics of your contribution. They must do this as part of their preparation for the questions that will arise from outside discussants about your work. These questions will occur at all levels. Your colleagues will not (and should not) be embarrassed to ask their questions of you. Anticipating their questions, you should not be embarrassed to ask your questions of them now in the beginning of this project so that you are prepared for the intense intra-project scrutiny at the end.

Commonly, as a new member of a research program that is being conducted by senior scientists, I will interrupt a conversation that is conducted in my presence, but whose content I am expected to absorb, with the statement:

"I'm sorry to interrupt here, but I have a couple of dumb questions".

I then proceed to ask these questions. I ask them as plainly and as clearly as I can, ensuring that there is no evidence of frustration or impatience in my voice. Uniformly, every time that I have done this, there have been the same three responses. The first response is that my question is answered. It is answered without sarcasm with a voice that, instead of dripping with acrimony, is instead gracious and charitable. If I have any other questions, I then ask "Can you suggest where I can read more about this"? The response to this question has, again, always been generous and informative.

The second response is that someone else who was also present during the conversation, but who remained mute, will quietly say that they are glad that I asked what I did because they had my same question. It always turns out that my "dumb" question was not so dumb after all!

Lastly, an additional effect that is produced by asking a low-level question during these important conversations between the more senior investigators in the project is the effect that the question itself has on the conversation. Asking "the dumb question" does not reduce the intellectual level of the discussion, but it loosens the conversation. No one was willing to ask their set of "dumb questions", that were different than mine until I chose to ask my set. Once my question was out on the table and answered collegially, the other investigators relaxed enough to ask their questions. It is as though the ice has been broken, and others are now free to reveal their ignorance and vulnerabilities to each other as well without fear of rebuke. The conversation becomes more collegial, more relaxed, and more importantly, a true educational experience for everyone. Much good product is produced when you courageously ask your simple question. Your choice to ask the question is not just good for you, it is good for the study.

Here's the bottom line. You will probably be embarrassed to ask the question. Go ahead and be embarrassed, but ask the question anyway. Feel abashed, but don't let that feeling stop you from gaining the knowledge and understanding that you need to be a full participant in the research project.

4.3.4 Teach in Addition to Being Taught

During this early phase of your work in your new project, you will, in all likelihood not be the only investigator who is absorbing new material. Since you will be making a contribution to the program, the other co-investigators will need to learn of your contribution as well. Just as the program is stronger with your knowledge of what it is that the project is about and what they will be doing, the project will also be stronger with these scientists' understanding of what it is that you do in the project. You may be able to avoid their critical misunderstandings of your contribution by giving them a lecture, the purpose of which is to provide a brief primer in your area of expertise.

As with many areas of their interactions with these more senior investigators, junior investigators can be easily intimidated by this experience, and understandably so. The idea of providing a brief lecture on your area of expertise to the senior investigators can be one of the most anxiety-ridden occurrences that you can experience. However, it need not be that way. Chapter Five will focus on how to make presentations to audiences of all sizes. You can use the skills that you gain from that discussion to drain the stress out of this presentation. At the conclusion of your talk, you will have accomplished two things. The first is that your discussion will have been well absorbed by an attentive audience. The second is that the senior workers in this research effort will gain a new appreciation of both your courage and your capacity to communicate relevant and perhaps complicated information.

4.4 Reliability and the Junior Investigator

"Nothing astonishes men so much as common sense and plain dealing"

Ralph Emerson

The productivity of your cooperative program is essential, and your work as a junior investigator will contribute to that effort. In fact, your product will have to dovetail with that of others in order for this joint effort to generate a noteworthy result. With each investigator working toward a common result (or set of results) for the joint program, each investigator's work effort must fit together with that of the others. Given the independent work efforts and ideas of the participating investigators, this collaborative and interactive effort requires careful planning by the project leaders. During this planning effort you will be asked to produce a result or deliverable as your contribution to this effort. An important measure of both your maturity as an investigator and your stature in the program will be your reliability.

4.4.1 Do What You Said That You Would Do

At the bear minimum, reliable investigators do what they said that they would do for the project. They deliver work-product on time, and in the anticipated format.

Unreliable investigators can bedevil a project. They do not provide the deliverable that they claim they can supply, or provide the deliverable too late, or in an incorrect format. The investigator whose contributions are chronically missing, or late, or arrive in an unhelpful configuration commonly deny the impact of their effort's unreliability. He minimizes the impact of his nonproductive activity, and claims that he will meet the next deadline. However, with each passing unmet target date, the situation worsens, and the quality of the conversations degrade. Finally, it can be difficult for this unreliable investigator to make a persuasive point about any ongoing aspect of the project as long as the project is waiting for his required part. Like a lame leg, the project cannot put its weight and foundation on this unreliable investigator to aid its progress.

There are three keys to being reliable; planning, diligence, and, above all, attitude. Of these three, the first two are the easiest to attain. Anticipate that you will be asked about when you can provide the necessary product for this work effort and give careful, methodical, and prospective thought to this question. While the discussions of the aggressive timelines of other dynamic investigators in the project can be infective, try to avoid losing yourself in this excitation; this enthusiasm can blind you from a clear view of what a reasonable timeline for your contribution will be. Only after you have given careful thought to your own various and critical time obligations should you commit to a specified date for your product. Think carefully before you speak, because you will be held to what you say.

A useful tool that is used among engineers when they plan complicated projects is to build into their development time the opportunity to deal with unexpected emergencies. Despite your best efforts, equipment can break. The arrival of reagents can be delayed. Hard drives fail. Computers are stolen. People get sick. These occurrences represent the unpredictable and volatile environment that surrounds you. Who among us would not take traffic patterns into account when they agree to an important commitment that requires them to drive across town? You may plan on a direct route, but you must also plan for the impact of others on your progress. Build in the time to deal with emergencies and other unpredictable events.

There are many electronic devices that are now available that allow you to plan and schedule your work, whether that work spans days, weeks, or months. From our point of view here, it does not matter which of these electronic assistants that you buy. However, whichever device you choose, it will only help you if you affirmatively and actively decide to use it assiduously. For me, this means making only the notations that matter. Regarding my own calendar, I only enter those items into it that I fully intend to do. Making a new entry on my calendar is my commitment to myself to accomplish the task that day. When the appointed time arrives, I work hard to accomplish the task. If there is an item that I am not willing to diligently resolve, it does not get into my calendar.

To help you stay on track with your production schedule, plan on providing regular and frequent progress reports to the program team. In fact, you may be required to update the team leadership, along with all of the other investigators on the team. If you are not, offer to give a short and terse summary of your work. The purpose of this volunteer effort is not self aggrandizement. If you have misunderstood any aspect of your role or configuration of your deliverable, you will certainly learn of it during these brief reports. Of course, the additional practice of speaking to the group, listening to and absorbing their comments and criticisms will help to build your growing confidence.

4.4.2 Meat Hooks

Once you have planned carefully, then carefully follow your plan. Find, an insist on an isolated time to work on the project. Ensure that you have the necessary tools to do the job. Create the environment in which you can bring your combination of knowledge, talent, intuition, patience, and consistent effort to the task at hand. If you have telephone/visual conferences, schedule them so that they do not interrupt your work. For a time, let your phone ring unanswered, and let your e-mail pile up. However, you probably cannot get away with what one famous scientist did.

> On a day when he was receiving visitors, Albert Einstein allowed a fellow scientist to enter his home and come to his work parlor for a friendly discussion. When they entered his office, Einstein asked his colleague to please wait for a brief time while he finished up a small matter. As the visitor waited in Einstein's presence, watching the great man work, his eyes were drawn to the features of Einstein's workroom. Prominent among the trappings of the room suspended from the ceiling, was a huge iron meat hook. Stuck onto the hook appeared to be a collection of papers. The papers did not appear well organized at all, each sheet being pierced by the hook in a haphazard fashion.
>
> When Einstein wrapped up his distraction and turned to face his visitor, the visitor asked him what the papers hanging on the hook were. Einstein replied "They are letters and correspondence that I have received, but have not yet had the opportunity to answer". Noting the depth of the pile of papers, the visitor asked Einstein what he did when their were so many letters that they no longer fit on the hook. Einstein mirthfully responded "I burn them".

While we can't get away with this behavior, there is no lasting harm in shutting down your email client for a time or having your phone messages go to voice mail, while you quietly prosecute science. Remember — working on the science is supposed to be the fun part of the job; the portion that you should enjoy. Devote yourself to the task, while simultaneously dedicating yourself to completing it in the allotted time. While you are working, keep a running tab or list of new ideas that you get* but cannot act on because of your concentrated effort on the topic at hand.

Finally, enjoy these few hours, because as you have already seen, much of your time is spent in necessary, but not necessarily scientific, endeavors. Relish the moments you get to bring the full strength of your scientific talents to bear on science questions.

4.4.3 Above and Beyond

As we have seen, an important goal for you as a member of the team effort is to produce the required contribution from your work effort on time and in the proscribed and expected configuration. However, this is only your first goal. As a maturing investigator you should also have the goal of helping your colleagues produce their required contributions on time as well. This additional step is above and beyond the call of duty as a junior investigator, but is a worthy goal for a maturing scientist who wishes to be a valued member of the research team.

This second goal requires devoted and consistent effort on your part, working to ensure as best as you can that your contribution will be ready ahead of schedule. As you planned your productivity schedule, recall that you built in time that would be required to deal with the vicissitudes of life. If you were fortunate enough to have a peaceful and unhurried period of time for you to do your work, and you were diligent in your effort, then you may have some time to pitch in and help others who either did not plan to carefully, or were overwhelmed by other occurrences. If so, then step in and help. After all,

---

* For me, I have a voice recorder that will allow me to collect and store these ideas as I get them. Later, I can listen to them, sorting, developing, or discarding them at my leisure.

there will in all likelihood soon be a time when the world catches up with you, and you will need all of the help that you can find.

Be the type of scientist on whom your superiors can rely. If they don't notice this strength of yours, then others will.

4.5 Falling Behind

However, just as there are times when you will be ahead of schedule, there are, of course, also the times when you will fall behind. Through no fault of your own (or sometimes due to a scheduling difficulty that you did not manage correctly) there will be circumstances when your day is too full and falls apart. Work that you had planned to do, and that needed to be completed, does not get the attention that you had hoped to provide. As you rise in your career, you will have face this distressing event with increasing frequency. Thus, you need coping mechanisms for falling behind your carefully planned schedule.

A clear and useful way to deal with this chronically occurring source of dissatisfaction is to adjust a sometimes rigid mindset. As a young scientist, you are interested in developing diligence and completing all of your tasks. This is because task completion brings you closer to your goal. No doubt, you have memories from graduate school, college, and even earlier about the importance of completing your work in a timely fashion. In fact, many of us take great pride in completing a job on time. And, of course, we know and remember some of our fellow students and acquaintances in school who were lazy. These friends did not get their assignments turned in on time, waited until the last minute to prepare for an exam, and always struggled with completing a paper up until that report's due date. They were chronically behind, and chronically under pressure because of it. Your observations of these colleagues may have driven the notion of timely task completion even deeper into you. The following three strategies, when used together will allow you to defeat destructive reactions to this frustrating problem.

4.5.1 Coping Strategy #1

Completing work on time can, in and of itself, rise up to become an all important goal. Thus, the researcher may criticize herself when it appears that she is not able to meet the expectation of her calendar. By falling behind, she can sense that new required tasks will not be completed on time, and that new opportunities cannot be explored. As the backlog builds, the worker falls irretrievably behind schedule, and fears that her career progress is beginning to stagnate.

Also, lurking in the shadows is the link between your assessment of your own daily performance and your self-worth. Intense days that spiral out of your control can painfully rob you of an important sense of self-satisfaction. This is a dangerous trap that can all too easily ensnare you. In fact, you may indirectly build this trap yourself. On those days when your work has been particularly good, productive, and fulfilling, it is all too easy to let your sense of self-worth soar. You are buoyed by your own performance. However, the price that you pay for this self-image construction on good days is self-image destruction on disappointing days.

Thus, the combination of the increasing occurrence of days that do not permit you to reach your performance goals with the strong link between your daily performance and self-worth is a destructive one, robbing you of the some of the excitement and enthusiasm of your young career.

There are two important realizations that are available to you that, when viewed, can reverse your reaction to these particularly bothersome days when you are unable to meet your performance objects.

The first, and perhaps most important of the two, is to separate your assessment of your own value from your performance. Performance is an external metric that changes from circumstance to circumstance, and from day to day. Commonly, it is out of your direct control. Linking your own sense of self-worth to your ability to complete your task list is like strapping your sense of self-value in for a jolting roller coaster ride. There will be dramatic highs, and disorienting, disruptive, and painful lows. Your schedule, and the execution of your abilities might certainly enjoy this ride, but it should not be inflicted on your sense of value and adequacy.

Instead, your appraisal of your sense of self-worth must be insulated from your day-to-day activities. Consider the most expensive and valued diamond. It has high, perhaps immeasurably high, value. This value is constant, in the face of sun or rain, war or peace, prosperity or poverty. Regardless of its external environment, the diamond retains its value. This is the unwavering measure that you should ensure be placed on your self valuation. Your sense of adequacy should be well supplied, remaining even, constant, and steady.

By decoupling your self-worth from your performance, you are free to watch your day come apart without fear of self-condemnation. In fact, being free of self-condemnation, you can apply the best part of your nature to repairing or salvaging the day because you need not dread that your failed attempt will lead to the self-judgment of poorer performance and lower self esteem.

Thus, in some sense a "bad day", or a day that unravels right in front of your eyes is not just a challenge to your organizational skills; it is also a barometer of your source of self-worth. If, as your day begins to unfold and then to unravel, you begin to feel the pangs of inadequacy, recognize that these first pains are an indication and a warning signal that your source of self-value is at risk. This is an urgency that requires your immediate attention to correct.

Finally be aware that your sense of value is not just vulnerable on a bad day. Good days can be their own source of trouble. It is just as important on these rewarding days that you not allow your self-worth to be affected by the temporary boost that comes from these favorable external events. The tighter you permit this link to become in the good times, the more difficult it is to break during the bad ones. Insulate your sense of self-value from the exhilarating feeling that comes from a day well spent. Consider the following anecdote.

After his General Theory of Relativity was proved in 1918, Einstein found not just recognition in the scientific community, but also attracted the interest of the public as well. The growing recognition of his intelligence and insight and the demonstration of the veracity of his findings delighted a war-weary world. His sense of humility, when combined with Einstein's harmless banter and genuine childlike charm catapulted this heretofore obscure and quiet scientist to the epicenter of media attention. The statement "It's all relative" became a popular expression of the time. However, Einstein himself was not prepared for this onslaught of adulation. He did not know how to react to the crowds that greeted him and the blizzard of interviewers that pursued him.

During a dinner party, he met Charlie Chaplain, a popular movie star who was also the center of attention at the time. Since Chaplain had been a famous actor for several years, and Einstein needed an experienced perspective on the media frenzy, Einstein asked Chaplain "What does it all mean"? Chaplain replied simply "Absolutely nothing".

Guard and protect your sense of self-worth from outside performance. Allowing it to feed and grow on the sweet but non-nourishing product of good days allows it to starve during the poor ones.

4.5.2 Coping Strategy #2

After guarding your self-worth from the influence of your performance, take the opportunity to examine the chaotic environment in which you work that so quickly spirals out of control.

Despite my best attempt to lay out my activities on either a paper calendar or digital schedule, my day almost never proceeds as I planned. The analysis that I thought would take one hour actually takes two, and I don't get to complete it. The meeting that was scheduled to last for 45 minutes, spawned a following short, urgent meeting that took another half hour, itself producing an additional thirty minutes of paperwork and telephone calls that wasn't on my schedule. This is followed by an urgent call from the budget office that embroils me in an intense discussion because of a misunderstanding by an investigator about a project's budget. In the meantime, a nervous colleague, anxious about the anticipated departmental debate about her upcoming promotion, would like to urgently speak with me about strategies and tactics that she might follow that would be the most influential. Of course, all of these events occur in the climate of intense connectivity created by incoming telephone calls and emails. At the conclusion of this day, I review my schedule and find that, of the five items I wanted to accomplish, I worked on only two. Additionally, I now find that new activities need to be frontloaded on tomorrow's schedule. But, of course, tomorrow will be much like today.

The dizzying, unplanned, even chaotic work days are disconcerting. However, the problem is not the disorienting days, but my reaction to them. In fact, the days are exactly as they should be. It is my flummoxed reaction to them that requires adjustment.

The hectic days with their simultaneous and multidirectional activities are the days that promising junior scientist are supposed to have. The forward movement generated by a progressing career produces unpredictable activity and chaos. Chaotic days are to be anticipated and faced not with stupefaction, disappointment, and self-criticism but instead with resilience, strength, and curiosity.

Unpredictable activities that force their way into your schedule are the hallmarks of a career in motion. Think of your career as a rapidly moving river, producing rapid currents and strong eddies at is splashes forward. Its movements are unpredictable, sometimes fearful, but there is power behind it. Of course, one way to control this river-force it is to dam it up. converting it into a quite lake. However, the placid lake, while peaceful, is not powerful. It shapes nothing but is itself shaped. It is both platonic and motionless. That is not what you want for your career.

Forward progress needs command and movement, and these characteristics are translated into frenetic and unpredictable activities that don't make it onto your calendar, but nevertheless make there way into your activities. While chaos should not be produced for its own sake, it is the expected byproduct of the natural good momentum of your own career movement.

Therefore, recognizing that predictable chaos is an anticipated byproduct of your advancement, and that your sense of your self-value is not linked to your daily performance, free yourself from the tendency to stop the chaos, and instead just divert and shape it for the good of your colleagues and yourself. You need not feel guilty for not completing your task list for the day. Begin your day by recognizing that the most important event that will happen to you is the one that is not on your agenda but one for which you must watch for. A new opportunity that allows you to influence and shape the ideas and work of others, or that provides a new path of progress will intrude on you and require your attention. You don't want to miss this merely because it wasn't pre-announced and not on your calendar. Staying on schedule is only worth your total commitment if nothing can be gained by deviating. Your calendar is not your career, the events that swirl around you are.

4.5.3 Coping Strategy #3

You accept the fact that an important part of your day will be caught up in important and unplanned activities. However, this needn't be your entire day. Insist that at least a small component of your be in your control taking a "productivity hour" for yourself. During this time, work on a scholarly, professional activity that you particularly enjoy. Spend some time considering the project that you will devote this effort to. Luxuriate in this decision process. More than a thesis or dissertation, more than a collaborative effort, this work will be entirely yours.

There are several advantages that accrue to you if you are willing to find and fight for this productivity time. Since we have seen that time is such a precious resource, choosing to keep some of it for yourself represents an affirmative recognition that you can not just sacrifice your time and energies for a project or for other people all of the time. You need attention and sustenance as well, first and foremost from yourself.

Second, time spent alone in quiet productivity helps to quiet the restless voice inside you insisting that, at least for some part of your day, you should be able to apply your best efforts in a direction that you choose and not merely to meet an obligation. You have spent many years training for, and have made many sacrifices for your ability to conduct science in a field of your choosing. Asking for one hour out of 24 to work on a topic of your choosing is not an undue demand. You may choose to expend this time on a book chapter that you have been anxious to start, or a manuscript in which you will explore a topic that has been inadequately developed in the literature. It may be spent on the design of a new device. You may work on a computation that has been bedeviling you. You yearn to work on these issues, but you just can't find the time. The only way to find the time is to just take it.

Additionally, it must be acknowledged that a source of frustration in collaborative research efforts is the decision making progress. One of the frustrations of collaborative work is that progress is properly and commonly based on compromise. However, this means that the investigator team that is working with you on the project will not be able to incorporate all of your good ideas. Some of them will be rejected. Fortunately, the project, or writing plan that you are independently pursuing during your productivity hour is a natural venue for these concepts.*

Finally, your secured time may be the source of independent productivity. Relying on collaborative effort for the evidence of your experience and expertise can be a problem if the effort fails. After you have invested many months in the project, the program may fail for a variety of reasons. The funding source may be lost. The principal investigator may leave. Advances by competing researchers may negate the purpose of the project. A senior author may have a very leisurely approach in writing the project's results. These are beyond your control. However, by having a second source of productivity, you are not completely attached to the productivity of the group project. Your secured time may be an unanticipated wellspring of productivity by which your career progress can be measured.

Therefore, create a temporarily but reliable atmosphere where you can quietly work. The duration of this environment may be only 1 to 1 ½ hours a day. Intelligently choose the time, but insist on finding it.† During this time, answer no phone calls. Turn your email client off. If people find you in your office and attempt to root you out, then go to the library. If you have an assistant, be sure to know that you are only to be interrupted in an emergency. During this time, totally immerse yourself in the project of your own choosing.

4.6 Accountability
In the complicated and unpredictable mix that represents your day, you will no doubt experience setbacks and occasionally have to disappoint your research team that was hoping for a timely contribution from you.

---

* I have to confess that my ability to explore some of these rejected ideas of mine actually makes me easier to work with in a group. I may lose a discussion with my collaborators on the value of a particular contribution that I had hoped to make in a joint effort. This defeat is easier for me to accept if I know that I can use and develop the idea in work that I am carrying out on my own.
† My secured time is from 6:45AM to 8:15AM on workdays, and from 5:30AM – 7:30AM on the weekends.

In these circumstances, take full responsibility for the setback that you caused to your project. You may have missed a deadline because of an event that was out of your control. There may have been an intrusion on your work schedule by your supervisor. Someone else may have needed help and you offered to assist, and that took more time than you anticipated. Whatever the reason, there will be times when you miss a deadline that your team anticipated that you would make. This will not be an isolated experience in this project since your co-investigators will have the same type of occurrences befall them.

When I have missed a deadline, I have found that the simplest, honest comment that serves me the best is:

"I am sorry. I have missed this deadline. It is my fault, and I apologize"

Time and time again this comment has produced more goodwill and more support for my efforts as an investigator. I may follow that comment with some of the specifics about why I missed the deadline. I will also work out a new timeline that I should be able to make. However, a clear, unambiguous statement of apology, responsibility, and accountability conveys the message to the investigators that this is an issue for which I am accountable, and that I will correct.

4.6.1 "It Is All My Fault"

In 1863, Robert E. Lee, the commanding general of the Army of Northern Virginia, was at the zenith of his military career. After taking charge of this army one year early, he produced a string of military victories that exhilarated the Confederate leadership while simultaneously confounding and demoralizing his Northern adversaries. Entering the campaign on the brink of a Southern defeat, Lee drove the Union forces back from the edge of the Confederate capitol. He then defeated one Union army after another, sending one Union general after another into retirement. From Second Bull Run, Antietam, Fredericksburg, and Chancellorsville, he wheeled, feinted, divided, and struck with his smaller force, defeating the larger Union forces arrayed against him.

In June, 1863, his momentum was shattered at Gettysburg. After three days of fighting there, Lee's army sustained a clear, staggering and undeniable defeat. Looking around, Lee saw many reasons for his loss. Habitually diligent cavalry leaders suddenly disappeared for hours at a time, denying him critical information about his adversary's movements. One of Lee's general, unable to find his courage, refused to obey an order when the execution of that order would have carried the day. A second general openly quarreled with Lee and, when finally ordered to carry out an order with which he personally disagreed, procrastinated until the opportunity for victory had passed. The Union army, fighting on its own soil, had stiffened its ranks here in Pennsylvania while Lee's forces were far from home. Northern forces were constantly receiving reinforcements and supplies while the Confederate army, on its own, received no succor.

There were much blame to go around for the first loss suffered by this army. However, Lee immediately assumed complete and sole responsibility for this seminal defeat that resulted in over 50,000 casualties. This man, who took great pride in exemplary conduct*, accepted full accountability for the catastrophic Gettysburg loss at once. Immediately after the conclusion of the battle, he told his generals (some of whom had clearly failed Lee) "It is all my fault". He actively circulated among many of the decimated units of his army, talking to small groups of tired, wounded, and dying soldiers, saying "This is all my fault". In the dispatches he was required to send to his political leaders, he made it clear that he and he alone was responsible for the defeat of his army. In that spirit, Lee offered his resignation to Jefferson Davis, a resignation that was not accepted.

This accountability and responsibility helped to protect the spirit of his Army, aided the development of his generals (who would never fail him again as they had on that day), and amplified the level of his soldiers' devotion to him.

Miscalculations, errors in judgment, bad observations, and the play of chance are as inevitable as tomorrow's sunrise. The occurrence

---

*He never received a single demerit for bad conduct while a student at West Point, a singular remarkable feat for a young man in the company of other young men.

of these ineluctable and unfortunate events does not determine whether you are a good versus a mediocre scientist. Your reaction to then does.

4.7 Becoming vs. Being

Once you have mastered the new material that was necessary for your comprehension of the program, move rapidly to take advantage of your efforts. Begin to see your own participation in this project not as the contribution of a junior scientist, but as a co-investigator.

Junior researchers commonly wonder when they can stop being junior researchers. The answer is that you are a full-fledged investigator when you perform like one. A mature investigator seeks all of the ways that her knowledge base can contribute to the project, then sees to it that her contribution is most clearly, attentively, and accommodatingly made. When you are functioning at this perceptive and incisive level, you can drop the "junior" descriptor from "junior investigator".

Having mastered the background knowledge base, do not hesitate to take quick advantage of your mastery by using it to serve the project. Make a full contribution to the project's effort. Be cognizant of what is going on in all aspects of the study, and act of your knowledge. Cease trying to become an investigator and start being one.

Many junior investigators try to remain as quiet and as inconspicuous in a new project. While they may believe that there is safety in silence, in fact there is only the false peace of being content with their level of knowledge (and ignorance), and the sham serenity of assuming that the problems of others in the project are not their problems. This is a mistake. Specifically, by not being a full participant in the discussions of the project, by intellectually walling themselves off from and separating themselves from the ongoing activity, they are not testing their own knowledge base about the material. Remaining inconspicuous and quiet stunts the junior investigator's growth, and prolongs his maturation period in the research grant.

Gain experience. It is experience that gives you the sensitive feel of action that in turn leads to solid and reliable intuition. Extend your influence in the project by identifying ways that you can work with co-investigators for the good of the group effort. Look for every opportunity to expose your education and background to others in a way that supports them. Not only will this benefit the overall research effort, but it will reveal critical weaknesses in your own developing thought processes, allowing you the opportunity to repair them.

It is, of course, important to avoid the rash statement and the thoughtless action. By the same token, avoid the mistake of the opposite extreme. While rashness should be avoided, irresolution should likewise be shunned. If you have something useful to contribute, then make the contribution.

My first role as an investigator was with a group of forty cardiologists who had designed and were involved in the early stages of the execution of a large clinical trial in heart failure. My transition was a quick one; I received my PhD on a Friday, and was involved in discussion with this group the following Monday. A few days later, we were planning a presentation of the initial experience of the study. I knew relatively little about this modern therapy for heart failure that was being tested, and did not know the investigators at all. However, this group recognized that I was working to master this material, and patiently answered each of my "dumb questions". Six weeks later, it was decided that I would present our data to an audience of physicians. There is no doubt that I was overwhelmed by the prospect of presenting to a roomful of cardiologists who knew more about the disease and its modern treatment than I did. Nevertheless, I was also conversant with the materials and felt that I would be supported by my colleagues who had been participants in the study for longer than me. In any event, one thing was sure. Regardless of the outcome of the presentation, my knowledge base on the subject matter would be much stronger after my appearance because of all of the effort that went into my preparations. It only remained for me to control my own nervous faculties and energies in order to give the talk.*

4.8 Engage in the Action

To a great extent, how you conduct yourself in a collaborative project is how you will be treated by your colleagues. Professionals engender professionalism in others. However, a professional demeanor is not a

---

* Dealing with presentation anxieity or "stage fright" is the topic of Chapter Five.

rigid one. It is not isolationist, but participatory. So by all means, always be appropriate, but appropriately plunge in and take part in the activities of the group.

Your activity and participation in the scientific exchanges with your co-investigators produces several good products. First, it is good for the group. If your co-investigators are to benefit from your knowledge and training, then they must hear from you, and hear from you on a regular basis. If your area of expertise is complicated and/or technical, you may have to elaborate on the details repeatedly until they understand, and can begin to integrate this knowledge with that of their own. In

In addition, engaging in the brisk give and take of the group discourses allows you to educate others about the utility and tools of your own field. Experience in these dynamic dialogues gives you the sensitive feel of action, an intuition that will be invaluable in your writings and presentations.

4.8.1 Be Persuasive

There is much to be said for the art of debate in science. An active discussion between scientists who have different points of view can be a enlightening experience for each of them. Commonly these are short exchanges that occur and disappear like eddies in a stream. Be ready to inject important, pivotal issues when they occur and to defend your statements.

You may find that, on occasion, you will sharply disagree with other co- investigators (some of whom are more senior than you). Don't begin the discussion until you are clear in your own heart and mind that, regardless of the outcome, your value as a junior investigator has not changed. Because your self-esteem is not at stake you can fully engage all of your faculties in the discussion without fear of failure, since your self-worth is separate and apart from your outside experiences. This quick, simple affirmation before a meeting or discussion serves as a useful reminder helping to center you, preparing you for what is to follow.

The central characteristic of a good persuader is not so much her ability to speak as it is her ability to listen and to understand. Many times, the discussion can have at its root a misunderstanding. Before the discussion proceeds, first rule out any misunderstanding by listening carefully to the other argument. Since your self-worth it not at stake, you can absorb the opposing point of view with no harm to you. Examine it carefully, and ask questions about it until you completely understand it. Give its supporter every opportunity to correct and clarify it. Demonstrate to him by your questions, your review of his point of view, and your tone that you respect his position. Try to avoid any brisk point-counterpoint engagements until you fully understand the opposing position. In fact, it may take all of the available time at a meeting to discuss this other point of view. This is time well worth taking, so do it in an unrushed, fashion. Go out of your way to both learn and demonstrate your willingness to listen. Also, do not be quick to anger. As we said in Chapter One, respond kindly to a harsh word. Your role on the team is solid. Admit your mistakes or misunderstandings readily and easily.

Many of the "debates" in science are based on different sets of assumptions. At the end of this part of the discussion, you will know whether this is the case. If not, then begin your response, educating him about your perspective on the issue. State your point of view in language that he can understand. Do not lapse into techno-babble. Speak slowly, carefully, and clearly. If it would be useful for your fellow discussant's understanding, provide some helpful, clear examples that he will be able to accept. Focus on the concerns that he raised, and overcome them with clear, evocative language. Use a point that he made to bolster your own position. Rely on your knowledge, training, and expertise to help you make a point.

Simple reliance on these tools can provide the basis of a profoundly convincing argument, as in the following, hilarious example.

> After stopping for drinks at an illegal bar, a Zimbabwean bus driver found that the twenty mental patients he was supposed to be transporting from Harare to Beltway Psychiatric hospital had escaped from his bus. Not wanting to admit his incompetence, the driver went to a nearby bus stop and offered everyone waiting there a free ride. He then delivered the passengers to the mental hospital, telling the staff that the pa-

tients were very excitable and prone to bizarre fantasies. The deception wasn't discovered for 3 days.*

At the conclusion, with both parties understanding each other's points of view, the correct position, or a compromise position may be self evident to all. However, sometimes, the outcome is different, as in the following true story.

Immediately after the election of John F. Kennedy as 40th president of the United States, his father, Joseph Kennedy, a tough-minded patriarch who had done all that was possible to get his son elected, insisted on helping to select the new president's cabinet of advisors. Chief among the father's demands was that John Kennedy's younger brother, Robert F. Kennedy, be chosen as the new Attorney General of the United States.

This selection sent shock waves through JFK's advisors. The selection of a close relative of a president for such a high cabinet position was unheard of. This was nepotism at the highest level, and would certainly lead to severe and punishing criticism of this young president early in his administration. However, these advisors were well acquainted with Joseph Kennedy's stubborn streak and temper, and therefore began searching for the right person to dissuade him the president's father from his point of view.

They settled on Clark Clifford. The prestigious Washington DC lawyer had connections to the president's party, had served past presidents, and knew the Kennedy family personally. Clifford accepted the task and started his research. Several days later, when he has completed his review, he called the president's truculent father.

Clifford started the discussion with an acknowledgement of the important role that Robert Kennedy had played in the election of the president. He complimented Bobby Kennedy on his intelligence, his perception, and his acute political

---

* The Darwin Awards, 2003.

instincts. Clifford then reviewed the office of the Attorney General of the United States. He mentioned some of the key Attorney Generals in the history of the country, and described many of the pivotal times in US history when the office of Attorney General was singularly influential. He discussed the times that he, as advisor to presidents for more than twenty years, had seen the Offices of the Attorney General and the President work for the good of the nation. Clifford then returned to the topic of Bobby Kennedy, saying that there were many jobs in the government in which the president's brother would be visible, exert influence, and remain in communication with his brother on a regular and frequent basis. It was one of these other jobs that would be best for Bobby, best for the family, best for the President, and best for the nation.

Joseph Kennedy listened quietly, almost reverently to this series of arguments. When Clifford was completed his thesis, the father complimented him on his fine review and clear exposition of the argument, and then said "Clark, Bobby Kennedy is going to be Attorney General of the United States"!

4.8.2 Sense of Humor

Persuasion is not a science; it is an art. Being persuasive doesn't mean that you always argue as though you are immune to criticism. The art of being persuasive requires that you demonstrate your own vulnerability. Once of the most satisfying and useful ways to do this is to retain a sense of humor about your own work. Be easily entertained by both your own comical missteps, and the comical errors of others. After all, there is no scientific tenet that denies us the right to have fun being colleagues.

One common mistake that many junior investigators make is that they embrace their own work with almost religious solemnity. Remember that your self-worth is not based on your work thesis or product, but instead finds its roots in an internal source that is protected and inured from the daily swirl of your activities. Look to strengthen this foundation, inspecting it for any weaknesses or damage that the experiences of daily life can inflict. A useful indication of a healthy self-assessment is the ability to make fun of yourself. The more serious the argument, the greater the necessity of a sense of humor.

This last comment may be surprising. Actually, some scientists may even be insulted by it. However, having a sense of humor about your work does not mean that your work is frivolous. The statement's justification is that, while your work is very important, it is not all-important. And, while you derive a deep and lasting satisfaction from your work, it should not be the source of your self-justification. Consider the following.

> Most of the battles during the US Civil War in the border states were not engagements over the titanic issues of the rights of men vs. the rights of states, but were instead smaller fights between neighbors. In one little affair, an intense fight was waged between a small unit of Union men against a smaller unit of their neighbors who supported the Confederacy. After this engagement in which several men were killed, and many were wounded, a hush fell over the field of fire. A few minutes later, the young Confederate soldiers heard tremendous new noises coming from their surviving adversaries. The youngest of the southern soldiers, being unsure of the reason for this strange digging, grinding mechanical noise, could restrain himself no longer. In a shrill, clear voice that was heard across the small battlefield he called out "Hey Yanks...What are you up to?
>
> The reply from the Union side of the line was brusque, official, and all business "Shut up Reb, it's a military secret".
>
> A moment later the southern soldier responded " Awwww...we know that. But, surely, you can tell *us*?" Laughter erupted on both sides of the battle line...

Although friends aren't always friends, enemies are not always enemies, either. If these men could retain a sense of humor in their deadly, killing business, surely we can find something amusing in our own more gentle affairs.

In science, we work to make contributions to an immense, and rapidly growing body of knowledge. However, each of our contributions, while not negligible, can be relatively small. I have had the opportunity to make some useful contributions to statistical methodology. I devoted important energy to this work, and am proud of it. Yet, I must confess that I would be surprised if these innovations and advances were in active service 100 years from now. Furthermore, I have also had the opportunity to work on the development of new and important medications in the treatment of cardiovascular disease. These medications are helping people today. Yet, I would be amazed if these medications were still being prescribed fifty years from now.[*] As a junior scientist, you must commit your effort to work that is timely, but who among you can say that time will not pass your contribution by? A sense of humor about your work helps you to keep this in balance.

As a statistician, I commonly must work with investigators who enthusiastically accept my presence on their team. They know that their work product will ultimately be reviewed by a statistician before publication, and, in order to avoid any lethal criticisms at this final level of review, they engage my services early in the development of the research project. My colleagues accept the fact that I will make an important and necessary contribution to their research program, yet it is one that they do not really understand. There is therefore a detectable level of suspicion about my contribution. At the end of a mathematically intense demonstration of an analysis that is required for their work, I sometimes encourage my nonmathematical co-investigators to keep in mind that, despite the rectitude of the mathematics.

'Statistics is like a bathing suit. What it reveals is interesting, but what it covers up is critical'... "

---

[*] After all, how many of the medications that were developed with great fanfare and acclaim in the 1950's are still used today to prevent heart attacks? For example, at that point, a health diet was a daily regimen of breads, eggs, bacon, butter, meat, and milk, a diet that many would criticize today.

What makes this so funny is that, my statement reflects their thought processes. They would have never thought to frankly articulate these to me because they feared that I would take offense at their perceived denigration of my field. The fact that I can myself make fun of my own area of expertise demonstrates to them that I have the same types of thoughts about the applicability of my work to their project as they have. By sharing this concern, I can be better trusted to guide them through this mathematical wilderness.

4.9 Subcontracts[*]

As a student, it was desirable for you to gain as much experience as possible in your chosen field. This commonly meant that you would spent time working on a project for an investigator. Sometimes this work was for money, other times you would volunteer your time and effort to gain this valuable experience. The relationship was a simple one. You would supply your time and effort for training and knowledge.

As a junior investigator your contribution to the project is somewhat more complex. There is no doubt that there is basis work to be accomplished for the project for which you are responsible. This may include devising a new instrument, working with animals, carrying out analyses, or developing computer simulation packages. This is the body of the work that the project relies on you to complete. However, there is also the opportunity for you to make additional, intellectual contributions to both the specific research project, and also to your chosen field. So, although you have the responsibility to accomplish some basic research tasks, you also should plan to move beyond that by making your own contributions to the research field. This is the important difference between the student perspective on research, and the investigator's point of view. The student appropriately focuses on getting the work done. The investigator, while insisting that the work be completed, also looks for the opportunity to have a lasting impact on the scientific field.

---

[*] This section was developed with the help of Dr. Craig Hanis, Ph.D. and Dr. Susan Day, Ph.D, both colleagues at the University of Texas School of Public Health.

A common mistake that many junior investigators make is that they bring the student perspective to their collaborative research effort. This is reflective in the administrative mindset that they bring to the research project. The junior scientist may mistakenly believe that she will only contribute time and the development or use of special equipment to this research effort; thus that is the only support that they request from the project's grant. She does not consider that she should allow for the time to develop her own contribution to the field through her work on this research project. One way in which this time can be available to the junior investigator is if a student or post-doctoral fellow actually works on the project with the junior researcher. The role of this additional person is to carry out the basic work of the project, work that the junior researcher will supervise. With the burden of carrying out the basic work lifted, the junior scientist is now free to engage in deeper, more advanced work for the project that would strengthen the contribution that the project makes to the scientific field. Additionally, the junior collaborator may not give careful consideration to the need for physical resources. While the special needs for equipment may be obvious, someone must pay for computing and communication support (e.g., telephone, email, fax) as well as basic supplies.

A useful way for the junior investigator to obtain the support that they need for their project is through the development of a subcontract. The subcontract states the formal relationship between the junior investigator and the collaborative research project. It is the responsibility of the junior scientist to complete and negotiate the subcontract with the principal investigator of the study. On this subcontract, the percent effort of the junior investigator is provided. In addition, the effort of the student, colleague or post doctoral colleagues are also provided. Finally, the support for equipment, supplies, and travel are also requested. When approved[*], this subcontract will formally state the role of the junior investigator in the project. Completing the subcontract negotia-

---

[*]These subcontracts require formal administrative approval by the institution's research project office, so be sure to set aside time in the grant submission process for the appropriate oversight committee's involvement and approval. Also, if patient care is involved, or patient records are to be collected, there is commonly a human subjects protection committee or institutional internal review board that must also provide approval.

tion makes an important contribution to the junior investigator's developing administrative skills. However, most importantly, the junior scientist receives the support that she needs in order to oversee the basic work the collaborative research team requires of her, as well as permit her to make a deeper, more cerebral contribution to the research effort and her field in general.

4.10 Documentation

Perhaps one of the most burdensome, but most necessary aspects of your work is clear and adequate documentation. These important notations are good for both you and the research program.

Specifically, documentation is a lucid, decipherable record of the development of your work product. Its caliber and clarity should be such that a specialist in your field who is not part of your research team should be able to examine it and, based on a review of this work, determine exactly what you have developed and how it evolved. This documentation record should be clear, legible, and be stored in multiple, safe locations. Your institution may have standing rules on the documentation of work product, just as it, no doubt, has regulations that guide the presentation and development of an audit trail.

Documenting your work product is critical. Document the development of an idea that you have. Document the progress that you are making on the design of a new instrument. Document any computer code that you write. If your work involves the complicated use of a spreadsheet or an electronic formula sheet, then document that. A simple rule of thumb that reveals the importance of the documentation process is

"If you do not have time to document your work, then you do not have time to do the work".

4.10.1 Three Reasons to Document

Documentation is not a mere inconvenience, like washing the car after you go for a long, enjoyable drive. Documentation is an essential part of the work process and effort. Identifying the reasons for the documentation can help you plan exactly how you are going to organize your records.

Documentation is essential for at least three reasons. The first is that it is most helpful for you. The process of documentation requires that you carefully consider and assimilate the progress on the work that you have completed so far. This summarization process can be the catalyst for your identification of important new ideas and procedures that can spur further project development. Thus, a documentation record that includes periodic, brief reviews of the work that you have accomplished thus far can be very helpful to you as you write it, as well as an aid to future readers as they work to understand your ideas and the state of theses ideas' development.

The second reason documentation is necessary is that it helps to jog your memory. As your career develops, you will find yourself making contributions to several different projects simultaneously. Each of these projects will apply a different application of your skills, and requires a somewhat different work product from you. In all likelihood, you will be able to successfully partition these different projects in your mind now, avoiding confusion between what report is required for Project A, and what analysis is required for Project B. However, will you be able to remember the important details on your currently active projects when you are asked questions about them six months from now after they have ended? How will your memory be five years from now? Without clear, easily understood documentation for you to rely on, you will find yourself forgetting the minute details of your work.

Perhaps, over a period of one year, I may carry out 125 different analyses and derivations. Over the course of fifteen years, this is approximately 1,875 evaluations. It is not the involvement in so many analyses that is surprising. What is surprising is that commonly I am asked about some of the details of an analysis that I carried out many years ago. The reasons for the renewed interest vary. Nevertheless, with no warning, questions about the intricacies of an evaluation arise, and, since I am the author of the analysis, I am quite reasonably expected to have the answers. While I could provide an overview of the analysis from memory, the absence of clear documentation would cripple my attempts to report on the small but important details of the old evaluation. Good notes are critical to help "jump-start" my memory.

This realization has implications for the work in which I am currently involved. Since, I don't know whether my current enterprise will attract pointed queries from the future, I must assume that each one will. This prudent assumption requires me to document it clearly now for my future convenience.

A third reason for documentation is to provide protection for you. In collaborative research, misunderstandings are regrettably common. You may find yourself in the unfortunate position of having to dispute a comment describing your work that others have made. Having clear documentation provides the clearest record of the matter. The following is an example.

The conclusion of a large clinical experiment is hectic since many presentations of different aspects of the trials results are sought. As the main statistician on the project working with the investigators, it was my responsibility to provide the required analyses for these scientists. The results were sent to the investigators who incorporated them into their presentations. After a particularly stormy question and answer session that followed one of the presentations, the presenting investigator called me to irately complain about my work. He stated that the analysis was not what he had requested; furthermore, it was not correctly labeled. After telling him that I would look into the matter, I returned to my file on the topic. My records on the matter consisted of his original request to me stating what he required in the analysis, and the analysis material I generated in response to his evaluation. I was therefore able to quickly contact the investigator stating that, 1) the analysis complied with his request, and 2) the analysis was properly labeled. This ended the matter. In the absence of that documentation, I would have been forced to rely only on my memory, a memory that had been taxed with the execution of a rush of different analyses looking at different aspects of the same clinical question. Clear documentation quickly dispatched the dispute.

4.10.2 Hard Copy Documentation

Some work can begin and end with electronic documentation. Other work is initiated not electronically, but with paper and pen. The product of each effort should be documented.

Commonly, my first development work on a project in statistics begins with the purchase of an artist's sketch book, costing about $10.00. This spiral bound book is composed of simple clean unlined pages. Any and all work that I do for this project is first written in this book. The documentation begins with the initial idea of the statistical development. From there, it proceeds to the development of the particular mathematical notation that I require*. The body of the book is then filled with my development of the mathematics. Commonly in the first exposition of an idea, I will make mistakes. When I find them, which typically requires repeating part of the development, I state clearly what portion of the work must be repeated, and then restart the derivation or calculations. Toward the end of the development, I will include an outline of any of the computer code that is required for the project.

An additional step can be taken when the book containing the handwritten development is complete. The contents of the book are scanned into a computer. These image pages† can then be written to storage media (e.g. hard drives, compact discs, or DVD's), backed up, and archived for storage. This process fixes in place a complete record of your involvement in the project's development.

There are useful alternatives to consider. One useful archival device is the digital camera. You can simply take pictures of the notebook pages with an inexpensive, relatively low resolution digital camera, keeping a digital record of your progress. Another useful procedure is to take digital pictures of certain aspects of the development of a project. For example, when I work with a collaborator, we commonly jointly use a single blackboard to develop the work. After an extensive session, the blackboard is full of ideas, notations and formula. Several clear digital photographs of this blackboard capture the notation that we used, allowing us to study it, reproduce it, or reduce it to text. These

---

* This is usually a very time consuming part of a complicated process. However, stopping to take the time to develop the write notation can pay a handsome dividend by streamlining the following mathematics.

† Be careful to stay away from propietary image pages, since in the volatile software industy, the company that makes the software can go out of business, and the images may be not be readable by future operating systems. Since operating systems have provided continued support for images saved as bmp, tiff, or jpeg files, these files are likely to be readable and accessible in the future.

can be stored with the other digital documentation of the work's development. However, there is another advantage of this approach. A clear digital photograph of the blackboard does more than just capture the content of the work. Seeing all of the formula's laid out as we jointly wrote them helps to capture the atmosphere and spirit of the labor as well.

4.10.3 Computer Record Documentation

Most all of us use computers in our daily work. Some of us may use word processing, spreadsheets. Others use specially designed and custom written software. Some of use statistical and analysis software. Others of us are devoted to hand held devices. Some of us write software. Whenever you use software for a project, you must back this data up, and store it in a location that is both accessible and safe. The three mantras for computer work in science are backup, backup, and backup. We are going to go one step beyond that, insisting that it be a useful tool for us as well as those who follow us.

4.10.4. Residentialism

Residentialism is the unfriendly acts of inanimate objects. Examples of residentialism surround us. In fact, we cannot get away from them. Running into nothing but red traffic signals when you are late for work is an act of residentialism.* Your eyeglasses falling and breaking just before you have to appear in court is residentialism. When your car's "Check Engine" light comes on 250 miles from the nearest town and garage, you have experienced more stomach-churning residentialism.

   Obviously these machines are not working against us. It is just that the random failure pattern that they follow ensures that they will sometimes fail when we need them the most. Our interactions with computers have deepened our experience with residentialism. Random failure means failing at harmless times† and also failing when the fail-

---

*While a student at Purdue University, the only time my commute was unpredictably delayed by a train crossing railroad tracks in Lafayette, Indiana were the mornings I had an 8:00 AM test.

† Sometimes computers fail at humorous times. To prepare for the Y2K problems that were expected to affect computers on January 1, 2000, I turned my

ure can do the most damage. We therefore have to be prepared and back our systems up.

It is perhaps best to think of backing up your work not as one more maintenance job you have to perform, but as part of your mainstream computer activity. Backing up is part of the system and environment that you have created to ensure productivity. Clearly your productivity will be slowed, perhaps even halted by a computer failure. Not only will you have to replace the computer, but you will have to replace the data as well. With a system that is backed up, restoration of the computer, the software, and the data can take a matter of days, sometimes hours. On the other hand, without adequate backups, you may never completely recover.

When it comes to backing up off site, be sure that it is truly off site, and not just a nearby locale selected for convenience. The experiences of a man who backed his data up from his home computer, storing it on CD's in his garage, only to lose both this house and his garage in a torrential flood is evidence enough that "off site" means you choose the storage location not for its proximity, but for its distance.

4.10.5 Generating Quantitative Reports

One of the most common functions of an investigator is to use software to aid in the generating of a report that her co-investigators will read. This software could be statistical software, database software or spreadsheet software, among others. If you are responsible for generating the report, the process may work as follows. You receive a request (commonly by email or telephone). You engage in a dialogue with the inquisitor, ensuring that you understand the question. Having a clear understanding of the question, you then carry out the analysis and generate the report. If this is an important aspect of your work requiring your effort several times a year, then you will need a reliable procedure to document it all.

---

computer off the night before, the first time I had done this since I bought the machine in 1998. When I returned to work on January 2, 2000, I turned my machine on. While I did not experience a Y2K problem that was anticipated, I did experience the simultaneous failure of three hard drives. This act of exquisite, triple-residentialism is a personal record that I have yet to beat.

Documentation works best if it is an integral part of your analysis effort. This means that the citation of your work should proceed in real-time, as you are actually doing it, rather than be relegated to a rushed, *post hoc* documentation effort that only begins upon the project's conclusion. Therefore, as the analysis projects grows and expands, so does the documentation.

My certification procedures have become increasingly intricate over the years as I have come to understand the true need for a clear record of my work. Fortunately, software has evolved to substantially reduce the organizational aspect of the documentation. The process is not effortless. However, this certification effort is a natural outgrowth of the project work that I do. The key to my procedure is to create an electronic link between the request for the analysis, the code that I must write to carry out the analysis, and the software's output. Essentially, I link the request from the investigator to the code that I write. This code is then itself linked to the raw output of the software, that is then linked to the report that I write. Hypertext is critical to this process, substantially adding to the convenience of this approach.

The analyses that must be carried our require many steps, and several interactions with the investigators. I begin by creating a directory entitled "Exercise and LDL Project". Within it, I will create the following folders

> Code folder
> Database folder
> Raw Output folder
> Reports folder

The Code folder will contain all of the code that I generate for the project. This code can be programming for statistical software, or programming for a database or spreadsheet. The Database folder will contain all of the databases that I create during the many anticipated analyses for the project. The Raw Output folder will contain the output exactly as it is produced from the code, and the Reports folder will contain the reports that I write based on that raw output. Any spreadsheets that I create based on the raw output are stored in the Reports folder.

In the Code folder will reside one word processing document, simply called CodeDoc. CodeDoc will hold all of the code that I write for this project. When I begin the project, CodeDoc is blank. As I write code that first examines the database, checks the quality of the data, creates new variables, and verifies the accuracy of new variables, this code is saved in CodeDoc. When I have verified that the programming code works, I place that code at the end of CodeDoc. As time passes, and I write more code, CodeDoc grows. By the conclusion of the project, every single line of code that I have written for this project resides in CodeDoc.

The first entries in CodeDoc, that contains the first code that I wrote for the project, are very simple. These introductory entries commonly just verify the appropriate connection to the database, followed by some data extraction and variable creation. As one proceeds to read through CodeDoc, the analysis becomes more complicated as I work my way towards the more complex analyses that the investigator requires. Thus, scanning through CodeDoc is reading a chronologic history of my work on the project.

The project will consist of many aspects as data is collected, check and transformed. This work is executed by the code I write, and each of these tasks and subtasks creates output. Many data listings and tables are created in this process The output from each block of code is saved in its own document that is in turn saved in the Raw Output folder. Thus, for each new subtask, a file of output is created and placed in the raw output folder. Thus over time, as more work is carried out in this project, the amount of code that is written increases, and the number of documents in the raw output folder also increases. By the end of the project, there can be over a hundred documents in the raw output folder.

Although the process as described thus far permits a complete record of all of the code that is written for a project, and all of that project's raw output, the utility of this information can be improved by creating a link between the code that generated the raw output document and the raw output document itself. This is accomplished with a hyperlink. At the end of the several lines of code that have produced output. I will add a text comment line "link to raw data". I will then set up a hyperlink within the word processor that hyperlinks that text comment to the actual file in the raw data folder that contains the data analysis that the code produced (Figure 4.1).

This device allows me to read through CodeDoc, find the code that interests me, and click on its text-comment line to immediately open the file that contains the output that the code produced.

Continuing, I link in the report the same way. When the output will be the basis of a report that I will send to the investigators, I create the report in the Report folder. I then add a comment line to the code (e.g., "link to report") that produced the raw output that in turn produced the report, hyperlinking that line to the report in the report subdirectory.

```
libname v8data v8 'd:\sasdata\care\data\v8data';
options linesize=75 pagesize=60;
Title1 'The SAS System';
Title2 'ACAT Design';
data v8data.l1;set v8data.analysis;
if tx_group=1;
if (strok = 1 and d_strok < 365 and d_dth > 365 and d_dth > d_strok + 30)
or (pep=1 and d_pep < 365 and d_dth > 365 and d_dth > d_pep + 30)
or (exp1=1 and d_exp1 < 365 and d_dth > 365 and d_dth > d_exp1 + 30);
Title3 'Treatment Group Events within first year with post event survival >
30 Days';
proc print data=v8data.l1; var pep d_pep exp1 d_exp1 strok d_strok d_dth ;
run;
proc freq data=v8data.l1; tables death strok fmi_cmi pep exp1; run;
*link to raw data
```

Figure 4.1 Example of programming code with hyperlink to output

Comments that I get back from the investigator that lead to the generation of more data and reports are placed in the CodeDoc as a preamble to the code that I write in response to the investigator's message. Thus, I can see at a glance, the comment of the investigator immediately followed by the code that I created to respond to her query. A click on the first hyperlink reveals the output of the code, and a click on the second hyperlink opens the report that I wrote based on that output (Listing 4.1)

At the conclusion of the project, I have a collection of subdirectories whose entries are hyperlinked in a logical fashion. When the time comes, I can write the entire subdirectory tree to a permanent storage and archival device that will provide a complete analysis history of the project complete with all intermediate results.

While this is not the only type of documentation system, it has proven invaluable to me, having several advantages. There is no paper; all documentation is electronic, allowing it to be easily stored. The system is also completely transferable to other media in a way that preserves the hyperlinks. If there are any questions about the analysis that arise years later, this style of documentation is readily available and easy to decipher. In fact, I have come to view this quality of documentation as just as important a product of the project as is the report that the investigators require.

Listing 4.1 : Code from CodeDoc, providing initial investigator request, responsive code,
and hyperlinks to raw data output and report

(From Investigator). Please run univariate and multivariate renal slope models (change in CrCl and GFR over time) without the interaction term

```
libname v8data V8 'd:\sasdata\care\data\v8data';
options linesize =80 pagesize=60;
Title1 'The SAS System';
Title2 'GRF Quartiles';
proc univariate data=v8data.renalfol;var gfr_b;run;
Title2 'Creatinine Clearance Quartiles';
proc univariate data=v8data.renalfol;var creacl_b;run;
Title2 'GRF Slope Model Stratified by Subgroup';
data v8data.l1; set v8data.renalfol;
Title3 'Entire Cohort';
Title4 'Univariate Analysis';
```

```
proc reg data=v8data.11;
model betagfr = tx_group;weight wtgfr;run;
Title4 'Multivariate Analysis';
proc reg data=v8data.11;
model betagfr = tx_group race_w gender gfr_b acei_b sbp1214
sbp1416 sbp16 dbp7080 dbp8090 dbp90 hdl37 ldl125 chol209
tri144 i_diab uprotein;weight wtgfr;run;
link to raw data
new GFR report link
```

4.11 Respect Your Own Judgment

Junior scientists frequently make the mistake of disrespecting their own good judgment. Sometimes they prematurely give an opinion about a scientific issue before they are prepared to simply because they have been asked to provide one and they are "on the spot". Other times they do not provide an opinion because they do not know how to formulate one after a review of the data. Since criticism commonly follows the delivery of an opinion, the junior investigator who hopes to shun criticism chooses to remain quiet.

It is perhaps all to easy for you to debunk your own judgment. After all, after living with it all of your life and being fully cognizant of the difficulties that it has cause, you are painfully aware of its shortcomings. However, others may have a very different perspective of your judgment. While you may not value the words that you utter very highly, others can hold them at greater value. Do a good service not just for yourself, but for others as well, by carefully formulating and then carefully articulating your opinions.

If you are not ready to make a judgment, simply say so. While you are formulating your judgment, make sure that it is a complete judgment, not simply a narrow, scientific one. Expand its base. For example, while there is no doubt that an important part of the analysis of the question at hand is scientific, is there no room for compassion? For humility? For respect for work that is not your own? For the desire to strengthen the work of others? Integrate these perspectives as well into your scientific analysis so that your evaluation reflects the important non-scientific as well as scientific perspectives. Cultivate your judgment. Think about it, examine its basis, and challenge it. When it is complete, practice providing your opinion lucidly, unhurriedly, and gently. Also, be prepared to defend it without fear. Criticism does no harm and provides the greatest benefit to the scientist who has a healthy sense of self-value.

Keep in mind that people who don't know you very well tend to believe that you are putting good thought and effort into what you are saying. A comment that you toss out cavalierly or thoughtlessly can be seen by strangers as being representative of your point of view. And, of course, once the statement has been made, it cannot be unmade. When you speak, keep in mind that more people may be listening to you then you know.

This latter point is important with institutional email. The contents of an email message that you write can help to elevate you, or lead to your ridicule. Once you send an email containing an opinion, you have lost control over the dissemination of that message. Offhand comments that you make in an email to a friend can be routed to the attention of others. Emails are commonly sent to the wrong person. You may have perhaps intended it for one person, but sent it to many more. Additionally, the person to whom you did send it forwarded your message to others, perhaps by mistake, perhaps not. A message that you sent that you hoped would be harmless can, through a circuitous route, wind up on the computer or PDA of your supervisor. Sometimes they wind up in the office of the Dean or the Chief Executive Officer.

Be wise, and wisely use your email. Compose your email with the idea that it could be read by your principal investigator, the state legislature, or a regulatory commission and not cause you embarrassment. Be sure to read each email message you send two or three times to ensure that it says exactly what you mean. Never think that you are too tired to do work, and therefore you will catch up on your email. Sending messages in this state is as bad as sending them under the influence of alcohol. If you are too tired to write representative, defensible email, then you are too tired to read any. Shut your email client down and find something else to do.

Your judgment is held in high regard by others. Make sure that you accord it the same status as well.

4.12 Senior Investigators and Castigation

Out of the blue, you get a phone call from the administrative assistant of the program's senior investigator. Although the language is polite, the tone is unmistakably clear. The principal investigator of the project needs to see you at once. The reaction of the junior investigator is immediate and common. Hearts beat fast. Palms sweat. Stomachs churn. If the meeting is not to take place for a day or so, you may have some restless nights in front of you.

Since these types of meetings will punctuate your career, you will need some usefully coping skills to help you prepare for and get through them. One of the first skills that you require is one that effectively deals with the issue of intimidation.

4.12.1 The Intimidation Factor

First, deal with your intimidation. It is not your superior, but instead your intimidated reaction to them that is your greatest adversary in the upcoming meeting. Take this enemy head on by first recognizing what intimidation does to you. The internal pressure and fear generated by intimidation disconnects you from the best of your abilities. Specifically, fear steals your memory for details and your ability to calculate. Trepidation causes your fine intuition to escape you, and your capacity for articulate comment may be nowhere to be found.

Of course, these fine faculties are still present, but the anxiety has built a wall up between you and your talents and capabilities. In a very real sense, fear has caused you to disarm yourself when you need these abilities more then ever. Letting fear into your heart and mind is like letting a thief into your house. The result is that you are going to be robbed. What makes it worse is that you are complicit in your own robbery.

In order to have command of your own talents at the upcoming meeting, you must remove your reaction to intimidation. To defeat this, first recognize that fear (like fungus) grows best when it is left alone in the dark. Deny fear its strength and hold over you by pulling it out of the shadows and into the light. The upcoming meeting holds the fear of judgment. You fear being judged and found wanting in the judgment. This is the beginning of the cascade of failure that fear produces. You fear being ridiculed. You fear the loss of status, the denial of a recommendation in your behalf, the fear of job loss, the fear of an uncertain career, and, ultimately, the fear of a damaged life.

However, these fear-melded chains that ensnare you are made not of iron but of vapor. The reality is that, even without facing your superior's wrath, your career is uncertain. In fact, you cannot even guarantee that you will have a safe drive to work tomorrow. If that cannot be assured, how can your future career, affected by forces that you cannot see and may never know, be assured? The reality is that your future will always be unknown and uncertain, regardless of how your boss feels about you at the moment.

However, there is a second, balancing reality. It is that your inevitably uncertain future is no threat to endowed workers such as you. This is because capable people develop the strength and spirit that they require to deal with the stresses and challenges in the future. Specifically, the gift to talented people is that, if they are willing to look, they can find within themselves a new combination of strength, insight, discipline, vision, and energy to confront future problems. You can therefore be assured that, for the unseen problems of the future, you will have new and heretofore unseen strengths. Being therefore assured that the future will be handled by these abilities, fully energized when the need for them arises, you can be confident in the face of future uncertainty. This confidence for the future releases you to focus today's energies and abilities on today's problems.

Thus, the way to defeat fear is to simply see that fear is based on a lie. Destroy it with the simple truth and assurance that your growing, developing natural talents and abilities can overcome uncertain problems waiting in your future. You are more than a match for whatever will face you. No senior investigator or boss, no matter how demanding or intimidating can take this realization from you. You may rob yourself of it by giving yourself over to your fear, but no one else can rob you of this truth. Only you can do that. Put another way, anything that your superior can take from you is something, that, in the long run, is not worth having. Accepting this truth when you walk into the room to meet your boss can profoundly affect your discussions with her.

4.12.2 Listen

Once intimidation and your fearful reaction have been rubbed out, you
are free to bring your best faculties and talents to bear in the meeting.
One of the most important of those is the ability to listen. It is much
easier to fully listen in the absence of fear. Listen carefully to what
your senior investigator is telling you. Be sure to ask questions to make
sure that you understand exactly what she wished to convey to you. Try
to appreciate her point of view.

This is particularly useful if she is criticizing you. Even
though you may disagree with what she has to say to you, make sure
that you understand the position that she is taking. As a senior investigator, she is likely to have more experience than you do, so allow yourself to give full consideration to the possibility that she might be right.
With your sense of value being unaffected by the discussions, you can
afford to slowly and carefully consider her comments. If a response is
not required right away, take a day or so to consider exactly what you
have heard. Keep foremost in your mind, that a lecture from your senior investigator is, above all, an opportunity for you to learn. Like a
short-term loss on a smart, long-term investment, be willing to accept
small, measured steps backwards on a good, well planned career path.

As a junior scientist, you have not earned the right to respond
to constructive criticism with arrogance. Do not resist receiving an instructive and useful lesson out of stubbornness or insecurity. An occasional corrective lecture, while never really enjoyable, can promote
your character growth in an important and necessary new dimension.
The fact that the events occurred that led to this undesirable setting may
reflect a weakness on your part; a weakness that has now been forced
into the open for you to critically review and examine. Evaluate this
flaw carefully and take deliberative steps to ensure that 1) you
strengthen this weak area of yours and 2) that you are vigilant for the
circumstances in which this failing may be put to the test again. This
second point is critical Although it is understandable to attempt to
avoid the circumstances in which the weakness was revealed, you may
have to continue to confront it during your career. Learn to anticipate
these circumstances, overtly considering what your correct and appropriate response should be. Since this is a weak area for you, its repair
and restoration requires your careful consideration and attention.

4.13 Conclusions

Collaborative work is one of the most exciting and challenging activities that you will take part in as a scientist. Whether the collaboration is for an administrative or a scientific task, the essential ingredients for your successful participation remain the same.

First, carefully examine your sense of self-worth, guarding and protecting it from performance and other external metrics. The daily recognition of your value, separate and apart from your surroundings and daily circumstances, keeps you tightly tethered to your talents, strengths and abilities. With this link in place, you can quietly face the upcoming day with confidence, endurance, and charitable trust.

Secondly, learn the material that you need to learn in order to contribute to the project, while simultaneously instructing your coworkers in this project about your expertise and how it will be applied.

You only need your education and a solid, stable sense of self-worth to be a full participant in the collaborative venture. Being assured that your self-value is independent of your performance, you are free to participate and engage in the project, using all of your talents and abilities to support the group effort. Don't shrink from, but instead, actively seek out opportunities to help other coworkers in the project. Be willing to extend yourself, and even put yourself at risk to provide support for a colleague.

Recognizing that these activities may wreak havoc with your calendar, allow your good but unscheduled activities to dominate your calendar, and not the reverse. Be prepared to receive the unanticipated email or phone call that provides an opportunity for you to engage your talents and capabilities for the good of the project. When you make a mistake, apologize clearly and easily.

Your interaction as an intelligent, young scientist with your institutional environment will produce a swirl of unplanned activity that will demand action on your part. It is up to you to keep some of the fun and stimulation that pulled you into science into your days. For that good end, inject a "productivity hour" into your day so that you might work quietly with satisfaction on a scientific matter of your choosing.

The product from these efforts is a well-balanced, focused, and knowledgeable investigator who recognizes the importance of the project, and communicates effectively with all of the team members. Additionally, you will also have the important combination of vigilance coupled with the willing attitude that permits you to shoulder not just your share of the work effort, but to help with the burdens of others as well.

References

1.   Monahan BP, Ferguson CL, Killeavy ES, Lloyd BK, Troy J, Cantilena LR Jr.(1990). Torsades de pointes occurring in association with terfenadine use. *Journal of the American Medical Association*. 5;264(21):2788-90.

Chapter 5
The Investigator and Presentations

5.1 Introduction

There can be no doubt that, as a scientist, you will have to make presentations before audiences. These lectures will be to colleagues, co-workers, and sometimes competitors. You will make presentations to both advocates and to skeptics. In each of these settings, as the presenter, you will have to publicly open yourself to the comments and criticisms of others.

To be an effective speaker, the ability to communicate openly and clearly with strangers in public requires uncommon strength. While there are "natural speakers", the majority of us must work at developing this skill. The aim of this chapter is to present you with the idea that you, as a junior scientist, have the internal strength that you need to be

an effective and persuasive public speaker, and to provide guidelines on
how to harness that strength.

5.2 Sources of Information

There is a wealth of information available about the art of giving presentations. Among the most helpful are

http://www.public-speaking.org/public-speaking-stagefright-article.htm
http://www.brookes.ac.uk/student/services/health/presentation.html
http://www.gita.org/events/annual/27/Seminar Presentation Guidelines
2004.pdf
http://clubs.mba.wfu.edu/speakindeacons/Resources1/Ways to Control
Presentation Anxiety.doc
http://www.aacc.cc.md.us/com111/mod3.htm
http://totalcommunicator.com/jitters_article.html
http://www.bradford.ac.uk/acad/civeng/skills/pubspeak.htm

This is by no means an exhaustive list. These websites provide useful,
clearly understood discussions of the fear most people have of giving
lectures. In addition, they offer useful mechanisms in helping to plan
for a presentations. Some of the discussion in this chapter will draw on
the content of these resources.

5.3 The Rise and Fall of Stage Fright

Any honest discussion of the art of giving presentations must acknowledge that most people rebel at the idea of public speaking. In an often
quoted news article, the London Times reported a study in which 3000
interviewees were asked to list their greatest fears[*]. Many of the stated
fears were easily anticipated, e.g. fear of flying, fear of heights, fear of
disease, as well as fear of animals, insects and loneliness. However,
41% of the respondents reported that they feared giving a public presentation above any other. They actually rated this fear greater than their
fear of death.

---

[*] *Taken from http://www.aacc.cc.md.us/com111/mod3.htm*

5.3.1 The Reasons for Presentation Anxiety

While it is hard to envision that people are better prepared to part with their lives than to ascend to a podium, clearly, many people have a deep and sincere fear of speaking in public. In fact, the anxiety leading up to the experience is as bad, if not worse than, making the presentation itself. Each of us has experienced part of the constellation of symptoms association with presentation anxiety, more traditionally known as stage fright. This complex include blushing, sweating, shaking, rapid speech, and stuttering. In some people, stage fright produces a mental confusion, and the loss of their ability to articulate in front of the audience.

These symptoms are a response to a physical fear reaction. The adrenal glands, in concert with other hormonal symptoms, react to our fearful response. This reaction of our body is as though the threat felt by us is a physical threat, and not an emotional one. Responding to this perceived physical threat, epinephrine, norepinephrine, and other hormones are released into our systems, priming us to prepare for a powerful attack. Our heart rate increases and our blood pressures rises as the cardiovascular system prepares for a physical danger that is actually not present. Blood rushes from our gastrointestinal tracts to our muscles, giving us the sense that "butterflies" are in our stomachs. Our breathing rate increases, and our palms begin to sweat. This is a strong, concerted reaction to a material menace. Your body is preparing you to survive a physical assault. But, of course, there will be no attack, and there is no physical threat. There is only the fear. Stage fright is the emotional complex that is triggered by fear.

Of what is the speaker so afraid? There are many opinions about this, and most likely each of them is right in one circumstance or another. The common explanations for this fear is that the speaker is in a new and unfamiliar situation. Another is that the speaker is fearful of being the sole focus of an audience's attention. This is commonly linked with a fear of isolation. As the speaker, you and you alone are the cynosure—the center of attraction. With the observers concentrating on you, the fear may be that they will concentrate on your appearance, your diction, and your idiosyncrasies. This can easily turn into the fear of being ridiculed. This concern goes together with the fear of looking foolish, of mental befuddlement, of speaking irrationally, of losing coherence. The anticipation of these joint outcomes can over-whelm the speaker before he actually speaks, producing the neurohor-monal changes discussed earlier. Ergo, stage fright.

5.3.2 The Response of the Audience

Ultimately, the anxiety-struck speaker fears being hurt and sustaining damaged by giving the lecture. But, an honest and fair appraisal of the usefulness of this fear reaction requires us to ask how likely is it that such damage will be sustained. An amazing fact about presentation anxiety is that, despite all of the fears that may consume the speaker, her audience usually don't receive the signs of nervousness that she fears are being transmitted.[*] In fact, each individual in the audience has a set of observations and a personal set of self-absorptions that keeps them from focusing solely on the speaker.

Consider your own reactions as an audience member. Aren't you too busy, fumbling with the agenda, or speaking to a colleague, or turning your cell phone off, to pay close attention to the speaker's man-nerisms for very long? Since the audience is not concentrating on every detail and facet on the speaker's countenance, its members miss the outward signs of her fear. In addition, since the audience does not know the speaker well, they cannot detect the subtle signals of nervousness that the speaker fears are being broadcast by her mannerisms and non-verbal cues.

Actually, as the speaker, your situation is better than that. The members of the audience share your deep rooted fear of making a pres-entation. They know how they would feel if the roles were reversed and they were on the stage. In fact, without saying a word, your simple cou-rageous act of walking before them to the podium engenders a sense of admiration in them. The audience hopes that you will be able to suc-cessfully complete your talk. More likely than not they are rooting for you, and they do not doubt your ability to complete the presentation successfully. In this regard, their optimism is closer to the truth than the low self-image of the panic-stricken speaker.

At its root, then, stage fright is simply a very real fear of a very unreal threat.

---

[*] http://www.aacc.cc.md.us/com111/mod3.htm

5.3.3 Defeating Stage Fright: The Hunk-papa Sioux

The Hunkpapa is a tribe of Indians that are part of the Sioux Nation.[*] This nation, along with the Oglala Sioux, Lakota Sioux, and Blackfoot Sioux, inhabited and freely roamed the great plains of the United States up through the mid-nineteenth century. Among their leaders and fighters were numbered Crazy Horse and Sitting Bull. Although the Sioux had produced many responsible and compassionate leaders, these two men were held in the highest regard by their countrymen. Crazy Horse and Sitting Bull possessed a different potency. They created and exuded a strong sense of self-identity and purpose, powered by a palpable and irresistible force. The Hunkpapa said that these men "owned themselves".

You can confront the challenge of presentation anxiety by resolving the issue of ownership. Overtly, consciously, and affirmatively decide who owns you, then act on that decision. If you reclaim ownership of yourself, then stage fright is dealt with through disassembly. It is a simple replacement process. Presentation anxiety works by filling you with self-destructive images and thoughts, leading to self-destructive reactions. When you actively and affirmatively replace this complex with positive, deep seated beliefs in your own merit, then you recover your sense of value and purpose.

Specifically, confront anxiety by reasserting your personal sovereignty. Reacquaint yourself with what you stand for. Establish again in your own heart and mind your irreplaceable value as the individual scientist that you are. Anxiety is a fear of chimera. The reality is that there is only one person, and, throughout the existence of mankind, their has been only one person with the unique combination of abilities, strengths, knowledge, curiosity, diligence, and intuition that you have. You are that person, and the instillation of these capabilities and insights within you first imbues, and then empowers you with value separate and apart from external concerns. Even if your presentation was an absolute, and complete failure, its failure does not diminish the value of

---

[*] *Sioux is an adaptation of the French word for "enemy".*

your talents, and must therefore not reduce your sense of self-value. Your sense of merit can never be taken—it can only be given away.

Retain and strengthen ownership of yourself. Stage fright is an attempt to rob you of your sense of purpose and self-worth. Observe, however, that the presentation and its associated stress will quickly pass away. Any audience reaction to it, good or bad, will rapidly go by the wayside as well. Your personal sovereignty, i.e. your appreciation and approval of the value that your unique personality and combination of talents and abilities represents, does not pass; it is constant. They are there for you to appreciate, to draw strength from, and to develop. Presentations are ephemeral. Personal sovereignty is solid and steadfast. Recovering and reasserting it is central.

5.4 Preparation

There is no substitute for knowing the subject matter for a talk. The positive impact of the previous discussion about personal sovereignty is minimized if the ultimate source of your discomfort as a speaker is that you simply do not know the material about which you are going to talk.

One common reason for inadequate groundwork for a lecture is that the speaker does not set aside enough time for this preparation process. It is important not to underestimate the amount of time this process will consume. The rule of thumb that I use is to first quickly estimate how long it will take me to prepare for the talk, and then simply double that estimate.

Adequate preparation is its own reward. It bears much greater fruit than just the mere product of rote practice. Preparing for a talk is the opportunity for you to review your own work, and to find the best perspective for its inclusion into the body of scientific knowledge. This effort is not without its own sense of well-deserved satisfaction to which you are entitled.

During your preparation, be sure to not just reference, but to understand the work of others. If this work appears in the literature, re-familiarize yourself with the material's contents. This can be invaluable, and not just for your own re-education. At the time of your presentation, the colleague who made an important contribution to the field may be in the audience. If this individual chooses to ask a question, being cognizant of his contribution places you in a perfect position to construct a responsive answer.

If any of your presented material contains mathematics or arithmetic computations, be sure to check the calculations again. Stop at different points, and recheck your assumptions. Do the calculations in a sequence that is different then the sequence in which you actually carried out the computations. For example, if you must compute $A(B - CD)$, then check your answer by calculating the equivalent $AB - ACD$. It is far too easy to have "your eyes disconnected from your brain" when you reviewing your own mathematics. Checking in a different way is refreshing and ensures that your calculating faculties are fully engaged in the review process. However all of this takes time, so find the time to do it.

5.4.1 The Layman Rule

The audience of your talk is hoping and expecting to be educated by you. Therefore, although you may have a good deal of information to share with them, you must focus on conveying that information effectively. Make your presentation lucid and digestible. You can learn a great deal from the audience's response to the presentation that you make. Their critical appraisal of your work can sharpen your own scientific focus. In fact, you may get a new research idea based on a discerning comment by a colleague in the audience. However, for these criticisms and comments to be helpful, your colleagues must first understand your presentation.

In my personal ranking of criticisms that my presentations receive, I do not mind hearing "I know what you are saying, and I think that you are wrong". This is a comment that leads to debate, the outcome of which is good for me and other members of the audience. The worst criticism that I can receive is "Lem, I have no idea what you just spoke about!" This indicates that I have wasted the time of my colleagues as they try to comprehend an incomprehensible presentation of mine. It is this criticism that I work hardest to avoid.

With this foremost in my mind during my preparation, I try to keep the points of my presentation as clear and as elementary as possible. I call this the "layman" rule". My goal is to make a presentation clear enough that a literate layman can understand it.

This rule's purpose is not to insult the audience; its execution does not imply that the audience is "no smarter than a layman". Patronizing the audience is an important mistake to be avoided. The layman rule is instead, based on the fact that the audience does not know my work as well as I do. Some components of my discussion will be new and unfamiliar to them. Sometimes, the concepts on which the talk focuses are ideas with which the audience is familiar; but they are just not used to having them expressed in the way that I have chosen. It takes the audience time to understand my perspective on the scientific question at hand. As the speaker, it my job to keep the audience together and "with me", rather than to "lose them". By presenting the material with the same clarity that I would for a layman, i.e. a literate non-specialist, I hope to make the talk transparent to everyone.

If you accept the concept that the speaker should make her presentation as clear and as lucid as possible, it then makes sense to apply the following guidelines. Begin your talk by telling your audience what to expect from you. End with a clean, crisp summary. Emphasize the important points, and de-emphasize the unimportant ones. It you are using variables, explain each one clearly. If you portray a graph, explicitly take a moment to describe the definitions of each of the axes. Avoid complicated tables and multicolored graphs unless you have a great deal of time to dwell on them and explain them. If you are saying something new that the audience has not heard before, then give them the opportunity to digest what you have explained before moving on.

If you are using slides, design them as simply as possible. Many times I have been in the audience of a talk that I am understanding and enjoying, only to have the presenter say "I know that you can't see all of the details on this next slide, but..." Why has the presenter inflicted this slide on his audience, if he knows the audience cannot see and understand the slide? Is this talk for the audience or not? Your goal is to work to keep your talk as simple as possible so that the ideas that you articulate are clearly communicated with minimal distraction. Respect your audience.1

Another advantage of the "layman rule" is that its invocation challenges my understanding of the material. After all, if I cannot explain the concepts presented in my talk at an elementary level so that an attentive layman understands them, then perhaps I do not understand the material as completely as I should. In this case, I have more work to do.

5.5 Walking the Plank

Rehearsing your talk is time consuming, but of great value. Preparation before practice concentrates on the small but necessary details of the talk. This micro-focus on the minute issues of your presentation is necessary to ensure the accuracy of the factual content of the lecture. However, the entire talk has to fit together as a complete mosaic. A practice session helps you to integrate your talk and see how well its component pieces fit together. The sections of the presentation must support each other. Its flow must be both logical and natural so that the audience is not confused or distracted. These features are nonscientific but aid and support the comprehension of the audience. Finally, the talk must be a certain length. It is hard to have a precise estimate of the duration of your talk without actually giving it.

The second reason for rehearsals is that they give you the opportunity to practice controlling your own nervous energies. Planning the presentation is one thing. Actually talking through it is quite another. Consider the following analogy.

Imagine a wooden plank, ten feet long and one foot wide. It is lying flat on the ground. When asked, almost everyone can walk that plank without falling off to one side or the other. Most people can walk the plank effortlessly, without any thought, particular exertion, or special skill. Now, take that same plank and raise it until it is one foot off the ground. Slightly fewer people can walk it without falling. If you raise the plank until it is ten feet above the ground, you will find that most individuals are not even willing to try to walk it. If you elevate the plank until it is one hundred feet off the ground you will find that it is the rare individual who is willing to attempt the walk.[*]

The proportion of people who can walk the plank shrinks rapidly as the altitude of the plank increases. Yet, the required skill to walk a plank ten feet long and one foot wide remains the same. What has changed is the required confidence in your capability to carry out what

[*] Taken from comments by Gen. George Thomas, 1863.

remains an easy task. Learning to trust in your own abilities, regardless of the external consequences, takes time and patience. This is what is gained in rehearsal. The more important the presentation (i.e. the higher the plank will be set in the end), the more important the need for rehearsal.

The ease of recording your performance on video tape can amplify the ability of rehearsals to improve your confidence. First, the use of video tape adds to the realism of your practice presentation. Secondly, watching the video tape gives you the opportunity to be in the audience of your own practice presentation. This perspective will permit you to make some countenance observations. Do you speak too fast? Do you speak in a monotone? Do you look down too much, paying no attention to your audience? Do you move your arms too much, distracting the audience? Do you stand like a statue? These mannerisms are clearly revealed in a videotape of your practice presentation.

Continuing with this issue, you can use the video-rehearsal to aid in changing any of your bad habits that appear during a presentation. For example, I found that, when left to my own natural tendencies, I speak too fast. While I wanted to correct this, moving to the other extreme would be intolerable. I needed a way to calibrate my speaking speed. By using a videotape, to tape, then view, then re-tape, then review a short reading session of mine, I was able to find the best speaking speed, and practice it until it became effortless.

5.6 Final Preparations – 72 Hours to Go…

Every scientist's last minute preparations for a presentation are different. I am best served by the following. Three days before the actual presentation, I bring my content preparations to an end. I have completed my reviews. I have prepared my slides. Rehearsals have come and gone. I know where I am to give the talk, and how to get there. I have a reliable estimate of the audience size. I have found the audiovisual equipment that will be used to support my presentation, and have tried it out, assuring myself that I am comfortable with its basic use. If I need to, I can give the talk without much in the way of audiovisual support. All of this planning work has been completed. Now, three days before the scheduled presentation, this preparatory component ends and a new readiness phase begins.

During this second, final phase, I consciously and deliberately remove my focus from the science and reseat it on myself. Specifically, I recover, strengthen, and reassert ownership over my life and its guiding principles. I overtly review what my career stands for. I reflect on the better natures of my personality. I recount the times that, in a moment of despair, a family member, colleague, friend, or senior scientist said exactly what I needed to hear, perhaps without knowing that I needed to hear it.

During this period, I shun new manuscripts, I avoid studying email, and distance myself from last minute advice. Instead, I insist that I get adequate sleep and rest. I watch a favorite movie, or read a chapter from a beloved book. Having already mastered and controlled the science in my presentation, I now choose to reassert mastery over myself, and enjoy some of life in the process.

Now, being centered and secure, and, in full recognition that my purpose, value, and merit are unaffected by my actual presentation or any reaction to it, I am prepared to speak to my audience.

5.7 Reverse Radar

Sometimes in preparation for a pivotal lecture, it is easy to be plagued by new distractions. These distractions come disguised as questions that have no good answers. Examples are "What if the president of the company comes to my presentation when I am discussing the most difficult part of the talk?" "What if no one chooses to attend the session"? "What if someone interrupts my presentation, consumed with violent disagreement"? "What if they laugh at me"? These types of tormenting questions can be gut wrenching and interminable. If you are not careful, these Lilliputian concerns can tie you down.

In a moment of frustration, I decided to put these questions to the test. I spend some time considering whether these early monitories provided any useful warning to me. I asked the question "Do these 'what if' questions predict actual occurrences"? I then started to track their performance as warnings. Specifically, before a presentation, I would make note of these self-afflicting questions (a warning that invariably involved someone else's action, and not mine.) After the presentation was complete, I would take a moment to review whether the warning came true. In no case did the event that was predicted by these admonitions come to pass. In every case, the issue raised by each of the "what if" questions failed in its prediction.

Of course, unplanned events do occur during presentations. Slide projector bulbs can and do go out. Hard drive performances become erratic. Media storage devices are incompatible with each other. Operating systems still crash. These unfortunate events do occur. [*] However, the key observation is that the predicted events do not. Thus, as a practical matter, these early monitories are not really warnings at all; they are merely distractions from what actually will occur. By placing your focus on a false prediction that is most commonly the product of anxiety, you can be caught unprepared by the occurrence of an unpredicted event.

In the face of these observations, I decided that it would not be sufficient for me to ignore the "What ifs?" Instead, I have gained assurance that what they warn of will not occur. Since they have always been false, they can be treated as a "reverse radar", not pointing toward the direction of danger, but instead pointing away from it. Thus, a pre-presentation "thought alarm", attempting to warn (or frighten) me about the danger of a question that would be put to me about whether I had read an obscure manuscript years ago can be treated as an alarm about a question that will do me no harm. I can therefore discount it, and return my focus to more pressing and helpful considerations.

5.8 Two Minutes to Go...

There are only a few minutes to go before your talk. The prior speaker is concluding her presentation. This is the most agonizing time. Commonly, after my labors and preparations, I find that my pulse has, nevertheless inched perceptibly upward. However, I know that in less than five minutes it will be back down to its regular, steady, and reliable rhythm. I therefore take my mind off this useless pulse-monitoring activity, and instead choose to place it in the following story.

---

[*] At the beginning of a presentation that I gave at a major corporation, I scanned the audience and identified my college advisor from thirty years before in attendence. While this was not bad, it certainly was an unanticipated surprise. I had no idea that he was no longer in academics.

A young officer during the US Civil War was given his first assignment. With several hundred soldiers under his new command, he was ordered to take his troops ten miles (half a day's march) and from there, to dislodge an enemy force from its position.

This officer, after organizing and informing his troops, started them on the march, himself in the lead. As the march got underway, this young officer realized that, although he wanted to be an officer, he had never actually led soldiers into battle before. Although he knew many of the frequently used unit formations, and had memorized many of the orders that commanders commonly gave in battle, he had never given them in a fight. It occurred to him that he was very inexperienced, (perhaps too inexperienced, a quiet voice whispered) to be given this command...

As he led his columns of troops over the hilly terrain toward his objective, he reflected on other issues in his life. Aside from his military education, he had not done well in school. In fact, he also performed poorly during his military training. He had developed a taste for alcohol that he had been unable to control, and occasionally, he had to be revived from a drunken stupor by other officers. He had tried to be a farmer once—and had failed. In fact, he reflected, every business he undertook in order to support his family had ended in failure. Ultimately, he wound up working in his father's tannery before the war because he had failed at everything else. His life, so far, was filled with failure...and now this...

He revived himself from his brooding, facing the recognition that he could not go on. As he and his soldiers approached the last rise between them and the enemy, he opened his mouth to give the order to halt the advance and return to camp. However, at that moment, when he knew within his heart he was going to fail as a soldier too, he gained his first unobstructed view of the enemy. He saw that they had seen him too, and that they were moving rapidly, but moving rapidly *away* from him. As he sat in amazement, watching the last of his adversaries disappear from sight, it occurred to him that they had been just as afraid of him as he was of them. This was a turn of the question that he had never considered before, and did not forget thereafter.

The young officer was Ulysses Grant.

5.9 Giving the Presentation

When it is time for you to give your presentation, you simply need the strength to follow through on your commitment to yourself. Don't think — simply do what you planned to do.

5.9.1 Countenance

When I first started speaking publicly, I used to spend time memorizing the first one or two minutes of my planned remarks to the audience. This maneuver helped me to relax and to settle down. However, although it was a useful exercise, I no longer use it because it inappropriately changed my concentration. I am not well focused on my audience during this recitation, but am instead focused on steadying myself. Thus, I now make my final, settling adjustments before I speak to the audience, helping to ensure that, when I begin speaking, the audience has my full attention.

An important key to relaxing your audience to what you have to say is your use of vocalisms. Vocalisms are not the words, but the sounds that accompany your speech. Specifically, they are the tones, pronunciations, speech rates, pitch and inflections in your voice. The philosopher Friedrich Nietzche thought of vocalisms as the most intelligible part of language. When you are confident, your voice has one sound. When you are hesitant, it has another. It has been said that, just as lyrics need music to come alive, spoken words need vocalisms.

The challenge for the speaker is to produce the right vocalisms in order to engage their audience. To answer this question, consider that, just as vocalisms are the music behind the words, there is emotion behind the vocalisms, and a person behind the emotion. Therefore, to correctly influence vocalisms, the speaker has to be the right person, i.e. has to have the right attitude. From the right attitude flows the right emotion, and from the right emotion comes the right combination of vocalisms.

The right attitude is commonly an open one. In order to open up your audience so that they can hear what you have to say, you must open yourself. When you relax and open up, your audience follows suit.

Actually, a very simple process can produce the timely transformation that you need. As I approach the podium, then turn and face the audience, I ask myself how would I explain the material that I am presenting to my most special loved one. How would I educate, convince, and persuade her of the content and implications of my work? Immersing myself in this context produces the change in my attitude and outlook that I need. All sense of anxiety, of resentment, of frustration, and of anger drain away. In full anticipation of being trusted, and with the certainty of forgiveness for any mistake that I might make, I cannot help but relax. Relaxing, in turn, reconnects me to my best faculties. My memories, my vocabulary, my sense of humor are all once again under my control and command, and I can enjoy the experience. My vocalisms adjust to my attitude and emotions, and I have created the environment in which I have the best opportunity to reach my audience.

Actively choosing to submerge myself in this mindset evokes from me the perfect countenance. When, as the speaker, I relax, the audience members themselves respond by relaxing. When the audience is relaxed they more easily learn from my presentation. The rest is anticlimactic. The presentation proceeds easily and is over much too quickly.

5.9.2 Slideshows

Although I am compelled to use slideshows in my discussion, I do my best not to rely on them. All of the practice that I have engaged in during the early preparation for the talk permits me to essentially give the lecture without the slides. If I allow myself to rely on them, then I find that I drift into concentrating on the slides, and not the audience.

The appropriate focus is typically the result of a balancing act. It is, of course, useful to have the slides available to you. Certainly, in a technical talk, you don't want to have to force yourself to memorize many small but important details that you will provide in the lecture. Also, if you get distracted, for example, by an unanticipated question that temporarily interrupts your train of thought, the slide is there to help refocus you. However, by simply reading your slides to the audience, you lose a potentially important connection with the audience.

My goal in giving a talk is not reading my slides, but reading my audience. I want to gauge their reactions to my talk. Are they upset? Bored? Energized? Focused? My sense of how the audience is reacting helps to guide the words that I use to reach them. I may need to alter my voice cadence or volume. I may make a point that I had not planned to make, or I may pull back and not extend myself as far as I had planned. Staying and remaining calm is the key. Focus on the audience, and discover what moves them.

5.9.3 When You Make a Mistake

Eventually, you will make a mistake during a presentation. You will forget a detail. You may garble your description of material covered by one slide. You may be sternly corrected by an audience member who has identified an inaccuracy in your presentation. There are two useful steps that you can take to handle this type of occurrence.

The first is to anticipate them. You are delivering a presentation to an intelligent, attentive, and discerning audience. Anticipate that they will find something critical to say about your lecture, and that they may interrupt you to make their point. Be prepared for it, if and when it occurs. Similarly, expect that you will make a mistake working through a slide. Although you hope to complete the presentation perfectly and without error, expect that you might misstep. Don't be surprised if, despite your best effort, you make a mistake.

Secondly, keep in mind that mistakes are common and everyone makes them. What distinguishes you is not the error, but your response to it. React by quickly correcting the mistake. One of the best ways to do this is repeat your review of the slide that you garbled, this time saying it correctly, then pausing to make sure that everyone understands the correction before you move on. For example, during a presentation, I said

> "In this sample size estimate, the use of the dependency parameter decreased the total sample size of the trial by increasing the sample size for the analysis of the primary endpoint that had the largest variance of the estimator."

However this was a wrong statement that I realized a moment later. I then tell my audience

> "I need to apologize because I may have misspoken a moment ago. What I meant to say was 'In this sample size estimate, the use of the dependency parameter decreased the total sample size of the trial by *decreasing* the sample size for the analysis of the primary endpoint that had the largest variance of the estimator.' I just want to take a moment to make sure that everyone understands my error, and the correction."

Try not to rush through making a correction. Despite your best efforts, the audience may find your presentation difficult enough to follow if it contained no mistakes. Mistakes obstruct their views of your main point. When you make a mistake, go back, correct it for your audience, giving them a moment to collect themselves, and then move them forward through the rest of your talk.

Secondly, after you make the correction, proceed with the remainder of your talk as though the mistake did not occur. Don't let the mistake fatally disrupt your equilibrium.

Even the best of prize fighters, on their way to a victory in a fifteen round fight, will lose a round. In fact, he may lose more than one round. The eventual victor may even get knocked down during the fight. However the good boxer keeps his sense of balance, purpose, and courage. Despite these temporary setbacks, he come back to fight the remaining rounds hard, that was his goal all along.

You expected that mistakes may occur. You have acknowledged and corrected it. All there is to do now is to move on.

5.9.4 Finishing the Talk

As the end of the talk approaches, the speaker commonly and correctly recognizes that they are nearing the end of the experience (or the ordeal). This sometimes leads to a new accelerated speaking pattern as he hurtles to the end of his talk. This is an unfortunate reaction that you should resist.

   This last minute rush can undo the fine, first part of the presentation that you completed. By racing through the final component of your talk, the audience quickly senses that you do not want to speak to them anymore. As you detach from them, they can disconnect from you, and some of the more valuable points in the last part of your lecture can be missed. Pace yourself and check your speech pattern as you near the end of your presentation. If you need to, make yourself pause for a moment to re-center yourself before finishing the lecture.

   If you have carefully planned and clearly delivered your presentation, you can anticipate that there will be several questions at the conclusion of your talk. Questions are a blessing, not a curse. Their presence often affirms that people understood your talk, and that they want to engage you. You can gain, and impart important new knowledge in this interchange that follows the lecture. If you can answer dynamically, the question and answer session can become a spirited repartee that everyone enjoys.

   When answering questions at the conclusion of the talk, be sure to answer the question. Speak in a voice that can clearly be heard. It commonly helps if you can first answer the question directly, rather than give an elaborate re-presentation of your work. Consider the following question asked at the conclusion of a statistical talk that I gave:

> "Is the sponsor of the study, who contributed tens of millions of dollars to this research effort, more likely to be happy with the conclusion of the experiment if they chose to follow your plan"?

A common answer might be

> "These research efforts are complicated. They involve many considerations and many factors have to weighed. Some of these factors were presented in my talk. However, the selection of more than one possible prospectively declared endpoint

can increase the likelihood that the sponsor will be pleased with the result."

In my view, a better response to the question "Is the sponsor of the study, who contributed tens of millions of dollars to this research effort, more likely to be happy with the conclusion of the experiment if they chose to follow your plan" would be

"Yes. By prospectively declaring more than one endpoint, and with the *a priori* allocation of type I error to each of the endpoints, the sponsor is more likely to be happier with the outcome, everything else being equal."

Both answers are defensible, but the first is indirect, and frankly does more to protect the speaker than it does to educate the audience. It is what I call a "non-response response". The second answer is clear and firm. It puts the speaker on the spot, in the sense that he may be asked to defend his assertion. The answer doesn't have to be provocative. But if a question can be answered clearly and directly without being provocative, then answer it clearly. On the other hand, if you are ethically bound not to answer a question, then simply say "I cannot answer that" and explain why.[*]

Additionally, answer all questions respectfully. If a question asked by an audience member appears silly to you, don't let any trace of your attitude enter your voice. In this case, that attitude is likely to be transmitted as arrogance to the audience. If a question is asked angrily, then respond with an answer that is both firm, and soft spoken. When considering your answer to such a question, take a moment to drive fear and anger out of your heart; this will ensure that these emotions do not betray themselves in your voice.

Finally, when you are all done, take a few moments alone to reflect on what you have accomplished. You have just completed an important presentation to a large audience. While you may have felt

---

[*] An example would be if you are asked about the results of an experiment that cannot be released yet because of obligations to your coinvestigators, who have all agreed to announce the results jointly at some time in the future.

fear, you were not moved by it. Instead, you remained purposeful, steadfast, and true to your conviction that you had something of value to impart to the audience. You deserve to feel good and thankful for a moment, so be sure to take a moment to do so.

Later, take some time to reflect on the usefulness of the preparations that you made for your lecture. On what should you have spend more time? Were you over-prepared on some issues? What maneuver helped you to retain control over your own nervous energies? Did you focus on the audience during the talk? Did you control your speaking cadences? Did you make any mistakes, and, if so, did you respond well to them? Did any of the "what if's" come to pass?[*] This short, solitary review will be helpful as you begin to prepare for the next presentation.

5.9.5 Final Comments

Preparing for a presentation tests your true knowledge of your own work by requiring you to clearly explain it to others. Giving lectures provides a way to disseminate your work. Defending your work in a question and answer session can instruct you about the utility of your work and its contribution to science, while sharpening your debating skills.

If there is an enemy to be faced in making presentations, it is not the interaction with the audience, but the fear of failure. Don't let presentation anxiety stunt your development as a junior scientist.

References

1.   Feibelman PJ. (1993). A Ph.D. Is Not Enough: A Guide to Survival in Science. Cambridge MA. Perseus Books.

---

[*] Discussed in Section 5.6.

Chapter 6
Ethics and the Investigator

6.1 The Scope of This Chapter

You will very likely face an ethical dilemma as a scientist. You will certainly face important ethical decisions during your career. This chapter will help to prepare and strengthen you for these inevitable challenges. It is not the purpose of our conversation to repeat the content of the many excellent general treatises on ethics that are easily available to you. Instead, our focus will be on the ethical issues that junior investigators must commonly address, concentrating on the unique vulnerabilities of these developing scientists.

6.2 Ethics

Ethical conduct is the demonstration of your respect for the work, contributions, and sacrifices of others. General discussions and treatises in ethics have been written[*], but these rulebooks neither identify all good ethical behavior, nor do they delineate the complete universe of ethical misconduct. Rules may describe ethics, but ethics are a way of life. Ethical conduct is derived from a mindset, and flows from an attitude. It is not the mere memorization of a collection of rules.

For you as an investigator, it may be more useful to think of ethics not as a collection of documents, but instead as a body of "living principles". These principles, growing and adapting over time, govern your interrelationships with others in science. These interactions are complex and interactive. They consist not just of actions, but of words, and not just of words but of vocalisms and "body language". These complicated dynamics, occurring at many levels, cannot be completely detailed in writing. In this sense, trying to codify the ethical behavior of others is like trying to photograph the wind. You can observe its effects, be it gentle and pleasant on the one hand, or destructive on the other, but you cannot observe the driving force behind these manifestations. Ethical conduct is not determined by rules but is governed and calibrated by an ethical character, itself undergoing continuous renewal.

Ethics is commonly reduced to identifying the right thing to do, and then having the strength and courage to do it. However, it can

---

[*]Many sources are available on the web. A compendium of resources can be found at http://www.csu.edu.au/learning/eis/ethxonline.html). Concern for ethics, as might be expected, reaches down to the high school science level (http://www.nzase.org.nz/ethics/animal.pdf). There are ethics centers on line (http://onlineethics.org/). In addition, there are now journals devoted to ethics (http://www.opragen.co.uk/).

be hard to know what the right thing to do actually is. Consider the
following[*]

> Germany was in ruins at the conclusion of World War II. A
> young American physician who arrived there at the war's end
> observed that Germany's urban foundation had collapsed.
> With no effective administration, communication or transpor-
> tation infrastructure, the ability of the German municipal gov-
> ernments to deliver food and medicines to its citizens had dis-
> appeared. In this vacuum, diseases of poverty and poor sanita-
> tion arose to attack the old, the young, and the infirmed.
>
> Particularly virulent was an outbreak of pneumonia
> that was especially lethal among German infants. Fortunately,
> this infection was successfully treated with penicillin. How-
> ever this antibiotic, then a relatively new drug, was in short
> supply.
>
> Simultaneously, an outbreak of gonorrhea and syphi-
> lis broke out among young American soldiers who were con-
> sorting with prostitutes. Gonorrhea, without therapy, would
> produce a life of pain and misery. Untreated, syphilis would
> lead to insanity and death. The definitive treatment for each of
> these diseases was the antibiotic penicillin.
>
> This young physician did not have enough penicillin
> to treat both cohorts, and he had to decide to which he would
> administer the drug. The German infants who had no respon-
> sibility for the 50 million deaths that the war produced would
> be its newest, last, and perhaps most tragic victims if the doc-
> tor treated the soldiers.
>
> However, the GI's had not wanted to come to Europe
> and fight, but were compelled by the actions of a country that
> had given itself over to a tyrannical despot. Thousands of
> Americans had died or been maimed by choosing to fight in

---

[*] This scenario was provided during a lecture while I was a medical student at
Cornell University Medical College in the Spring of 1996. I have long since
forgotton the identity of the lecturer and so am unable to give him an appropriate attrribution. However, perhaps it is credit enough that almost thirty years
later, I still remember.

order to set other people free. They were not clerics; they were simply young men acting like young men commonly did. Were they to be punished by withholding treatment?

   The physician did not have enough medicine for both. Who should he treat?

Some honest and generous people can quickly determine what "the right action" is. However "the right action" might be different from one commentator to the other. Still, for others, equally honest and ethical, the decision is perplexing and difficult. Rulebooks on ethics are of little value in these types of situations where the best of ethical conduct is required, and required immediately.[*]

6.3 Innate Value

An important part of our discussions thus far in this book have focused on the manner in which the investigator should treat himself. The importance of self-esteem, of prizing your own value despite the nature of external circumstances, is a core principle for the scientist. In a manner of speaking, the recognition that you have great value regardless of how your colleagues or superiors treat you is the ethical treatment of yourself.

   The ethical treatment of others is based on the principle that they have innate and special value, irrespective of their external circumstances. Good ethical behavior flows easily from your decision to accept, with approval, the belief that your colleagues, adversaries, critics, experimental subjects (human or animal) each have special and unique significance. Their worth remains unchanged regardless of how they are treated by others, or how they treat you. This is the basis for reacting to them and their work product with deference and dignity.

   Recognizing the innate value of others reinforces your drive and desire to respect them, their efforts, their time, their work, and their opinions. This is a very high standard, and one that requires consistent

---

[*] The physician chose to use the penicillin to treat the GI's. He said "Every morning, outside my office, the young German mothers would line up, clutching their coughing and dying babies to their chest, and spit on me as I walked by".

effort and character development from you to achieve. However, this core principle of the innate value of yourself and of others provides clear direction for you as your gauge your relationships and interactions with them.

6.4 Undertows

It is unlikely that the reader will dispute the importance of moral rectitude and good ethical conduct. It is also reasonable to assume that your peers and colleagues shun unethical behavior as well. When I was a medical student, I cannot recall a single episode when a fellow medical or graduate student ever affirmed publicly or confided in me privately that they wanted to be an unethical physician, or that they aspired to become an improper scientist. By all observations, their motivations for conduct good science were as genuine as mine. Nevertheless, some of them have, sadly, given themselves over to poor ethical conduct.

Examined from another perspective, senior scientists who are currently engaged in unethical conduct today, started their career, in all likelihood, with the attitude that you have or had as a junior investigator. They did, as you do, cling to a firm believe in proper professional conduct. Yet they too have gone astray. A relevant question for you is, "What is it about me that will make me different from professionals who have come before me and who have lost their ethical way"?

Why do some junior scientists with the best and most wholesome of intentions ultimately engage in unethical conduct? Part of the reason is that young workers are not looking in the direction of the attack. As a junior scientist, you can't help but be attuned to sensational issues in ethics that may be in the news (e.g. falsifying data in a manuscript, or stealing authorship of an abstract, or withholding therapy from ill patients to make a research observation). However, large ethical difficulties in oneself do not spring up *de novo*; they inexorably develop from character and personality flaws that the scientist allows to go uncorrected. These defects, either hidden from view (or hiding in plain view), emerge to exert their overt influence during a time of duress, anguish, frustration, or fear. Thus, the scientist must consciously develop a talent of self-discernment in order to recognize their own small vulnerabilities. Recognition of these flaws is the first step toward their removal, or, more accurately, replacing these weaknesses with new found strength.

The ethical nature of your character requires constant attention and must be guarded. However, recognize as a junior scientist that rarely will your personal ethics be overcome in one hurried assault. Your boss will not storm into your office one day, interrupting your quiet deliberations to demand that "you must carry out the following flagrantly unethical task...". Instead, your ethics will be overcome slowly over time. This corruption, like the slow stream of poison sliding into a clear mountain lake, is a process that occurs over years, and produces a predictably sad outcome.

The temptations and opportunities for unethical behavior are all around us. The promises of money, prestige, promotion, and grant awards sometimes seem closer to reality if the investigator is willing to engage in only a little unethical behavior. For example, including an inaccurate and favorable summary of an experiment in a grant application to strengthen the argument for an award can appear to be the smallest of violations; the investigator decides to "let it go". In a collection of your work, the incorrect attribution of the ideas of a student is easy to get away with, but is poor ethical conduct.

We, as investigators, are surrounded by these temptations every day; like a strong undertow, these forces work to pull us away from our ethical base. If we are passive, this unethical undertow will sweep us downstream. Your vigilance is required to detect these circumstances, and your affirmative energy is necessary to resist the temptations that they offer.

Damage to your ethics through enticements or distractions can occur in any career field. In some environments, the distraction is money. Of course, everyone is concerned about money, and commonly money is a good reward for good work. However, in some environments, workers fixate on money. Although the ongoing central activity at the institution is supposed to be science, much of the conversation that take place is about money. Discussions of stock prices, estimations of the sizes of year-end bonuses, computations of the impact of a new product on one's wages, conversations comparing the salaries of different people can be ubiquitous and appear to swirl around you. Even the most charitable and least material people can be carried off by this monetary maelstrom. Dissenting voices are overruled. Everyone in the organization agrees that ethics are important; however, if an outsider were to judge what is the most important principle by the prevalent topics of conversation, the most important concept would be seen to be not ethics, but money. The atmosphere is not seasoned with money, it is poisoned by it.

In other fields, the focus is not on money directly, but on publications. In a field where publications are intended to serve as simply a method of communicated scientific information, they can unfortunately become an end unto themselves. Colleagues discuss and compare the number of publications that they have. Researchers consider the advisability of working on projects based on the work's "publication potential". Of course, publishing is important to the scientist, but the love of publishing (i.e. the idea that publishing has great value regardless of its content) threatens to poisons the ethics environment.

Working and hoping to become successful in these environments can first disorient, and then overcome your sense of ethics. As an investigator, you may not recognize the harm that will befall you. However the combination of pressure and acceptance ("everyone is doing it") can overcome the better nature of your ethics.

6.5 Case Histories

Unfortunately, there have been many cases of ethical misconduct in science. It is instructive to examine a small number of case histories. The two following examples were chosen primarily because they involved junior investigators. The histories are reviewed here not just to provide the facts of the case, but to help you as a developing scientist to generate the vision to see the seeds of unethical conduct. By watching it develop in others, you may develop the inner sight you need to identify and rub it out of yourself.

6.5.1 Case History 1: Childlike Emotions

John Roland Darsee was a 33 year old fellow in the lab of a prestigious professor at the Brigham & Women's Hospital at Harvard University.[*]

---

[*]This account is taken from http://www.unmc.edu/ethics/data/darsee.htm.

By 1981, he had published over 100 papers and abstracts while at Harvard and at Emory University.[1] This young scientist was considered one of the most remarkable of the researchers who were working in a prestigious cardiovascular laboratory. His seniors anticipated that he would be a shining star in the field of drugs and other interventions that speed recovery from heart attacks and heart failure.

However there were suspicions that Dr. Darsee's work was not all that it appeared to be. Over a period of time, two of his colleagues, along with a laboratory technician who worked with Darsee, harbored suspicions about his accomplishments in the laboratory. Fearing that an abstract that Darsee was preparing contained no actual research, but only fabricated data, they went to the director of the lab to request an investigation. The director asked Darsee to show him the raw data that was the basis of the thesis of the abstract, a request to which Dr. Darsee acceded. He then returned to the laboratory and started some recordings on a single animal. He charted and dated these recordings in such a fashion as to make it appear that the data from this single experiment was from several experiments. Seemingly unaware of his company, he executed this fraud in the presence of several colleagues and a technician. They accosted Darsee who, in the midst of this confrontation, admitted to his falsifications. In the face of this confession, Darsee was stripped of his important National Institutes of Health fellowship. In addition, the offer of a faculty appointment was withdrawn. However, Dr. Darsee denied any other falsifications, and was permitted to continue to work in the laboratory and to proceed with his publications.

Later that year, additional research difficulties were encountered. The lab in which Darsee worked was part of a multi-institutional study. When the multi-center study was analyzed, an evaluation revealed that the data that were collected from Harvard's lab was discordant with that of the other institutions. An ensuing investigation revealed that Darsee had falsified the Harvard contribution to the multi-center study as well.

The spreading investigation revealed that nine of Darsee's papers and 21 of his abstracts that he had authored while at Harvard were false and had to be withdrawn. Darsee stated that, although he had no recollection of falsifying data, he acknowledged the review panel's establishment of the fact of falsification and his personal role. Delving deeper in Darsee's past, it was determined that eight of the papers that he published while at Emory were false; these were retracted from the literature. In addition, 32 of his authored abstracts from Emory were found to contain manipulated or fabricated data. In fact, some of the coauthors on several of these abstracts did not know that their names were on the abstracts. An examination of his record while an undergraduate student at Notre Dame demonstrated that he falsified data at this pre-graduate level. Darsee was debarred from NIH funding and sitting on advisory bodies for 10 years.

To simply recount the sad story of a promising but young scientist is not a sufficient evaluation of this troubling case. The question that each junior scientist must answer is "How can I be sure that this will not happen to me".

As Darsee came to grips with his own tragic record, he tried to explain why he has chosen to take the unethical path. At one point, be referred to the death of his father, and his admiration for his mentors. At another point, he asked "forgiveness for whatever I have done wrong." Perhaps most revealing of all, he said, "I had too much to do, too little time to do it in, and was greatly fatigued mentally and almost childlike emotionally. I had not taken a vacation, sick day, or even a day off from work for six years.....I had put myself on a track that I hoped would allow me to have a wonderful academic job and I knew I had to work very hard for it."

6.5.2 Case History 2: The Patchwork Mouse

A major scandal at one of the most prestigious cancer research centers erupted in the 1970's.[2] and is also illustrative of the level of pressure to which junior scientists are exposed.

The idea of treating major human organ failure with a transplanted organ from another human was becoming an increasingly attractive idea in the mid twentieth century. In the 1960's, the concept moved from theory to reality, as surgeons mastered the monumental task of keeping the patient and the transplanted organ alive during and after surgery. For the first time, the ability to treat end stage renal disease with a new kidney, or to ameliorate heart failure with a new heart was moving from the experimental phase to a place as a useful therapeutic option for patients with these fatal diseases. However, it soon became clear that, most times, the body did not react well to the implanted organ. The immune system of the patient receiving the new organ reacted to the transplant as it would to a foreign body, mounting a brisk and fulminant attack against the new and unrecognized tissue. This reaction would destroy the new organ in a matter of days or weeks. This "host vs. graft" reaction was not generated when the transplant occurred between close relatives or in those people who, through chance, were determined to be a "good match" with the new organ. However, for the vast majority of the population who could find no such match, organ transplantation would not be a viable option. Solution to the host vs. graft reaction became the new imperative in transplantation research.

Attention turned to the Memorial Sloan-Kettering Cancer Institute, where a young and promising scientist was brought in to solve the problem of transplant organ rejection. The junior scientist, William Summerlin, focused on the problem of skin grafting, where skin from one patient was grafted onto that of another. The skin was well recognized as a tissue against which a host vs. graft reaction would be immediately launched and easily visible. Thus the outcome of the procedure could be quickly observed. Furthermore, a solution to the skin transplantation problem would not only open the door to the solution of the host vs. graft reaction for other organs, but would allow skin grafting procedures to be more readily used in unfortunate burn victims.

Dr. William Summerlin began his work by attempting to graft the black skin of one mouse onto the flesh of a white mouse. There were high expectations for his efforts, and it was hoped that he would be able to produce this patchwork mouse free of any evidence of host vs. graft disease in short order. Finally, he claimed that he had succeeded by incubating the graft in a nutrient medium outside of the body. This simple solution had apparently been missed by contemporaneous transplantation researchers. However, fellow researchers were having difficulty reproducing his results. In order to reassure his colleagues that he had indeed solved the problem, Summerlin showed his chief a collection of mice with a patchwork of black and white skin.

This impressive display stayed his critics, and the transplantation community began to breathe a collective sigh of relief, believing that the host vs. graft reaction had been solved.

Problems arose at once when other researchers requested Dr. Summerlin's protocol and were unable to duplicate the results and produce a patchwork mouse. Further investigation and interrogation of Dr. Summerlin revealed the magnitude of the fraud. Unable to get his procedure to work, Summerlin had used a felt pen to color white-skinned mice black in a patchwork fashion, simulated dark skin grafts on white mice. This, in combination with the assertion that operations had been performed that had not been carried out, was the basis of his claim. His career was over.

The scientific community was flummoxed by this tragic and desperate act. Several explanations as to Dr. Summerlin's possible motive were offered. It has been suggested that Summerlin actually believed that he really did solve the host vs. graft problem in the way he described, i.e. using the simple nutrient bath; however, he mistakenly grafted the skin of one mouse to the skin of a related mouse. Unable to reproduce this successful graft, but self-assured that his results were correct, he resorted to the felt-tipped marker. He may have seen no harm in this because of his belief that his initial results were correct.[3]

This situation was complicated, but once again, the combination of high expectations and character weakness produced a personally destructive and sad result.

6.5.3 All Human Together

The question is not whether you as a scientist agree that the preceding case histories are lamentable. Here is the relevant question: do you have a background in which, during a moment of fatigue or ambition, you can falsify (or have ever falsified) information? If an honest reflection of your history reveals the presence of this weakness, then react, not with self condemnation, but constructively and with an understanding of why you committed the fabrication. Specifically, resolve to 1) correct the record, and 2) ensure that you take action to avoid this problem's recurrence.

This second step is critical, and requires a closer inspection. If you have difficulty with honesty when fatigued, then affirmatively take the following measures. Specifically, give up the career advancement track, the stress, and the lifestyle (as well as the benefits that accrue to that lifestyle) that engender your weakness. Until your character grows, and you can maintain steadfast honesty in the face of fatigue, choose to be content in a lower echelon position in which the best of your talents can be brought to bear and displayed, rather than work in a more prestigious position that will bring out the worst in you, destroying your promising career. Don't progress as fast as possible, but instead, as fast as is consistent with your ability to work reliably, dependably and honestly.

Additionally, (when rested) examine yourself. Force to the surface the deeper issues that command your unethical behavior when you are fatigued. What is it that you fear will happen in revealing the truth? Why are you so frightened of failure that you are driven to the extreme of falsifying data? The fear is real, and, if it is a fear of self-condemnation, then you have a great deal of company. It is commonly not the failure at a task that we fear, but the accompanying self-loathing that we cannot bear. The simple but revealing truth is that you, with your intelligence, insight, and capabilities, are far more valuable than your experiment's outcome. Begin to replace the self-condemnation with self-respect. Sometimes this requires counseling, while at other times just the time for self-reflection. These are simple steps that you can take to strengthen your character and, perhaps, save your career.

Also keep in mind that if you do not have the particular weaknesses revealed in the previous two case histories, then you have others. We are all human together. We do not each have the same flaw, but we each have some flaws against which we must struggle. Come to know your particular set of weaknesses and work to strengthen yourself against them.

6.6 Cite your work carefully

With the intense competition for grants, publications in prestigious journals, and even media coverage, it is all to easy to view career progress as a zero-sum game; a tournament in which every victory achieved by one research group is felt as a defeat by another. This is a remarkably prevalent mindset in endeavors that are, by definition, collaborative. While very few motivations fuel our productive efforts like healthy competition does, rarely does the scientist working alone and in isolation miraculously produce a stupendous result. Competition is only a device, and while scientists are commonly and sadly caricatured as a collection of magicians on a stage racing against each other to see who can pull the rabbit out of their hat the fastest, the nature of our work remains collaborative.

As a junior investigator, there may be two areas of your work in which you will have the opportunity to put your ethics on this issue to the test. The first is your ability to resist taking credit for a capable student's good idea. The second is your reaction to the good idea of a colleague that you come across in reviewing a manuscript that is not yet published, or by evaluating a grant application that is not yet funded. The common thread that connects these situations is that the originator of the idea is in a disadvantageous position. The naïve student cannot adeptly protect herself from intellectual property theft, nor can the manuscript or grant author defend himself from the malevolence of an anonymous reviewer. Each circumstance provides the opportunity for theft, precisely because the victim's work product is open and exposed. Specifically, it requires ethical strength to recognize and resist the temptation of stealing from a vulnerable colleague.

6.6.1 Deft Thefts

The work of students is especially vulnerable to intellectual theft. Students develop freely in a trusting intellectual environment that encourages the flow and interchange of ideas. If you have been assigned to a student as their advisor, mentor, or have been asked to sit on a thesis/dissertation committee, you will find that you will be exposed to many good and innovative ideas. Commonly, very little thought is given to tagging each idea to its correct creator in this intellectual cauldron. Several of these ideas may be important and useful to you, and, when properly developed and described, would make a worthy contribution to your field. It therefore should come as no surprise that the temptation can be great to take the student's idea as your own. The student may not recognize this deft theft as such, and, in their naiveté, may believe that your action is appropriate.

However taking the student's ideas and work product as if they were your own is naked intellectual theft. Like any crime, several people are damaged in the process. One is the student (and, indirectly, the student's family), and the second is you and your character.

Commonly, the student's goal is not just to find a topic, but to gain the widest possible experience in developing that topic. They are looking for new and formative experience with cerebration, instrumentation, computation, but, most importantly, collaboration. They have worked hard and patiently to put a committee of advisors together in order to produce the highest caliber of scientific and professional interchange. They assiduously pursue every lead that you provide for them, and excitedly share with the committee any new ideas or breakthroughs that they believe they have experienced. They are anxious to make progress, but that progress is built on a bedrock of trust and loyalty that develops between the committee and the student. The student draws freely on that trust, using it to shape their scientific capabilities and advancement.

Intellectual theft demolishes that foundation of trust. The student's work productivity is thwarted by the theft. Additionally, and perhaps most importantly, the student herself is damaged by the encounter. Her ability to work effectively with others is impaired, and only with great difficulty is she able to trust other collaborators again.

Overcome the temptation to usurp the student's work as your own. Avoid the trap of thinking that you will do a better job than the student in placing the student's work product in its best context and in its promulgation. Who can do the better job is not the point. The student has earned the right to complete the development herself. The value of her work product is secondary to the value of the experience she will gain in taking the lead in publishing and disseminating the result. If you are concerned about a successful integration of her work into the current fund of knowledge, then the best role that you can play is to support her by letting her draw on your expertise in crafting her report or publication. The student benefits immensely from this concerted effort on your part, and in the process, gains a remarkable experience in seeing what a good professional collaborative writing experience can produce.

A second thought-trap that investigators fall into is the belief that they need the acknowledgement of the work product more than the student does. The investigator may think that the student has a wealth of opportunity in front of them, while they do not. This is a remarkably pessimistic and self destructive thought process to which the investigator should not succumb. Both you and the student are better off if you devote your support efforts to helping the student to publish their work in their own right, with them as first author, and you as supporting author. This can be a seminal experience for a student researcher while simultaneously rejuvenating your career interest.

6.6.2 Theft During Grant and Manuscript Reviews

Grant reviews can be dynamic if the subject matter is of great interest. As a grant reviewer, you can learn a great deal about the subject matter under investigation. The literature reviews are commonly excellent, and the interchanges that take place among the reviewers are dynamic and provocative. Involvement in grant reviews is a wonderfully productive activity for junior investigators, providing the opportunity to both learn, discuss and debate contemporary issues that surround your research interest.

However, reviewing a grant is essentially looking closely into the ideas and intellectual repository of a fellow investigator. Sadly, when the work of others is open and unprotected, the temptation of theft is near at hand. Unscrupulous grant reviewers can pirate an idea, or technique, or style of analysis from the grantee whose work they are reviewing, taking the idea as their own. This theft debases the reviewer, the grantee, and the entire review process. When the grantee discovers that his work has appeared in an unacknowledged form, a dispute can break out, further eroding scientific relationships, and wasting valuable time.

This is an unfortunate sequence of events, made all the more so, because the coveted ideas will commonly become available later in published form. If the reviewer finds themselves unable to wait, they can call the grantee and discuss the issue after the grant review has been completed (including formal notification of the scores the grantee received on the review). This kind of post-grant communication can be very productive and lead to a new collegial relationship between the reviewer and the grantee. By exerting discipline, the grant reviewer has elevated the work of the grantee and the nature of his relationship with the grantee.

Similarly, when the peer review process for a manuscript is complete, and the reviewer has received the final decision of the journal to which the manuscript has been submitted, it is quite appropriate for the manuscript reviewer to contact the author to discuss the idea suggested by the author that intrigued the reviewer. Issues of acknowledgement should be covered to the author's satisfaction. Once this is accomplished, new collaborative efforts can be professionally and ethically forged.

6.6.3 Cite Honestly

Modern problems that scientists are compelled to solve are by nature constructed so that no one working singly and in isolation can solve them. Instead, the sustained, combined efforts of different individuals with different talents is required to attain the final solution. It is sometimes difficult to see where one scientist's contribution ends and the other begins within these collaborative constructs. Which of two men who are both struggling to move a heavy piano up a flight of stairs can take credit for completing the task at the expense of the other? The burden of labor may shift momentarily from one worker to the other, but the joint effort of each is required. In the end, the feat is accomplished and both share in the achievement.

Since your work product's luster has an important contribution from the reflected light of the accomplishments of your colleagues, learn to take a singular delight in acknowledging the work of others. Be careful and specific in detailing the contribution that others scientists have made to your work in your own writings, and presentations. If you make a mistake in a citation, move rapidly to correct it, as you would hope that others would react to a mistake in the citation of your own work. Work openly and collaboratively, freely acknowledging the work of others.

Finally, those who attempt to usurp what in reality belong to another can be in for quite a surprise, as demonstrated below:

When a man attempted to siphon gasoline from a motor home parked on a Seattle street, he got much more than

> he bargained for. Police arrived at the scene to find an ill man curled up next to a motor home near spilled sewage. A police spokesman said that the man admitted to trying to steal gasoline and plugged his siphon hose into the motor home's sewage tank by mistake. The owner of the vehicle declined to press charges, saying that it was the best laugh he'd ever had[*].

Being less than honest can produce its own unpredictable collection of unfortunate surprises.

6.6.4 Spinning Results

Your work must be promulgated if it is to be received and integrated into the current fund of knowledge by the scientific community. You will have the primary, if not exclusive responsibility in this affair, and therefore bear a special and sometimes solitary burden. As we all have observed, there are alternative ways to place your work into context.

Unfortunately, research results are frequently described in a mawkish, rather than circumspect manner. This is understandable. There are only a small number of presentations that can be made at highly visible plenary sessions occurring during prestigious national and international meetings. Similarly, almost every scientific field has a limited number of distinguished journals, producing a natural and healthy competition for publication slots. In order to gain the widest readership (and, perhaps the greatest notoriety) the temptation is great to state the research results in their most provocative manner. These overstatements are misleading and reprehensible. The environment is further worsened by the sensationalism of scientific results by the lay media.

The price science pays for this sensationalization is inaccuracy and ultimately, loss of credibility. The greater the stretch from the reality, the greater the potential to mislead the community. It is clearly critical to describe the implications of your work product. However, it is also important to describe these results cautiously.

---

[*] Taken from The Darwin Awards 2003 which may be located at http://www.binarywrangler.com/archives/000063.php

Consider the case of a clinical trial in health care. The Lipid Research Clinics (LRC) study was an examination of the role of cholesterol reduction therapies in reducing the risk of clinical events. Designed in the 1970s by lipidologists working in concert with experienced clinical trial methodologists, the LRC trial set out to establish with some finality the importance of cholesterol level reduction in reducing clinical sequelae of atherosclerotic cardiovascular disease, whose primary manifestation is a heart attack. It was designed to randomly allocate men to standard acceptable risk factor management for heart disease (diet and salt control, blood pressure control, and exercise), or this standard therapy plus an agent to reduce serum cholesterol measures. This cohort was then followed over time, counting the number of fatal and nonfatal heart attacks that occurred. LRC required over 3,500 patients to be followed for seven years to reach its conclusion, incorporated into a pre-specified hypothesis test.

These investigators did not underestimate the importance of their work. They knew the field was contentious, and that their study would be criticized regardless of its findings. The researchers designed their protocol with great deliberation and care. Upon its completion, they converted their lucid protocol into a design manuscript, publishing it in the prestigious *Journal of Chronic Diseases*[3]. This was a praiseworthy effort. The investigators prospectively and publicly announced the goals of the research effort and, more importantly, disseminated the rules by which they would decide the success or failure of the experiment for all to review before the data were collected and tabulated. This is one of the best approaches to reducing experimental discordance.[*]

In 1984, the study's conclusion were anticipated with great excitement. When published in the *Journal of the American Medical Association* [4] the paper revealed that active therapy produced an 8.5 percent reduction in blood cholesterol levels. Furthermore, there were 19 percent fewer nonfatal myocardial infarctions and 24 percent fewer deaths from cardiovascular disease in the active group. They declared that the study was positive.

However, a comparison of the analysis plan that the investigators stated that they would follow with the one that they actually used

---

[*] Study discordance was defined in Chapter Two.

and published at the trial's conclusion revealed an important difference. Using the original analysis plan, the results of LRC would be negative. However, the analysis procedure that they used produced a positive result was different.[*]

As we might expect, there are many plausible explanations for the diluted finding of efficacy for LRC. The cholesterol reduction therapy chosen for the trial, cholestyramine, was difficult for patients to tolerate. This difficulty led to fewer patients taking the medication, vitiating the measured effectiveness of the compound.[4] It must be said that, even with this weak cholesterol reduction effect, the investigators were able to identify a trend for a reduction in morbidity and mortality associated with cholestyramine. The study produced much new information that would have served as a firm, scientifically-based foundation for the next clinical experiment. However, the investigators chose instead to fly in the face of their own prospective rules for assessing the strength of evidence in their study, resulting not in illumination, but in withering criticism from the scientific community. This finding resulted in much controversy, distracted the community of lipid metabolism scientists, and was a basis for the concern that the US government was disseminating the notion that cholesterol reduction therapy was good for patients in the absence of firm, incontrovertible evidence that is now available.

Journal readership and audiences can clearly be mislead by an author's incomplete explanations and disingenuous descriptions. Imprecise descriptions and inaccurate statements are certainly disrespectful of your colleagues and the scientific community, and therefore are un-

---

[*] How was this possible? The critical region for the hypothesis test was $Z > 2.33$ according to the original, published protocol. The achieved value of the test statistic was 1.92. Since this was not greater than 2.33, the study should have been declared null. However, the investigators claimed at the end of this study that the best critical region for the hypothesis test was not $Z > 2.33$ but $Z > 1.645$. They changed the significance level of the test, based on the findings of the trial. The fact that the investigators published a design manuscript prospectively, highlighting the rules by which the trial would be judged and the standards to which the trial should be held, makes the *post hoc* change in the required test significance level singularly ignoble.

ethical. An investigator cannot claim to simultaneously hold his audience in high regard while he deliberately deceives them with the use of purposefully inaccurate statements, that, through their ambiguity, suggest more than the research methodology warrants.

There are two useful approaches that you as a junior investigator can take to purge your work product of this detritus. The first is to affirm that you will be satisfied with nothing but your best scientific effort. As a young scientist, you have developed and demonstrated scientific intuition and capability. It takes practice and consistent, patient effort to wield these in the right combinations. Now, develop the internal discipline and strength that you need to suppress your work if it not the product of your best effort. Only when you have satisfied yourself that you have before you is the result of your finest work product, then disseminate it clearly, letting it stand on its own merits.

Secondly, consider who your research effort will serve? Is its purpose merely to increase the citations in your own resume? Is your purpose in writing to speed you along your career trajectory? When you write, let your writing be motivated by the need to serve. When you make a contribution to the literature, let it come from spirit of service, not of the need to feed your own curriculum vitae. Service, not self aggrandizement, is central to making a solid contribution to science.

When you begin writing, ask first how will the results of your work best serve the readers. An honest answer to this question will purge any hint of intellectual dishonesty from your papers. It also creates the intellectual atmosphere for you to write freely about the limitations of your work that will help your colleagues best determine what the implications of your findings truly are.

6.7 Sexual Harassment

There is a wealth of material on sexual harassment, and the advice that is so readily available elsewhere will not be repeated here.* There is no

---

* See for example, http://www.eeoc.gov/facts/fs-sex.html. A statement of the federal law that governs this is http://www.eeoc.gov/policy/vii.html, and an interesting discussion of the complexity of the topic may be found at http://www.menweb.org/throop/harass/commentary/hostile-env.html.

excuse, and no person (junior scientist or otherwise) should ever tolerate or inflict sexual harassment or abuse.

Make no mistake. Your first obligation to your colleagues is to develop and sustain a professional relationship with them. This involves treating them, their opinions, their work, their personalities, their emotions, and their bodies with dignity and respect. This is an unceasing, irreplaceable obligation that you must face and discharge regardless of whether you have the desire and your colleague's permission to explore a nonprofessional relationship. If you do pursue a personal relationship with a colleague, then that personal relationship does not replace your professional obligation to them. Any personal aspects of your relationship must be in addition to your responsibility to treat them professionally.

These complications can be overwhelming and destabilizing. Emotional and sexual involvement is very complicated, and only a very few people are able to develop and sustain them while maintaining the true interpersonal dignity that professional relationships demand and require. It is rare couple that can work together as vibrant professionals, yet develop and retain personal and intimate relationship, an observation that acknowledges the particular emotional balance these couples must have. The rest of us are better off avoiding the entire matter by keeping our emotional and sexual interests separate and apart from our professional relationships.

6.8 Community Research and Obligations

Many investigators are interested in carrying out research in a community of patients. After developing a scientifically valid protocol and gaining Internal Review Board (IRB) approval to carry out the research, these investigators then face the daunting task of entering the community and recruiting patients to agree to participate in their study. This can be a particularly daunting task, and investigators have become very imaginative in persuading patients to participate in their research efforts. In these efforts, there are both individual patient responsibility, and, it can be argued, community responsibilities as well.

6.8.1 Patient Obligations

The principle that subjects who are recruited for a study require the best possible treatment must not be reduced to a simple truism. It is inconvenient for a subject to participate in research. They volunteer their time their energy, and quite frankly, sometimes their health for taking part in our studies. Researchers are honor bound and obligated to ensure that the participants in their studies receive the best available treatment. Subjects are a precious resource that should not be taken for granted and never to be squandered.

Consider for example, a four hundred patient clinical study, designed to test the effect of an intervention to reduce mortality. In this study, all 400 patients are to received an intervention; 200 patients will receive an active intervention, and the remaining 200 will receive control group therapy. If we assume that in the control group, the mortality rate is 40%, then we would expect, 200 x 0.40 or 80 deaths to occur in the control group. If we expect the active treatment group would have a 10% mortality rate, then we would expect 200 x 0.10 or 20 deaths in the treatment group. The effect of therapy, and the ultimate contribution of the research effort, depends on the difference in the number of deaths between the two groups. This measurement rests on the experience of $80 - 20 = 60$ patients.

These sixty patients are clearly very valuable to the research effort, and if the investigator knew who they were, these patients would, no doubt, be the object of special care and attention. The investigator would ensure that these patients understood the importance of the research effort. The investigator would see to it that these patients received the therapy to which they were randomized, and explain as many times as necessary how important it was for the intervention (be it control or active) to be administered. These subjects would not be made to wait to see the investigator. If one of these patients did not have the money to keep an appointment for a prearranged visit, transportation would be provided.

However, the investigator does not know which of the 400 patients might be in this select set of 60. Therefore this investigator must treat *every* patient in the study like *that* patient is *the* patient that will make the difference in the research. This is one of the ethical obligation of the investigator to her patients.

6.8.2 Community Obligations

In the attempt to identify patients for this study, the investigator has several possible approaches that he can take. One is to pursue patients individually. He can advertise for subjects publicly through, for example, flyer distribution, radio and television advertisements, and internet communication. However, another, perhaps more effective tack that the researcher can take is to first pursue a relationship with community leaders. These local leaders are commonly tightly connected with workers, families, services, and businesses throughout the neighborhoods of interest. These community leaders are able to extend information about the research effort deeper into the community than by the general broadcast approach. More importantly, these leaders have important influence within these neighborhoods. The support of these influential people can be an important incentive to people to participate in these studies.

However, the most successful and long lasting relationships between investigators and their research communities requires that the scientist honestly represent himself. The investigator must convince the community that the privacy, lives and livelihoods of the subjects will not be sacrificed in the research effort. The important of this assurance is critical in gaining neighborhood support for a research program, made all the more crucial if the researcher is himself a stranger in the research community. In an increasingly cynical world, where the motivations of all are suspect, and strangers are not given the benefit of the doubt, this assurance must be more than ironclad—it must be the truth.

The heart of the difficulty is that, regardless of whether the research is to be executed in a disenfranchised and poor neighborhood, or in an affluent community, each community fears that the lives of its citizens are held to be of less value by strangers and outsiders. This fear is fed by sensationalist stories in the media (many of which are true), in which the innocent and trusting have been victimized. Therefore, if the researcher is to gain the support of the community, he must persuade the people of that community that he would abandon his research before he would allow harm to come to them. While the researcher must believe this, this belief is not enough; he must educate and persuade a questioning community of his concern for their safety and wellbeing.

This is a very time consuming effort, but, a sacrifice the investigator should be prepared to make if he hopes to gain community support for his research. While your explanations are useful, your sincerity is required.

In order to demonstrate the commitment of the scientist to the community's involvement in the project, researchers will offer services that might not otherwise be available. Some scientists provide screening tests for health conditions that may be prevalent in the community. A series of talks and lectures at schools, churches, or other neighborhood gatherings can be well received. However, give thought to your motivation for these activities. Consideration of these tactics is actually a reflection on your philosophical approach to the community. Are you a researcher who may not have, but is willing to develop a concern for the community that extends above and beyond your research interest, or do you want your relationship with the neighborhood to be limited to your investigational objective? If you take the latter course, you run the risk of being perceived as scientist whose acts of generosity, time, and money in the community are seen as a mere *quid pro quo* to the neighborhood for recruiting subjects.

Your involvement in community activities that extend from the belief that your relationship with the community is deeper than your research interest is a time consuming one. The researcher must cease being an outsider, and be recognized as a familiar figure and a local repository of knowledge and advice. Relationships with neighborhood leaders can be very helpful here, but don't be surprised if they call you for help or advice on a difficulty matter in which you are believed to have some expertise.

6.9 Difficult Superiors

Among the most vexing problems that junior investigators must confront is the problem of interpersonal difficulties between you and a chief scientist to whom you report. Successfully navigating these difficult waters requires self-discipline, balance, and superb interpersonal skills. In these disputes, your goal should be to address the difficulty sensibly and professionally. Choose a behavioral level that allows you to emerge from the situation with a stronger disposition and sense of balance. You cannot guarantee a satisfactory outcome to the dispute;

however, you must ensure that your efforts to resolve this matter deepen and strengthen your character.

6.9.1 Delivering a Message

Chief investigators have many different motivations for being harsh with particular junior scientists; there are chiefs who are difficult, chiefs who are personally offensive, and chiefs who are unethical. What these senior investigators all have in common is that they each create a contentious and sometimes relatively unproductive work atmosphere. However, you must differentiate between these different personalities and styles because, while working with the difficult, tough boss can serve you well, working with the personally offensive chief or the unethical senior investigator can damage both you and your career.

The tough and unfair boss can choose to be a persistent irritant because he consciously singles you out for special, critical attention. He tends to be short on praise, but provides extensive critical discourses and elaborative disapproval. Despite your best efforts, he is unsatisfied and impatient, tersely demanding to know why you haven't taken the next step in your work. He seems to go out of his way to put you in situations (e.g. making presentations to audiences) in which he knows that you will be uncomfortable.

Central to your appropriate reaction to a hypercritical chief is your careful self-evaluation. It is common to wonder if you were misinformed about what your role would be in the project. Perhaps there was a misunderstanding about the talents that you would be bringing to the team. If you can, speak to other colleagues who have trained under him to see if they have been the object of similar treatment.

In this situation, it is very easy to give yourself over to despair because he may have damaged feelings. However, it is also possible that your chief has something valuable in mind for you. Possibly, his actions were calculated not to produce the best environment for you, but instead to create an atmosphere in which he commands your full attention. He has something to say to you, and would like your full concentration (perhaps in a way that you have never concentrated on anything in the past) before he can say it. This message is a core message, i.e. central to the development of your career. It may be that he has identified a penchant for the self-indulgent in you, or that he believes that you pay insufficient attention to your instrumentation. However, whatever his perceived shortcomings of you are, he believes that they are dangerous enough to damage your career trajectory. The persistent criticisms that you received from him so far are like the light but steady rain announcing the coming storm that, while tempestuous, provides the necessary water for good growth.

Now, of course, it would be better for all if your boss could just come to talk to you about this issue openly, honestly, and directly without this complicated behavioral preamble. However, interpersonal relationships, and frequently, inter-generational relationships are complicated by expectations and personality nuances. A boss who cared nothing about your character, scientific progress, or career would not take the time to identify your problems and share his perceptions with you. In fact, your chief recognizes your talents, and would like to see you make the fine adjustments necessary for your continued productive work. Since this type of chief has your best interest at heart, he is most likely to respond to your reaction to the environment in which he insists you work.

If this is the case, then your task as junior investigator is to prepare yourself to hear this message. This task begins with ensuring that you have a solid and reliable sense of self-worth and value, separate and apart from your external, critical environment. This strong sense blocks the conversion of harsh and helpful criticism of you into destructive self–hatred, as discussed in Chapter Four.

In preparing to meet with him, focus on two truths about yourself; 1) you are not perfect, and 2) you remain of great value regardless of your imperfections. Having protected yourself from the self–condemnation, spend some time with this hypercritical boss. Engage him in a conversation about his reaction to you. Be open to the possibility that, even though you may not appreciate the way that your chief has characterized your weaknesses, he may have clearly identified them. Respond affirmatively to that identification. Draw his specific concerns about you out into the open light where both of you can examine them clearly. By responding affirmatively to this critical but attentive chief, you can strengthen your character and scientific abilities. This permits a renewed relationship with him that is based more on positive responses to helpful suggestions than on an association that is shackled by the links of disapproval and self-condemnation.

6.9.2 Personal Abuse

Unremitting anger and hostility poured out by a chief onto her junior colleagues is a dangerous and destructive circumstance. This is not the situation presented earlier in which the criticism received by the investigator was instructive and constructive. Here, critical commentary is nonproductive, personal, and abusive. While it is a truism that you should not have to accept personal abuse in the workplace, it is also true that senior investigators are still provided a wide latitude and, commonly, are given the benefit of the doubt in many of these matters. Your institution should have safeguards and procedures that provide at least a modicum of protection for you. Frequently, however, these safeguards are imperfect.

Operating under a cruel chief in a personally and emotionally abusive atmosphere is damaging to you. Working in an environment that is full of anger is like taking a bath in caustic acid; without a good, thick, protective suit, you will be burned. Dealing with these painful circumstances requires firm and steady emotional control, qualities that you may not believe that you have, but that you must now develop.

Before we discuss coping strategies that you as an investigator can try, it is only fair to acknowledge that, in the end, all of the techniques that we will discuss here may fail you. Hopefully, this will be the rare circumstance, but we have to acknowledge this possibility. If, after your repeated efforts, you are not able to broker at least a ceasefire with your chief, you should leave her. Do not allow yourself to stay in a situation that is personally unhealthy for both you and your character development merely because working with her may be "good for your career".

The belief that you should remain in an emotionally toxic environment in order to keep the best productivity trajectory can be self-destructive. There is no guarantee that you will gain long term success by subjecting yourself to continued, daily, and unjustified abuse. Staying with an abusive chief may permit you to develop a work product that provides a temporary boost to your productivity, but in the meantime, other damage is done that offsets this small gain. Since your career is not your productivity, but also encompasses your principles, your standards, your character, your judgment, your conduct, your ethic, and your temperament, you must be equally vigilant in protecting them all. Staying in a personally destructive environment damages your perspective, alters your conduct, contaminates your professional judgment and unbalances you. Therefore, if your best efforts do not work—leave.

If you are unsure what you should do in this setting when all adaptive techniques have failed, ask yourself what advice you would give to your most special loved one if they were in your place. If your daughter, or husband, or nephew was the object of consistent personal abuse, would you not tell them to leave? Take the advice that you would give this special one, because you give it in the spirit of desiring nothing but the best for this good person; that is how you should advise and treat yourself.

6.9.3 Coping From the Inside Out

There are several strategies that you can follow to attempt to work effectively with a chief who is consumed with anger. Our goal, as stated earlier in the chapter, remains unchanged. You as junior investigator should handle this circumstance so that, regardless of the outcome (be it good or bad), both your character and your ethic are strengthened.

The foundation of each of the following strategies requires a solid sense of self-worth. Essentially, being the subject of ceaseless anger is the same as coming under attack. You meet this attack by fighting it off internally, in your own heart and mind first, before you directly deal with your vitriolic chief. This internal fight can be won by ensuring your sense of self-value remains protected and strong. Specifically, you must re-identify and strengthen your high self-value as the intelligent, capable, principled scientist that you are. Consider your ego-structure to be like a foundation for your aptitude, attitudes, and abilities. A house's good foundation does not require constant re-examination in quiet times; however, the occurrence of small quakes and tremors requires that this essential foundation be consistently monitored, inspected, and repaired. In these times of personal attack, pay critically close attention to your sense of self-value.

Your value as a scientist is greater than the valueless abuse being hurled at you.

Recognizing and reflecting this truth feeds and adds depth to your character. A firm sense of your own worth will provide the ballast and steadying support that you need for the coming struggles and confrontations. This solid sense may develop in a few days, or it may take several weeks. However, its growth is central to your ability to deal effectively with this growing crisis posed by your chief, a crisis that requires your special care and attention. Take the time now to get strong "from the inside out".

Being so strengthened, and armed with the recognition that the abuse offers no real threat to you, you can now more calmly evaluate the dynamic of the anger. Begin with the consideration of several possible explanations for the vitriol. For example, is it possible that the anger is situational? Has the angry senior investigator herself experienced a personal shock? Clearly the trauma of divorce, the death of a spouse, or new knowledge of the presence of a lethal disease can be expected to perturb anyone's sense of well being. So can the denial of a promotion, the receipt of heavy criticism, and the loss of institutional support. These are, of course, not excuses that justify the anger. However, if any of these situations are present, they would help to explain the outbursts and beg the question of whether a finite amount of patience on your part is all that is required.

If the anger is not situational, then consider meeting with her to discuss the situation. The meeting should not be an impromptu "hallway" conversation, but scheduled at a time when each of you can discuss this important issue. The purpose of the meeting is to educate her on what she has done, and to make it clear that while you are open to fair criticism, you will not acquiesce to verbal abuse.

If the senior investigator cannot find time to meet with you, then she must be persuaded to make time. In Chapter Three, we discussed the advisability of a mentoring committee. Your current circumstance is precisely that situation when this committee can be of great value because this group, made up not of your peers but those of your boss, can exert their influence. Meet with your committee, clearly explaining in detail your concerns about your boss to them. Your mentors

may have some insight into your chief's behavior based on their experience with her that you do not. After explaining your failed attempts
to meet with her, ask that they work to persuade your chief to meet with
you. If your boss is unwilling to listen to you, she may be open to hearing concerns voiced by her peers. It may be that the meeting must include your boss, your mentors, and you. Also, make every sincere attempt to oblige these honest attempts made by your mentors to resolve
this dispute.

Regardless of the presence of your mentors, preparing for this
meeting with your abusive chief will require special strength. After all,
she may take the opportunity to engage in further slander. Clearly, you
will need your best reasoning and interpersonal skills. However, you
are separated from them if you are lost within the tight grip of insecurity and self-condemnation. If this is your state, then your adversary is
not your chief; it is your own belief that you somehow deserve unremitting abuse because of who you are. If this is your feeling, then this is a
feeling that you must rub out. Answer the lie that you deserve unearned
criticism and punishment with the truth that your natural value and
worth is a greater reality than the stressful situation in which you find
yourself. Accepting with approval this truth about yourself is central to
your ability to communicate effectively in the upcoming meeting.

When the meeting occurs, stand your ground. By this time,
you have given important and critical thought to your relationship with
your boss. The purpose of the meeting is not to fight with your truculent chief. You simply want to educate her about what she is doing to
you and perhaps others around her. You have to find a way to transmit
this message in a non-threatening way. Since every investigator is different, the words and phrases that you need to speak will be unique.
However, it is most important to communicate clearly in a non-
threatening way so that she is not antagonized by the phrases you use.
In this situation, remember that you are in control if you control yourself.

You might consider saying the following in order to get
started.

"Thank you for agreeing to see me. I enjoy working with you
and being part of your scientific team, I have some concerns

about our professional relationship. If I have some specific deficiencies, I would like to learn what they are so that I can improve them. I am interested in being the best scientist that I am capable of being, and I believe that you can help me do that. However, lately, our discussions do not permit this, and I want to hear from you why our conversations have not been as professional as they might be."

This is submission through strength. Asking in this way demonstrates both your willingness to hear her side of the concern, but also serves notice that you expect a professional relationship with her and are willing to work to attain that. Remember you are not at the meeting to defend your actions, but to educate her about her own conduct. Accept criticism from her if, through this criticism, she is also being educated.

A good chief who has lost her customary good perspective on her relationship with her junior colleagues will hear the important message that you are conveying. Even though she may not say the words in response that you wish to hear, watch her actions over the next few work sessions to see if you have had an impact on her. Specifically, during this sensitive time, look for signs that she was educated by your conversation with her.

If she has been educated, the relationship may be rectifiable, and, you may choose to stay with the team. Your peers may want you to stay on the team as a stabilizing influence. Sometimes, junior investigators such as yourself may not react well to this use of your time, thinking that they should be focused on the science and productivity, and not on these emotion-laden activities. If you think this way, then I would encourage you to rethink your approach. Your value in collaborative efforts is not merely scientific; it is also to contribute to the collegiality of relationships that is the healthy conduit over which real scientific interchange takes place.

If your conversation was unsuccessful, and your chief was not educated, and the character of her relationship with you does not become more professional, then leave her group. Explain clearly to your boss what the reasons are for your departure. Leaving may be uncomfortable for you. In fact, you may have a boss who is vindictive enough, and small minded enough to attempt to damage your reputation by misrepresenting the circumstances of your dispute with her.

6.9.4 Lose-lose Scenarios

The previous scenario represents a deeply disturbing situation. Scientists do not like to abandon projects. You did not ask to be in this situation, and frankly, it is not fair to you to have to leave, and to have your career placed in jeopardy. However, since many of life's choices do not deal with fair interactions, you must set the caliber of your character in these lose-lose scenarios.

Essentially there are times in your career when you will have to choose between two egregious alternatives. Each requires you to pay a different but unbearable price. Prepare yourself to make the sacrifice to do what is right, making it in the belief that selecting the right alternative is its own reward.

Choosing to leave your boss requires you to pay a huge and painful price. You may lose any or all of the productivity dividend that would have come from the scientific work that you invested in her group. You are hard working and willing to earn the reputation as a scientist who can perform consistently as a reliable team member. You do not want the mark of troublemaker. However, the wrong choice requires you to pay a price from which you will not recover. A punishing pattern of abuse does permanent damage to your ability to function as a healthy, collaborative scientist in the long-term.

While you can and should give the best of your efforts to your chief, you must sacrifice your spirit of self-value and good ego-strength to no one. Also, remember that, as irrational as this world is, it is not so crazy as to waste good talent such as yours. While it is perfectly acceptable to be concerned about the damage done to your career by your dispute, also be reassured that the short-term damage will have no lasting value. Anticipate that new and good opportunities will find good scientists with good talent such as you.

6.10 The Unethical Chief

In this circumstance, we address the relationship between the junior investigator and the unethical senior investigator. Specifically, by unethical we mean a chief who does not value, and therefore disrespects the work of his colleagues and/or the sacrifices of his experimental subjects. This disrespect can take many forms. The fabrication of results is clearly unethical. The unwillingness to formally acknowledge the contribution of other workers is not right. Refusing to provide the best possible care to animals or patients that contribute to in vivo experimentation is also disrespectful and unethical. In addition, financial dishonesty is fragrantly disrespectful both to the granting agency, and to the people who provide the funds that the agency has the ability to disburse.

6.10.1 Ethical Lapse?

It is both a sad commentary and a reality that there are senior investigators who are involved in these, and other types of unethical behavior. However, unethical behavior can be hotly debated, and extremely controversial. Perhaps one of the most contested cases in recent years was the circumstances of Dr. Bernard Fisher, a distinguished cancer researcher. Dr. Fisher was chairman and principal investigator of the National Surgical Adjuvant Breast and Bowel Project (NSABP) for 27 years. At the head of a collaborative effort, Fisher first reported in 1985 that the less disfiguring procedure of removing the simple tumor from a women's breast (a procedure that has come to be known as lumpectomy) was as safe as mastectomy for women with early stage breast cancers.[*]

An audit was ordered for many of the patient records that formed the basis for the NSABP's lumpectomy study. The audit was originally intended to detect instances of fraud. While none was encountered, the National Cancer Institute (NCI) said, the auditors did find other discrepancies and ambiguities that resulted in the removal of more than 100 patients from the lumpectomy study. Furthermore, there were what appeared to be serious problems with the process by which patients were to provide their consent to enter the study. Specifically,

---

[*] Taken from Chicago Tribune, December 22, 1994 Thursday, Pg. 1; Zone: N Head Of Federal Cancer Institute Plans to Resign ; John Crewdson, Tribune Staff Writer.

information was collected on more than three dozen women after they refused to give their consent to be studied or had rescinded consent, a violation of ethical practices. Additionally, properly executed consent forms could not be located for several hundred other patients. Although there was no evidence that these women were harmed, the inclusion of these women violated federal regulations and medical ethics. The NCI asked that the experiment's analyses be repeated after removing those patients who had been inappropriately entered into the study.

Dr. Fisher reacted with indignation to these criticisms, complaining that "To go back to a database of a different era and to trim it and to change it and then do analysis is to me a very chilling thought." Likening the NCI's audit to "an audit of personal income tax returns from 1976 through 1984, based on 1994 tax laws", Fisher did not respond to a list of questions faxed to his office concerning why the patients had been enrolled, treated and followed. Dr. Fisher was subsequently removed as head of the Pittsburgh-based National Surgical Adjuvant Breast and Bowel clinical study for serious administrative failings.

The NSABP conducted numerous reanalyzes and shared with the government their findings confirming that the altered data had not affected the published results, concluding in 1992 that there was no "public health" crisis. In 1994, due to pressure from Congressman John Dingell, the National Cancer Institute insisted that an investigation commence on whether Dr. Fisher and his colleagues did anything wrong. At a June 15, 1994 hearing on data falsification, Dr. Fisher made the following statements:[*]

> "We didn't realize that the failure to publish our findings immediately would be misinterpreted by the public as an indication that we were concealing information....We should have been more sensitive to this possibility and we should have published our reanalyzes more promptly, and I truly apologize for that delay." (Page 170 of the hearing record)

---

[*] http://www.house.gov/commerce_democrats/comdem/press/105ltr45.htm

> "I accept my share of the responsibility for these administrative deficiencies that occurred." (Page 171)

> "I can tell you that I accept responsibility for any inadequacies that took place and I am very sorry for that." (Page 180)

Additionally, Dr. Fisher's testimony indicated that he delegated much of the administrative, audit, and statistical analysis of the breast cancer studies to the point of not 'Knowing what was going on.'[*]

In 1997, Dr. Bernard Fisher was cleared of scientific misconduct charges by the Office of Research Integrity (ORI) at the Department of Health and Human Services.

One can only imagine the whirlwind of emotions and reactions that affected junior investigators who were working under Dr. Fisher's authority during this tumultuous times.

6.10.2 Detection

Detection requires vigilance, and vigilance requires a metric.

While the presence of unethical behavior in a senior investigator can be flagrant, the suspicion arises slowly, and can be disorienting. To the junior investigator, the project's senior scientist is a person who has made the impact on the scientific community that the junior researcher hopes that she will be able to make. Sometimes, the senior investigator can be a hero to the junior researchers. This commonly means that the senior scientist receives his juniors' benefit of the doubt on issues (be they technical or ethical), and it is common for the junior researcher to defer to her senior in questionable circumstances.

A requisite for the junior investigator, however deferential they might be to their senior scientist, is the development of her own ethic. This development has its foundation in culture and family, but is further developed and refined based on the interactions the junior investigator has with others through discussion and readings. The development of this professional ethic is best nurtured actively rather than

---

[*] http://www.mith2.umd.edu/WomensStudies/GovernmentPolitics/CaucusUpdates/Update-vol14no4/hearings

passively and consciously rather than unconsciously. It requires good input from independent sources, as well as reflective thought. Just as your technical knowledge will never cease growing, so your ethical development should not stop. Also, challenge yourself. Can you articulate your ethical point of view? Can you describe the fundamental principles on which it is based? Can you calmly defend your ethical positions?

In science, we quickly learn how to form arguments in order to defend our technical point of view. Typically, we are not as able to describe and defend our ethic. While this may have been acceptable in the past, the time for ethically mute scientists has come and gone.

There are two important reasons to be able to articulate your own ethical point of view. First—you must have a point of view in order to enunciate it. Your initial failings at the attempt may point out that your ethical perspective may not have evolved sufficiently, a development that will require your attention and careful thought. Secondly, you will be required to clearly and cogently state and defend your ethical point of view when either your scientific work faces an ethical challenge, or you are required to comment about the ethical issues surrounding the work of others. Having already become accustomed to verbalizing your ethical point of view in a way that communicates your perspective in an informative, non- threatening manner will be valuable. Work on developing a concise statement that summarizes your ethical philosophy. After much practice, I have come to articulate my own belief in the following two sentences:

> "The ethical treatment of myself and others is based on the principle that we have innate, built-in value, regardless of our accomplishments or our treatment by others. This natural value requires that I treat the individual and their resources with respect and dignity, regardless of my opinion about their point of view or their accomplishments."

This philosophy has taken years to develop. It was not quite the same five years ago. No doubt, I will state it differently five years from now. However, I spend time thinking about and working on it, testing whether it is worthy of my adherence, and if so, whether I am adhering to it.

With your personal statement in place, you now have a metric against which the ethic of your own daily behavior and activities can be measured. However, this metric must be constantly challenged. The sources of this challenge are all around you. Since your colleagues will have an equally personal ethical philosophy that differs from yours, you may find that the conclusion that you come to in an ethical circumstance is different than theirs. It is most helpful if this produces an informed discussion between you and your colleagues. The point of this discussion is to provide you an opportunity to examine your ethical perspective from another point of view. Since perspectives in science and sociology are not static, it comes as no surprise that ethical values and standards must evolve.

6.10.3 Trust, but Verify

By working with a strong-willed chief who has far more experience and expertise than you have, it is natural for you to give this chief the benefit of the doubt in technical and scientific matters. However, this natural deference, can make it all too easy to replace your ethical sense of direction with that of your chief's. While trust in the ethical judgment of your chief may be appropriate, you must also challenge your senior scientist on ethical issues in which you believe you may have a different point of view. Therefore, ask and discuss the ethics of the troubling situation with your chief.

It is critical that your both retain and develop your own sense of ethics. Do not engage in a wholesale replacement of your ethic with that of your chief's sense of values. Of course, you will learn from the senior scientist and it is appropriate to choose to allow his experiences to shape your sense of propriety; however this process requires you to understand and affirmatively assimilate portions of his ethical sense of direction into your own. This is distinct from the wholesale embrace of his ethical values that is permitted to proceed because "he's the boss", and therefore must know best. The first is a careful assimilation process where you discard parts of his ethic that you believe may be wrong. It requires thoughtful consideration and careful integration. In the second, you accept all that is his, simply because it is his.

Fortunately, most chiefs are willing to spend some time talking about the ethics of a situation if they recognize that it is not your goal to threaten them. Make it clear that you would like an explanation to help further calibrate your ethical compass. It is more likely than not that the senior scientist's ethical perspective is better balanced than yours, or alternatively, that you are incompletely informed. For example, they may be some history behind the particular situation of which you are not aware but in which your chief took part. These past events can add a completely new dimension to the ethical issue under discussion.

If, on the other hand, your chief is unwilling to discuss these issues of ethics with you, then, frankly, you have a new problem, and one we will discuss momentarily.

6.10.4 Delegation

A well accepted and an admirable trait in a senior investigator is the ability and willingness to delegate responsibility. It is certainly proper for an advanced investigator who has too many responsibilities to avoid carrying them all out personally. Also, junior investigators who are looking for advancement opportunities gain valuable experience in carrying our new activities under the tutelage of their superior. In the overwhelming majority of circumstances, this relationship provides important benefits to not just the investigators, but for the project as well.

A difficulty can arise when the senior investigator asks that his delegate take a step in the discharge of the delegated task with which the junior investigator ethically disagrees. For example, a statistician working on a research project in a competitive research project may be pressured to produce "a significant result" and commanded to "get the significant result any way that you can". An investigator, interested in gaining some skill in reviewing budgets is told to "reduce the budget for the lab to $60,000 per year, and I don't care how you do it". A research physician may tell his resident "I don't care how you do it, but I want that patient in my study".

In these circumstances, it is best in these circumstances for junior investigators to do two things. The first is to recognize that their actions first and foremost must be governed by their individual sense of ethics. It is no longer acceptable for you to carry out an unethical request, a request that you know to be wrong, simply because your boss asked you to do it. When a final accounting for the event occurs, you will have to explain your actions. Let the motivation be something other than "I knew as a professional that the action I was asked to take was unethical, but I did it anyway because my chief told me to do it." In the end, if the action that you have been asked to take does not meet your own ethical standard, than don't carry out the action, and state clearly why you are refusing. This stand on your part will only rarely be demanded, but be assured that, at some time, it will be required.

Secondly, junior investigators have to learn to hear things the way they are meant to be heard. When a superior investigator says to carry out an activity and "do it anyway that you can", he commonly does not mean this literally. There is no doubt that this is what he said, but it is not what he meant to convey. What he meant to say was "Do this in anyway that is practicable and ethical". However the press of time, and his own frustration truncated the message. If you have a doubt about this, then challenge him by saying "You mean, 'Do this in anyway that is practicable and ethical', right?" This may lead to a moment of embarrassment, but far better to experience the moment, then to stay silent and find yourself on the horns on an ethical conundrum.

6.10.5 The Confrontation

If important ethical difficulties persist between you and your principal investigator, do everything that you can (that is practicable and ethical!) to have a series of open, honest conversations with your chief. Keep in mind during these dialogues that, in ethics, two people with diametrically opposed points of view can both vehemently believe that they are right. The only way progress can be made is if each is willing to look at the difficult question from the other's point of view.

It must be remembered that one of the considerations adding to the complexity of ethics is that ethics are dynamic. What was acceptable twenty years ago is not ethically acceptable now. If your boss was trained during an era in which the ethical practice that was acceptable at the time is currently not satisfactory, he has to be educated. This is sometimes not an easy task, and you have to use the right combination of tact and persistence to encourage his education. It may help to ask yourself how you would respond if a core belief of your ethic were overturned and no longer acceptable 25 years from now. How easily would you adjust to the new educational paradigm, growing to accept it as your own. In all likelihood, working with an imperious, arrogant, and demanding junior investigator would not help your adjustment. Once again, you may not think that it is part of your job description to provide an ethics update for your boss, but it can be one of the most helpful, collegial, and character building activities that you will engage in during your career. It also might save his career. If he think that you are being unkind, then remind him that you are being much kinder than a formal university, hospital, or institutional inquisitor would be.

Unfortunately, there are circumstances in which important ethical disagreements between you and your chief remain after all attempts at mutual education have been resolved. Keep your mentors closely informed of the situation, If they are able to add no new important advice to you, then you must leave the project. There is no acceptable alternative to working in an environment in which you are forced to conform to a standard of ethical conduct that is intolerable, and choosing to stay is playing with fire. You may pay an important and painful price by leaving, but you pay an immeasurable and un-payable price in the long term if you choose to diminish your standards and character by remaining in a morally unsatisfactory environment.

6.11 Final Comments

Familiarize yourself with the regulations that govern the definitions and guidelines of ethical activities at your institution. They serve by setting the appropriate standard for ethics. However, also recognize that trying to write rules that govern all matters of ethics is like trying to count the grains of sand on a beach; while many will be enumerated, many more will be missed. Ethics is an approach to life and not a mere collection of rules. Your ethical behavior is the living expression of your core principles that govern your relationships with people. Just as you have self-worth on which you rely, your sense of the worth of others regardless of their opinions and actions governs your ethical treatment of them. Institutional rules help you operationalize your beliefs.

Ethical behavior is dynamic. Therefore, as your field evolves, so to should your behavior toward others improve. If it is your intent, as a junior investigator, to be an ethical scientist, then challenge, re-inspect, and, if necessary, readjust your conduct. A scientific career that starts ethically will in all likelihood not end ethically if that scientist does not stay current with ethical issues and the impact of these issues on her field. If your central belief is to treat people and animals with respect, then small adjustments in your conduct that a developing scientific field requires should be easy to make.

Most importantly, remember that ethical researchers are not perfect. Ethical people make honest mistakes. However, what characterizes the ethical scientist is the response to their mistake. When they recognize that they missed an opportunity for ethical conduct, they apologize, make appropriate restitution, and, having learned the right lesion from their error, they move on. Ethical behavior is not perfect behavior. It is behavior that calibrates and self corrects.

Insist on working with other ethical scientists. Do not succumb to the belief that you are justified in working with an unethical individual because of the productivity boost that your career will get. This is like scooping scalding coals into your lap in the hope that you can stay warm; in all likelihood, you will be burned in the matter.

Also, when an ethical infraction takes place, and your "ethical alarm " goes off, do not treat it like the alarm that wakes you in the morning, hitting the snooze button and then going back to sleep. Treat your ethical alarm like a fire alarm. You have invested time and effort in developing and clarifying your ethical beliefs and sharpening your vigilance; do not ignore them when they attempt to warn you of an urgent problem. After recognizing the difficulty, think carefully before you speak on ethical matters. This is perhaps more important here than in other circumstances because the words and their implications can give offense where you don't want it to. In all matters, but in this matter especially, know what you are going to say before you say it.

Finally, good ethical decisions require good judgment, and good judgment is most easily found when you take care of yourself. You cannot bring the best of yourself to an important decision when your body is starved for sleep, your mind is starved for rest and relaxation, and your stomach is starved for food. Make these decisions when you are rested, well-balanced, sharp-eyed, secure, and confident.

References

1. http://www.unmc.edu/ethics/data/darsee.htm.
2. Hixson, J. *The Patchwork Mouse. The Strange Case of the Spotted Mice.* Anchor Press.
3 Medawar PB. (1976).*The Strange Case of the Spotted Mice.* The New York Review of Books; 23. http://www.nybooks.com/articles/article-preview.
4. Moyé LA (2000). *Statistical Reasoning in Medicine; The Intuitive P-value Primer.* New York. Springer. Chapter Six.

Chapter 7
The Junior Faculty Member

7.1 Academics 101

If you are entering academia as an instructor or as an assistant professor, then you are crossing into a world that is being transformed. While academia retains its distinctiveness from non-didactic institutes or corporations, the academic world is nevertheless ongoing tectonic shifts. These changes and alterations need not jeopardize your new career, but you need to be aware of them.

There was a time when the decision to enter academia involved the consideration of a relatively simple tradeoff. Plainly, the researcher had to choose between freedom on the one hand, and income on the other. A young scientist entering the academic community retained complete control of his career. He could work on what he

wanted, when he wanted. He could speak up in public, virtually unfettered. He could teach almost any course that he wanted. He could grade
students anyway that he wanted.[*]

What the academician gave up for this freedom was money. In
general, the salary of an academician was lower than that of the equally
trained professional in the private sector. However, these non-
academicians who were working in the private sector had grueling
work schedules. Commonly, they were compelled to work long hours
on scientific projects in which they had no fundamental intellectual
interest. They could be peremptorily dismissed from their job. Public
comments had to be vetted. So the choice was simple. While there are
always exceptions, in general, by working in academia you gave up
being rich for the ability to be independent. This independence was
called "academic freedom".

In our contemporary era, this paradigm has become complicated because the idea of complete freedom has been, for better or for
worse, successfully challenged by another idea – accountability. State
universities must be accountable to state legislators. Private universities
must be accountable to their governing bodies. The caricature of the
unproductive, tenured professor, drawing salary but generating no intellectual product has compelled universities to review the productivity of
their faculty on a regular basis. Faculty expenditures and positions must
be justified, and that justification is obtained through an evaluation of
productivity, as measured in three major areas; research, service, and
teaching. Thus, in the new environment, the academic scientist is never
far from justifying her work product to deans and other university administrators.

While this tightening of faculty oversight is not necessarily a
bad thing, close supervisory overview of faculty work is somewhat
new. In this chapter, we will discuss the modern metric of professional
measurement in colleges and universities, and then develop a profes-

---

[*] A example of this traditional view *in extremis* of academic life is the character
Indiana Jones (from the movie trilogy) who is an archeology department faculty member at a university in the 1930's. This "academician" teaches the
courses he wishes, avoids discussions with students by climbing out of his office window, and leaves the university on a whim to engage in scientific quests.
This caricacture shows academic freedom at its best and at its worst.

sional framework in which you may work, relatively untroubled in this new environment.

7.2 Defining and Evaluating Productivity

The core of the academic career is scholarship. Academic life is devoted to the pursuit of knowledge for its own sake, free from financial concerns, administrative requirements, and the need to always be right. The academic career is one of two professional classes of activities (religion being the second) where the metric of success is cerebral and not material.

By selecting a career in academia, you have chosen to benefit from, as well as contribute to, the creation of an atmosphere where scholarly pursuit and professionalism are ascendant. The three major areas of contribution in academics are teaching, research, and service. However these contributions are most effectively delivered from an attitude of service, strength, kindness, collegiality, discipline, charity, and leadership.

7.3 Teaching

In academia, to teach is to guide the learning of others. Educating students remains a key activity for faculty and is central to the measurement of academic productivity. However, even though teaching remains a core contribution, there typically are few, direct financial rewards for teaching. In fact, the dearth of pecuniary prizes for didactic expertise requires college and university faculty to continue to ensure that superior teaching is singled out for special attention and praise. The need for the clear, public recognition of these devoted teaching efforts is a perennial challenge before all faculty.

Continuing to place your best effort into teaching in the absence of material or financial awards requires a unique discipline and steadfastness; Typically, the teaching load of a faculty member is measured using a combination of three criteria; 1) the number of courses a faculty member teaches, 2) the number of students in each course, and 3) the percent effort that the faculty member expends in teaching. However, while these simple tabulations provide an evaluation of how much teaching you do, they do not yield an assessment of the effectiveness of your teaching. In order to gain this useful perspective, the students' evaluations of your teaching skills are obtained. This information allows an appraisal of your style, breadth of knowledge, and availability, permitting both you and those who oversee your teaching contribution to assess your ability to reach students.

In addition, your ability to work with students individually is evaluated through an assessment of your willingness and ability to advise students. Serving on MPH or M.S. thesis committees, qualifying examination committees, and the dissertation committees of Dr.PH and Ph.D candidates is an effort that is valued by the university and prized by the student. By working closely with your advisee, you are able to closely inspect and critique their individual research and investigational activities. Observing and then discussing the students' strengths and weaknesses with them provides invaluable commentary for the student to absorb and consider during this formative stage of their scientific development.

Secondly, by choosing to work closely with an individual student, you reveal your own personal study and research approaches to your advisee. Essentially, you open yourself up to your student, allowing her to carefully examine your style and technique, and permitting her to pick and choose which habits and perspectives of yours she would like to accept as her own. This time-consuming process is one that requires not just your voluble time and attention, but, additionally, demands strength of character. It takes a secure adult, with a good measure of their own self-worth to allow a student to openly make commentary or criticize their approach in a way that they are unaccustomed to hearing. Serving as an advisor requires patience, discernment, and self-discipline. Those faculty who can effectively train and mentor students in this most effective way deserve special consideration for these fine efforts.

7.4 Research

A second core contribution that you will make to academic scholarship is in the area of research. It is called research because rarely is a new idea completely novel in this complex, interactive world. The genesis of a scientific concept can most commonly be identified in an examination of the work that has preceded their efforts, that therefore must be examined again. In scientific fields where the best of scientific reasoning continues to be riddled by the absence of good knowledge, research and investigation must be a central component of your productivity.

While faculty can generally agree on the need for scholarly investigation, the generation of new knowledge, and the dissemination of that knowledge, there is commonly a healthy and ongoing debate on how research productivity should be measured. What follows is a collection of metrics that are used, and a justification of their use.

7.4.1 Publications

The publication of a manuscript is a declaration that the article's contents have reach a standard of quality that is worthy of dissemination to the scientific community. Lists of publications on which you are author are cited in your resume. Authors of publications are commonly ranked by their location on the masthead or title area of the manuscript. The value of a manuscript is measured by the quality of the research that generated it, the written description of that effort, an assessment of your role in the entire process, and the acceptability of the journal in which the manuscript appeared.[*]

The peer review process is an attempt to ensure that the manuscript's contents are objectively evaluated by outside experts in the field. Since outside reviewers are more likely to be objective then your colleagues or friends, the opinions of these external experts are, in general, more highly valued. The appearance of a manuscript in a peer review journal is a statement that the research effort and its description has met the current standard of science for dissemination. The more competitive the journal, the greater the number of candidate manuscripts there are that are vying for acceptance, the more grueling and

---

[*] This is not to say that manuscripts that pass the peer review test are correct. Sometimes, manuscripts are published because they represent new findings that must be confirmed before they are accepted. The appearance of a manuscript in the literature is a statement that the article has reached a minimum quality and that the results (in the editor's view), should be conveyed to the target audience, not a guarantee that the manuscript's results are correct. See Chapter Two for an example.

selective the external review, and the more rewarding the final publication.

A second, important consideration in the assessment of your scientific contribution to the literature is an evaluation of the role that you played in the research effort. This is difficult to accurately assess; however, the current state of these evaluative efforts focuses on the location of your name on the masthead of a manuscript. If you are in the middle of a long list of authors, then, although the research effort itself is laudatory, it can be difficult to assess your role in the project and almost impossible to view your performance in the development and authorship of the manuscript itself.

Typically, the scientist whose name appears first on the manuscript is the person who is directly responsible for writing the manuscript. Therefore, this "first author" is a scientist who has been intimately involved in the research project. This person provides an outline of the manuscript, and may develop writing assignments for the co-authors. The first author writes the sections of the manuscript that can be the most vexing. This scientist takes charge of the development of the bibliography. The first author accepts sections from the other authors, but these contributions must be carefully and critically reviewed before they are included in the paper; it is the task of the first author to ensure that the separately written pieces of the manuscript fit seamlessly together. When the manuscript must be edited in accordance with the demands of the reviewers and editors, it is the first author who takes responsibility for providing a response to each of their concerns and who also ensures that the manuscript is appropriately revised. The stamp of the first author's style is on the final manuscript, and its acceptance by a journal is substantial evidence of that author's ability to effectively communicate to the scientific readership.

While the responsibilities of the first author are generally clear, the specific activities of authors whose names appear after the first author become ambiguous. Therefore, as your names moves down the list of authors, from first to second to third to fourth, etc., confusion in the minds of your productivity evaluators about your specific role in writing the manuscript naturally rises. Thus these manuscripts on which you are not first author carry less persuasive weight about your ability to write effectively than other manuscripts on which you are the lead author, *ceteris parabus*. Senior investigators who provide important organizational support and intellectual leadership commonly appear last in the authorship masthead.

Of course, articles on which you are not first author, but in whose research you have played a major role have important value of a different kind. Specifically, these manuscripts speak to your ability to successfully participate in a collaborative effort. This is itself a critical skill and must not be ignored. However, these articles carry less positive weight in the argument that you can successfully write to the satisfaction of the scientific community.

Moving to the other extreme, published manuscripts on which you are the sole author are of great value since the research is yours and, in addition, you have sole responsibility for describing that research effort. This manuscript's acceptance in a high quality, competitive journal speaks volumes about your ability to produce solid work and competently describe that work in a way that is deemed worthy of dissemination to the scientific community by others.

Books and book chapters typically carry less weight than peer reviewed journal articles in science. This is not because these literary contributions require less effort, or are less persuasive. The reason that books and book chapters are discounted is primarily because the degree to which they are peer reviewed is uneven and difficult to judge. Articles and manuscripts that are submitted to peer reviewed journals are not accepted unless and until the external reviewers and editors have received a text which with they are satisfied. Books, on the other hand, are commonly accepted before they are completed. Many times, books are accepted for publication on the basis of a five page prospectus (or other writing plan), and one or two sample chapters. Additionally, although the work may undergo a rigorous review upon completion, typically, the author has a good deal more leeway in responding to the reviewers' demands. Specifically, since the book has already been accepted, the authors are not required to satisfy every concern raised by the reviewer. Thus, while the quality of books reaches a standard, and many outstanding texts have been, and will continue to be written using this standard, that standard is different than the one used by top quality peer reviewed journals. This is one reason why books and book chapters are not commonly authored by junior researchers, but are instead written by more senior scientists who can afford to be less concerned about the hierarchy of productivity measurement.

Judging verbal presentations offer the same difficulty to your evaluator as does assessing the contribution of a book. Making speaking presentations is always demanding, and commonly, a manuscript must be presented to the sponsoring body at or near the time of the presentation. However, it is difficult for an evaluator who has not attended your lecture, but only sees its brief description in your resume, to judge the standard to which the presentation rises. While there is a hierarchy of meetings in every field, just as there is a hierarchy of peer reviewed journals, a presentation is commonly held to be of less value than a peer reviewed manuscript, everything else being equal.

7.4.2 Grants

Being funded to carry our research is a central component of much academic work. Its major impact on your evaluators stems from the fact that 1) grants demonstrate your intent and ability to carry out research that extends scientific knowledge, the *raison dêtre* of a scientist, 2) they demonstrates your ability to successfully compete against other equally capable researchers in the eyes of external reviewers, therefore reaching the standard of an external peer review test, and 3) your ability to obtain research grants provides funds that benefit your university. While unfunded research meets the first of these criteria, and can provide valuable insight leading to peer reviewed publications, it does not meet these last two tests.

As was the case for the evaluation of publication efforts, there is a hierarchy among grants. Certainly, a grant on which you are the principal investigator presents the strongest case for your ability to describe your research plans cogently and persuasively. In this case, you are the primary person responsible for planning and conducting the science, and the main individual in charge of administering the research funds. It is anticipated that you, as the principal investigator, will play the key role in producing the manuscripts that describe the funded research.

The ability and the expectation for you to be the principal investigator on a grant (i.e. "have your own grant") can depend on your field. If you are in research medicine, biology, chemistry, genetics, epidemiology, you may be expected to obtain your own grant, for which numerous granting agencies are available.

Grants on which you are an investigator, but not the principal investigator, are also important demonstrations of your research expertise. These represent opportunities on which you can play a major roles in funded research. One way that you can do is by taking the lead on a subproject of the grant.

Thus, when it comes to assessing scholarship, manuscripts in the peer reviewed literature and funded grant research are among the most influential bodies of evidence. They directly speak to your ability to make scientific contributions that are competitive, well delineated, and relevant.

7.5 Community Service

Service is the process by which you place your own needs aside while you use your professional intuition, talents and skills to provide for the needs of others. While teaching and research are measures of your scientific prowess, service is a measure of your citizenship. There are almost uncountable number of service needs that you could satisfy. These exist at either the level of the university, or the local community, state, national, and international levels.

Your service contributions are certainly desired and appreciated at the university level. The successful and smooth operation of your institution depends on the willingness of faculty to play major roles in the oversight of the school. With the gift of academic freedom, faculty bear the important responsibility of creating an environment of productivity and development. This is an obligation that is successfully met with consistent energy and dedication. Academic programs are best developed by faculty. Definitions of academic scholarship are best defined by faculty. Junior faculty are best mentored by faculty. The most capable and diligent search for new faculty are executed by faculty. Guidelines for promotion and tenure of faculty are best set by faculty. These responsibilities require an important time commitment from faculty members who commonly already have a full teaching and research agenda. However, the fact that many faculty devote themselves to these actions speaks to their recognition of the importance of these tasks. Involvement in these activities not only increases your knowledge about the school, but demonstrates your willingness to put some of your own interests aside for the good of your fellow faculty and students.

The local needs of a community outside the university are varied, allowing you the opportunity to identify an activity in which you have a real interest that also requires your unique combination of understanding and capability. While you may feel somewhat isolated at the university, laboring under the belief that you are working separate and apart from any community activities, it is also true that there are many community groups who themselves feel cut off from the information and support that they need. These organizations have interests, or are charged with making decisions that require a scientific base of knowledge. However, they are unsure how to reach out for the required information. Municipal organizations, health departments, community hospitals, elder care centers, environmental agencies, and secondary school systems are but some of the many neighborhood activities that can avail themselves of your insight and knowledge. Each group commonly has very little in the way of remunerative resources, yet each can have an important need for your help and insight.

Service at the state, national and international levels provides an opportunity for you to work with other professionals through organizations with a broad reach. This service includes but is not limited to taking part in grant reviews, agreeing to participate in panel discussions, and serving as a referee for a peer reviewed journal. It also includes serving on oversight boards, writing position papers, and testifying before the legislature or Congress. These actions permit you to work with, and learn from, senior scientists and researchers as you work with them on the agenda issues at hand. You can gain important new experience, insight and skill by working with senior investigators as you contribute to their work on writing a position paper This activity can improve your visibility on the state, national, and international level.

7.6 Promotion and Tenure

In academia, the process of promotion and tenure has both simple and complex components. Every university has its own procedures. Most commonly this process includes the work of a Promotions and Tenure committee, whose job begins by gathering relevant information about the candidate faculty member. Determinations are made about each candidate's suitability for promotion, and when appropriate, the awarding of tenure. After these recommendations are reviewed by the school's dean, recommendations about promotion and the award of tenure are then made from the school to the university where they are again reviewed by higher university academic officials, up through and including the university board of regents. Despite changes and adaptations that have occurred over the years, the university tenure and promotion process continues to be one of the most serious and formal activities that these institutions undertake.

7.6.1 Promotion

Promotion is the process by which the candidate progresses through a series of well defined ranks. Traditionally, these steps have been from the rank of assistant professor to the rank of associate professor, and from the rank of associate professor to the rank of full professor. The criterion for these promotions is the candidate faculty member's scholarship record. Thus, the abilities of the faculty member to effectively compete for research dollars and to convert these grant awards into publications that appear in the peer review literature are central to the consideration of promotion. Also important is the demonstrated capability of the candidate faculty member to be an effective teacher for the university, and the candidate's commitment to the scientific community.

Many rules of thumb have arisen in the hope of providing junior faculty some guidance about the requirements for promotion. One example of such a "rule" is "a junior faculty member must have at least twenty peer-reviewed manuscripts in order to be promoted from assistant professor to associate professor". A second "rule" might be "an associate professor must have a national reputation in their field, and a full professor must have an international reputation". Such monitories, while informative, must be shunned as hard and fast rules, since one need not look far to find counterexamples to their predictive ability. What these guidelines attempt to embody is the sense that a faculty member who is both intelligent and makes sedulous use of her professional energy will demonstrate these traits and characteristics through well recognized and accepted demonstrations of academic scholarship and research. A junior faculty member who is well grounded, smart, accepts advice and constructive criticism, diligently works in her field, seeks new projects, looks for the opportunity to engage in research, actively conducts that research, persistently writes about that research for the peer-reviewed literature, and teaches will demonstrate that she have the traits worthy of promotion.

7.62 Tenure

Since tenure is a measure of the overall value of a faculty member to the university, its definition and criteria for award are less concrete and more nebulous than those for promotion. Traditionally, the award of tenure is the culmination of a long term commitment made between the faculty member and the university. The university awards tenure if it determines that the candidate faculty member has been, and can reasonably be expected to continue to demonstrate a consistent dedication to its mission. Thus the faculty member must demonstrate that her activities have been in alignment with the university goals. This includes, but is not limited to, service to fellow faculty, service to the school, service to the university and to the broader community. Through awarding tenure the university hopes to identify that relatively small number of faculty who are willing to put aside their own needs for the good of the institution.

7.7 Diligent Days

As junior faculty, the afore mentioned metric (or the particular relevant measures at your institution) should be kept in mind. The idea is for you to use your academic freedom to pick the activities that will allow you to use your insights, strengths, and talents to advance your field of science, and earn you fair recognition for your assiduous efforts by your peers.

However, now, swirling around you are a great number of activities in which you can become involved. Research activities may already be available for you to work in, or you may apply for new ones. While you may be handed an initial teaching assignment, once you have begun teaching and become comfortable with the task, handling the predictable problems of students with facility, you can expand (or, perhaps, contract to a degree) your teaching responsibilities. Service opportunities will grow as well, permitting you to pick what you would like to be involved in at a local, national, and even international level.

This freedom of opportunity provides a unique challenge. The early recognition of this challenge can lead to the creation of a rewarding and sustaining personal work-lifestyle that allows you to reach your goal.

7.7.1 Balance and Discipline

As a single, unmarried person, you learned that you cannot date all of the attractive people, simply because they are all attractive. You cannot choose everyone; you must instead choose someone. Similarly, you cannot be involved in all of the available university opportunities in teaching, service, and research merely because they are all appealing. You cannot select everything; you must select from everything. Doing the opposite, and being involved in all activities produces chaotic days. The fundamental difficulty presented by these inchoate days is that you cannot bring the best combination of your talents, ability, knowledge and intuition to bear in any one circumstance because of the continued distractions presented by other pressing priorities.

The best use of freedom is its disciplined exercise. The undisciplined use of freedom unfortunately can produce tumult in which, eventually, other people will determine your activities. That is the curious thing about discipline. You either exert it yourself, or, by not exerting it, you eventually must submit to the control of others. Thus, you will either discipline yourself or be disciplined by others.

As your productivity manifests itself, other well-meaning scientists will ask you to involve yourself in their projects. You must therefore strengthen your self-control so that it matches the increase in the number of opportunities for your professional involvement. First develop the will to say no. Then develop the skill to say no.

Develop the ability to say no by recognizing that no damage is done to you when you exercise your right to refuse. As a faculty member, you are not obligated to take part in every project that comes your way. This fact is not weakened, but is fortified when it is applied to junior faculty. As junior faculty, your time is even more precious during this critical formative period when you are developing new intellectual roots and grounding. Would you avoid deliberately overwhelming or burdening a colleague of yours, deliberately reducing their ability to function effectively, single-mindedly degrading their performance? Don't do this to yourself.

It you choose to accept responsibility for a new task, do it with the recognition that there will be other new opportunities in which you can now play no role. When these other opportunities come to pass, choose to let them go by because of your prior commitment to the task at hand.

The greater the freedom, the greater the need for self-discipline. Retain control of over how busy your days are. While it is important to work so that you get your work done for the day, don't frustrate yourself by insisting on being busy every moment of each day. While it is important to ration your rest, choose to ration your work as well. Allow enough flexibility into your day so that you can read, or have time to engage in discussions with colleagues. Permit yourself the opportunity to take advantage of small opening of opportunities that are of interest to you or to which you can make an important contribution without destabilizing your main efforts. You chose this career. It is perfectly all right to both work hard and to enjoy it.

7.7.2 Developing a Work-Lifestyle

The key to this productive but flexible approach is equilibrium. Devote your energy to creating a balanced, personal work-lifestyle. A personal work-lifestyle is the atmosphere and surroundings in which you work. It consists of your own attitude, your workspace, your time, your calendar, and your colleagues, The development of this personal work-lifestyle must appropriately weigh and integrate 1) your need to apply your professional talents to the fullest, 2) your need to be productive in science, and 3) your need to collaborate with fellow scientists, students, and administrators. Your daily efforts should allow you to do all three of these. There is no doubt that it is a challenge to build this work-lifestyle, but build it you must, and plan to build it to last. After all, you will have a forty year career or longer, and you want this structure to be one in which you are both comfortable and productive. Like any structure, it will need to be regularly inspected, repaired, and modified. However, this work-lifestyle will pay a handsome dividend by providing the foundation for your personal and professional academic growth.

The core pillar of this work lifestyle is respect for yourself. Recognize with approval that you have a combination of talents that are of great value to the university. However, you cannot apply these talents effectively to any of your endeavors if you are harried by a schedule that is too busy, or a workplace that is noisy and disheveled. Work for, and insist on, the environment that permits you the best opportunity to use the talents for which the university hired you. Then, take advantage of this lifestyle by applying your strengths and talents to the didactic, research, and administrative problems at hand.

Discipline the use of your time so that you have the opportunity to critically think about important and central issues that come up at the university. While it remains important to avoid lackadaisical and tepid efforts that must be repeated to reach a competent standard, it is also important to shun overly zealous activity in one area that takes your time and attention from more important matters. Develop a light touch on the steering controls as you navigate yourself through your activities. Let your goal be diligent days, not exhausting ones.

7.8 Teaching and Character

A central role of faculty at a college or university is teaching. While there are libraries of materials on teaching styles, philosophies, and approaches, we will concern ourselves here with the development of an over all strategy for teaching, and some tactical steps that you can take.

Developing a good teaching style begins with the recognition that students, their time, and their effort must be treated with respect and with dignity. As a new instructor, recognize that you cannot force students to learn. You instead must persuade them to teach themselves. You are not there to be their friend, nor are you there to intimidate or frighten them. Instead, you are there to provide instructional material to them, but, more importantly to persuade them to use the best of their talents to learn. This requires that you use all of your powers of persuasion to elicit from them the curiosity that they must bring to bear to master the course material. You will have to apply the best combination of firmness and tact, of prestige and of empathy to persuade them to learn, absorb, and integrate the course material into their knowledge base.

This requires a consistent supply of energy from you as you deliver your lectures to these students. These students won't be challenged unless you challenge them, and providing this challenge requires a consistent and dependable supply of spirited power from you. Most importantly, this begins with approaching the next lecture with the best attitude. Students are remarkably adept at determining whether you are tired or distracted. Their recognition that you wish to be somewhere else reduces the didactic experience for them because they believe that you hold them at a lesser, discounted value than they had hoped. Spending a few moments before class in emotional preparation for your lecture can provide handsome dividends for the class, and often for you. It is sometimes useful to remind yourself that you are not just instructing students, but future department heads, deans, judges, community leaders, and politicians. Those who will be charged with making controversial decisions in the future are gaining the foundation on which their decision will be made from your course of instruction[*].

Keep in mind that you are only one resource from which your students can learn. Illuminate for them the other sources of information that are commonly available. One of them is a library. Many students treat a textbook like a spouse, i.e. "to have and to hold until death do us part, forsaking all others". In fact, textbooks are useful, but imperfect tools. You will no doubt have chosen a text for your class that is useful for your students, but invariably, students will react to that text with varying degrees of dissatisfaction. One student may find that the chapter on intracellular morphology may make the topic of molecular biology come alive, yet the following chapter on the instrumentation used by researchers may be terrible. Encourage students to broaden their reading for the course. Spending part of the afternoon in the library will introduce the student to number of texts, each with their own strengths and weaknesses. At the end of the course, the student will have a per-

---

[*]Getting into the habit and practice of giving clear, well organized, and articulate presentations in class prepares you for giving clear and well organized presentations before different and sometimes more hostile audiences.

sonal library of material, that, taken together, provide the coverage of the material that the student needs to have mastered the course material.

Keep the students well oriented in the course. Students appreciate well outlined, well designed courses. A clear and lucid layout of the course can make an important difference, because students will not be compelled to take up valuable lecture time to discuss logistics of the course that could have been obviated with a clear statement of the courses prerequisites, lecture timing and content, and exam schedule. Remember that students commonly are challenged enough by the course material itself. They should not have to struggle to know what the material is that will be covered in the next lecture, or when the assignments are do. Spending a considerable amount of time thinking about the design of the course before the course is offered can pay handsome dividends later in the semester.

7.9 Publishing and Character

We have discussed the need for publishing in peer reviewed journals earlier in this chapter. In the university setting, you will have ample opportunity to satisfy this requirement. Some useful guiding principles as you develop your strategy are as follows.

Recall that the purpose of your career is not to garner the maximum number of publications. It is instead to practice good science on a regular and consistent basis, building up your knowledge base and scientific sophistication, and integrating these with the development of your character. An important component of that character is intellectual honesty. This calls for an honest answer to the question, "is this idea I have worthy of publication? Will it provide illumination of an important idea or concept?" If your critical appraisal suggests that the answer to this question is no, then suppress the paper. Discipline yourself to move forward into publication only those ideas, concepts, and analyses that you believe are worthy of dissemination to the scientific community. Doing otherwise is the equivalent of disrespect of your own good scientific judgment. When you make contributions, let them be contributions worth making. Your field of application should be better off, rather than merely more cluttered, because of your contributions.

Additionally, you will have the opportunity to make two types of contributions to the literature. The first will be based on collaborative effort. The second will be individual contributions that you can make. Typically, the collaborative manuscripts will come more easily. If you are competent, honest, articulate, and can easily admit your mistakes, you will find that you have several opportunities to be involved in collaborative research efforts. These efforts will produce manuscripts fairly easily, and, most commonly, these manuscripts will be authored by others more senior than you.

However, there are several disadvantages to collaborative manuscripts. First, they may not say what you as an individual would like for them to say. Collaborative manuscripts, by their very nature, are build on compromises that are made between the various authors, each with his or her own point of view. It is unlikely that you as a junior investigator will be able to have much of an influence on this complicated and subtle process. Your own point of view, regardless of how valuable, can get left "on the cutting room floor". Secondly, recall that, by not taking a major role in writing a manuscript, your evaluators cannot gain a sense of your skill in written communication to other scientists.

For these reasons, give serious consideration to the idea of publishing a manuscript in your field for which you are the sole author. Taking such a tack holds several advantages. First, writing a sole authored manuscript requires you to engage in a self-assessment in which you must identify the type of contribution that you wish to make to your field of application. Do you want to propose an idea, or call for a specific class of analysis? Do you wish to expose a troubling style of research evaluation in your area of expertise, and propose a replacement? A most rewarding experience can be spending some time reviewing the literature, specifically examining the publications in your field. It can be illuminating to discover that, while the literature itself is voluminous, the area of your specific and particular interest may not be well developed at all. This void can be filled by the contributory manuscripts that you wish to write. No one else has written them; they are for you to write.

Secondly, publishing your own manuscript requires you to develop your own writing skills. While it can be useful to observe the writing skills of others, work to develop your own by writing. This requires both time, practice, and patience. Progress comes steadily through practice, the more you practice, the greater the progress. The best way to learn how to swim is to swim. The best way to learn how to write scientifically is to write scientifically.

If you have not published a manuscript on your own, and are intimidated by the prospect, then start on a small project. Begin by authoring letters to the editors of some of the top journals in your field for publication. This activity serves a worthy purpose, because editors benefit from the calibration of their decision making process by the feedback they receive from their readers. Build your confidence and writing skills up slowly and steadily, until you are willing to write a manuscript on which you are sole author.

An advantage of working on a manuscript of your own is that you gain the valuable opportunity of taking complete control of the process. You and you alone are responsible for the text, tables, and figures. You and you alone decide on the submission date. You, and you alone must respond to reviewers, and negotiate with the editor. Assuming and discharging these responsibilities requires growth and the development of new skills on your part. You will gain valuable experience from the mistakes that you will make. In all likelihood, not all of your single-authored manuscripts will be accepted. However, since the topic you have carefully selected to write about is worthy of dissemination, make your manuscript stronger with each round of reviews that it must complete. Finally, do not give up when you receive a rejection notice. Instead expect rejection on your way to publication, much like a young ice skater expects to fall repeatedly as she perfects her skills.

The administrative and writing capabilities that are produced from these successful efforts will serve you well in the future. They will be particularly useful when you become first author of collaborative research projects. Your experience in selecting journals, your expertise in dealing with reviewers and editors, and your perseverance will ease your task of navigating the manuscript with its many authors toward publication.

Avoid ghost-authored manuscripts. A ghost-authored manuscript is an article that is written by individuals other than those listed on the masthead of the manuscript. These circumstances may occur when the true writers of the manuscript have a point of view that they would like to disseminate. However, since they do not have the same good and widely acknowledged reputation as others, they enter into an agreement with some of these other well known scientists. These latter, renowned scientists agree to have their names appear on the masthead of the manuscript, even though they were not the researchers who authored the manuscript. They essentially are paid to have their names appear on manuscripts that they did not write. This fraudulent practice misleads reviewers, editors, and ultimately, the journal readership. This is intellectual hypocrisy, and the perpetrators of these actions reduce the value of our collective profession.

7.10 Take Charge

Before you use your academic and intellectual freedom to drive your career, be sure that you first know where your career is going. As a junior faculty member, you will have many opportunities from which you much choose. How, specifically, do you want to use them? One of the difficulties of being a junior faculty member is that you do not yet have the metric to decide which activities you should be involved in, and which you should avoid. One of the most useful tools that you can develop to help you measure your available opportunities is to actively consider your long term career goal.

How do you want to spend your time twenty years from now? Do you want to be a theorist, or will you involve yourself in practical applications? Do you want to go into administration? Do you see yourself eventually as a dean? Will you be a full professor with an active research program? Will you spend your days teaching students, or will you be out on the lecture circuit? Will you be involved in politics? Do you see yourself heavily involved in doing community service? Will you be teaching and guiding students?

Few families start a vacation trip without a vacation destination, wandering randomly and aimlessly, having their direction chosen by weather, traffic patterns, and spur of the moment inclinations. Take some time now to plan your distant career destination. Pause to observe the senior faculty around you. Watch and ask them how they spend their days and time. Ask what they would do differently if they were starting out at the beginning of their career path, knowing what they know now. Use your mentoring committee as a sounding board for ideas and concepts that you have for your future. Educate yourself about the possible obstacles that you will face along that path, so that if you choose that path, you will be prepared to face them.

This is not a guaranteed path of success but it allows you to move in a well considered direction with your eyes well focused on your destination, being propelled by your own good talents and the intellectual and academic freedom that derives from being a faculty member.

Chapter 8
The Investigator as Leader

8.1 Seeing Yourself as a Leader

Leadership is the process by which an individual assumes responsibility for a goal-directed project or activity and, through his or her authority, directs the efforts of others to that goal. Leadership qualities exists in all of us, yet it seems that there are only a few people who can develop the right combination of the complex strengths and traits. While exercising their authority in completing the tasks, they rise to the attention of others.

At this early stage of your career, you cannot be blamed for removing considerations of leadership from your serious and thoughtful consideration. The daily whirl of your activities can easily require most of your attention and efforts, with little time and, perhaps little inclination, for deep thought on issues of leadership.

Some junior investigators are intrigued by the prospect of being a leader, but are also intimidated by it, comparing themselves to important historical figures in science, and concluding that they, as a junior scientist, do not and could not reach the stature of these icons. If you are one of these scientists, it may pay to borrow a page from a politician's book. When modern politicians consider running for President of the United States, they do not ask themselves whether they are of the same stature as George Washington, or Abraham Lincoln. Their perspectives are much more practical. Instead, they simply look at the men and women who have or are running for the job and say "I can do at least as good a job as they can."

You may have difficulty seeing yourself as a commissioner of a scientific body, or the head of a research institute, or the president of a university. While this perspective is understandable, consider that many good leaders did not actively seek out a leadership role for themselves. While leadership roles are sometimes created, they are commonly inherited. Retirements, resignations, and scandal can produce vacuums of authority that must be filled.

On the other hand, one need not be ambitious to develop into a good leader. If you enjoy your scientific career, are intelligent, can be charitable, and are well grounded, you will have the opportunity to become a leader. With these qualities, you do not have to point yourself in the direction of, and head for leadership. Leadership is headed for you.

8.2 Traits of Scientific Leadership

Leadership begins with responsibility. To be responsible means that you are liable for the project; you will be acknowledged for its success, and will have to account for its failure. It is as though you have something of value to lose if the project fails, and it is this link that ties you closely to the project's outcome. This tether of responsibility requires that you focus your active attention on the project, extending yourself to work for the project's success. The single recognition that you will be blamed for, and perhaps hurt by, the project's collapse requires special strength of character, a strength whose growth you can encourage now as a junior scientist.[*]

Leadership also requires authority. Leaders must have access to resources and the ability to control the application of those resources (money, equipment, and people) for the project's development and success.

You must accept both responsibility and authority in order to become an effective leader. Responsibility without authority is a recipe that generates frustrating and ineffective activity, frequently producing the project's failure. On the other hand, authority without responsibility can produce careless and reckless actions on the part of the leader who has no vested interest in the success or failure of the program. In order to function effectively as a leader, both your understanding of the importance of the project, in concert with your sense of responsibility, must guide your decisions to commit resources to the project. You must simultaneously consider the value of your resources, and their impact on the project's progress. Understanding your project and your assets, then skillfully applying these assets at the right time and in the right concentration for the successful completion of the project requires the delicate touch of a sensitive director.

8.3 Meeting the Challenge of Leadership

The granting of authority is only the beginning of leadership. How you exercise that authority is the true measure of your capabilities as a leader. This capacity is frequently revealed in your ability to a) be knowledgeable and resourceful, b) have administrative skill and diligence, c) have a good strategic sense, d) be imaginative, e) possess character, endurance, courage, and self control and f) have a spirit of benevolence. As you recall, these are the characteristics that we discussed in Chapter One, when you were taking stock of yourself. These traits, along with the ability to be persuasive, are important characteristics of good leaders. However, before you evaluate your abilities in this matter, we must discuss the one characteristic that is the foundation on which leadership skills are based – a solid sense of self.

---

[*] Developing this strength is the topic of the next section.

8.3.1 The Twin Challenges to Leadership

"No man is so brave that he is not surprised by the unexpected"
                                                                      Julius Caesar

The fear of failure is one of the greatest enemies of effective leadership, dissolving the will of a leader to be successful. This fear, striking as the result of a criticism or an unanticipated setback. can produce paralysis and ultimately the project's failure. Like an acid, it dissolves the bond between the fearful leader and the best parts of his own good nature. Decoupled from his resourcefulness and his strategic sense, the fearful leader flounders. His capabilities remain, but they have become disconnected and unsynchronized, producing dysfunction and emotional upheaval.

One of the clearest examples of this is the fate of Joseph Hooker. Appointed by Abraham Lincoln to replace General Burnside (who replaced General McClellan, who replaced General McDowell and General Winfield Scott), General Hooker was given supreme command of the Union Army of the Potomac in the winter of 1862. A tall man with striking features, commonly seen astride a magnificent white horse, he was imbued with both confidence and a bellicose nature. His soldiers called him "Fighting Joe Hooker", and he was known to say "celerity, audacity, and resolution are everything…".

In the spring of 1863, he marched his grand Union army south into Virginia, hoping to trap and overwhelm the smaller army of Northern Virginia, commanded by General Robert E. Lee. Hooker's movement of his army was inspired. It moved as one perfectly meshed force, executing complex river crossings with efficiency, moving forward first in one direction and then another. "My plans are perfect" Hooker said, and his men, filled with Hooker's confidence, believed once again in their own abilities to finally bring the war to an end with one total victory over an army half its size.

However, when General Hooker, now in Virginia, learned that the enemy was nearby and arousing to his challenge, he abruptly ceased being the aggressor. For several critical hours, Hooker issued a confusing series of orders, converting his aggressively advancing army to a confused collection of units getting in each others way as they formed an awkward defensive pocket.

When Lee recognized that the invading army was no longer on the offensive, he himself became the aggressor. Lee divided his army into two units, and Hooker did nothing. Lee moved one of these units behind Hooker, and still Hooker did nothing. Then, at a time of Lee's own choosing, his two detachments fell on the Union army. Hooker collapsed, and his army came apart. General Hooker, himself dazed by a cannonball, survived the debacle at Chancellorsville, that became the greatest Union defeat of the entire war. When asked later about his curious change in heart, Hooker stated, "I just lost confidence in Hooker".

The doubt produced by uncertainty, in combination with the burden of responsibility, are the twin scissors blades that severe the confidence of many men and women. However, your recognition of these future threats now, as a junior scientist, wins for you the opportunity to use this early portion of your career to prepare yourself to meet these twin challenges.

8.3.2. The Genius of Leadership

Anyone who is or has been responsible for a task or activity understands the burden of accountability. The idea of being held to account for, and sometimes having to pay a price for, a professional failure is understandably painful to many. Furthermore, responsibility commonly means not just being accountable for your own actions, but also for the activities and decisions of others. Thus, your career trajectory can be damaged by not just your own actions, but by the misguided and mistaken activities of those for whom you are responsible.

At its core, however, assuming responsibility also means that you are susceptible to a new danger. When the project is not going well, you are the one to blame. Being the point person, you are now vulnerable and easily criticized, despite your best efforts. How you are viewed by others is now in the hands of those whose actions you direct, since their mistakes will be seen as your mistakes. You are open to attack, an attack that can leave you hurt and damaged. When viewed in this harsh light, it is no wonder that the idea of responsibility is hateful to so many people.

In many people, much of the pain that is generated by blame is due to their sense that they have lost value. A leader who experiences a serious setback may believe (perhaps correctly) that others, learning of his failure, will believe that he is not as worthy as he once was. Perhaps, when he quietly come to grips with his own missteps, he also chooses to diminish his value in the face of his defeat, a point of view that amplifies this anguish. This corrosive process can be unbearable, and, ultimately, self-destructive. Fear of this sequence of events can destabilize a leader whose tenure is undergoing a particular period of difficulty. Additionally, this fear of failure is foreboding enough to repel those scientists who might otherwise avail themselves of the opportunity for leadership.

The genius of leadership is found in the ability to defeat the fear of failure. The heart of this ability is knowledge. While failure always remains a possibility, the good leader knows that she will suffer no lasting damage in the face of this letdown. Thus, she is able to replace this fear with the knowledge that she will sustain no great injury to herself in the face of defeat. This energizing knowledge permits her to apply her best talents freely and diligently to the project at hand with no core dread of the consequences of blame. This is the key, liberating step that many good leaders are able to take successfully. Having freed themselves from this fear, they can now stay connected to their core talents, drawing upon their best judgment, their best wisdom, and their best vision to prosecute the project for which they hold final responsibility.

This leadership genius does not contradict our previous statements about the necessity of a leader to accept responsibility and blame for a project. Instead, leadership genius recognizes that accepting blame does not mean that you are open to destructive self-condemnation. You accept the blame, while ensuring that this acceptance will do you no harm. You will learn from the defeat, but not be damaged or diminished by it.

While it is possible to inherit this leadership genius, most of us must learn it. As a junior investigator, the most direct way for you to develop this ability to remove the sting of blame is to decouple your sense of value and purpose from the performance of yourself or your team. Invest in self-significance, not performance-significance.

Performance-significance has two components. The first is allowing how you feel about yourself to determines your sense of self-value. You either "feel good" about yourself or not. You either "feel like liking yourself" or you don't. The second component of perform-ance significance is that you permit progress of your work-activities are proceeding to set your self-value. Because each of these components is based on a faulty assumption, your sense of self-worth is impaired, your ability to manage defeat is easily overcome, and in the face of defeat, you feel devalued, beginning a self-destructive spiral.

The snare of performance significance is particularly tight, and overcoming it, in the face of defeat, requires a monumental effort. As an example of the effort that this takes, consider the following illustration.

> By 1864, Ulysses S. Grant was the rising star for the Northern cause in the US Civil War. As a new general, he won clear victories for the Union in the Western theater when the poor performance of the northern armies in the east was exasperat-ing President Lincoln. During a period when the North lost one major batter after another in Virginia, Grant won deci-sively at Fort Donelson, Shiloh, and Vicksburg. These west-ern victories of Grant bolstered his own confidence and sense of significance. In the face of his fine performance, Grant was promoted to Lieutenant General, the first officer to receive that rank since George Washington, and given command of all of the Northern forces. It was expected that with this new title and authority, Grant would repeat his fine western perform-ance, this time in the east.
>
> Being buoyed by this acclaim, Grant rapidly went to work to build on his record of success. He ignored the mur-muring of some of his eastern subordinates, who, having ob-served a string of union generals have their armies and spirits broken against the rock of General Lee's Army of Northern Virginia, suspected the same fate was awaiting Grant. Anxious to put these doubts about his performance to rest, Grant launched a new major offensive against Lee's army.

The fight, known as the Battle of the Wilderness, lasted for three days. After intense combat, Grant was handed a spectacular and shocking defeat. The Union casualties were horrific, and the northern newspapers railed against this new, abominable leadership of its army. Apparently the quietly-voiced fears were well founded; Grant, like the other preceding Union generals, had been ground up by the sharp teeth of the Confederate army.

On the third night of the fight, when it was clear to all that he had suffered a major setback, General Grant retired to his own tent for the evening. When the enormity of his failure struck him, and he recognized that he was being held up to public ridicule, his taciturn spirit gave way to sobbing. Hearing this uncharacteristic noise emanating from their leader's tent, his aides gathered around outside, perplexed by these sounds of intense grief. Some officers, who by this time in the war had seen many men cry, remarked that they had never heard a man break down so utterly and completely as Grant was doing now. They prepared to give the orders for the army to retreat back to Washington DC, as they had done so many times in the past.

Next morning, Grant emerged from his tent, and quietly gave an order. The Army would not retreat north, but would instead move south toward the Confederate capitol of Richmond. For the first time in the war, a staggering defeat would be followed by advance, and not retreat. A night of agony was required for Grant to distance himself from the performance metric and the criticism of others. To Grant, it no longer mattered what people thought or said about him, his performance, or the sacrifices he would call upon his troops to make. Unleashed from a crippling reaction to the criticisms of others, he would follow his own best judgment.

When Lee heard that Grant's army was moving south, he remarked "I fear that this man will fight us every hour and every day until we are defeated".

The false assumption underlying performance-significance is the belief that your self-worth is not constant, and that it can be influenced by your activities. In performance-significance, your self-worth is evaluated against the metric of feelings and accomplishments. Since these two metrics are variable than their application to your self-worth suggests that your value also fluctuates. Under the rule of performance-significance, you have high self-worth on good days, and low value on bad days. You are measured by your accomplishments, and, since these vary, then so must your value.

However, self-worth is constant. It does not waver with feelings, nor does it increase or decrease with your sense of daily accomplishment. Your worth retains its same, constant, elevated value regardless of the external circumstances. Your performance can vary from day to day, based on events that are usually out of your control. Feelings are affected by many factors, including but not limited to stress, praise, criticism, hunger, fatigue, hormones, victory, and defeat. However, self-worth remains constant, and your valuation of that worth must also remain immutably high. In a tumultuous sea of anguish and activity, a clear and solid sense of your worth and value that is independent of external circumstances is a solid and dependable anchor for the developing leader.

Therefore, you can defeat the fear of criticism and blame that is generated by leadership with the recognition that their twin impact does not diminish your central value. The reality of your worth is greater than the reality of the criticism and blame that you face as the result of a failure. Being unafraid of criticism, you are free to accept its constructive aspects, and to develop and sharpen your leadership skills, because you are not harmed by the disapproval of others. A good sense of your high value allows you to maintain your balance when you sense that your project's progress is threatened. Without a good sense of self-worth, the threat of failure can unnerve you, decouple you from your best skills and insight. Alternatively, the absence of the dread that the project's failure will do core damage to you permits you to respond to a project crisis with alacrity, calling on the best of your vision, sense of timing, and judgment as you apply resources to get your project back on track.

8.3.3 Defeating the Peter Principle

A maxim from one of the more famous (or infamous) books of the 1960's states

"The Peter Principle: In a hierarchy, every employee tends to rise to his level of incompetence"[1]

This principle was the result of a study that examined possible reasons for the high level of incompetence that was observed in many corporations. In prominent companies, incompetent employees were present throughout the corporate structure, regardless of rank or the degree of expertise required for the job. The explanation that was offered for this presence was that the prevailing corporate culture promoted employees until they were in over their heads. These promotees, demonstrating competence at the lower rungs of the corporate ladder, earned promotion after promotion until they reached a level at which they could no longer demonstrate the proficiency needed for the task at hand. The demonstration of this new incompetence ended their continued rise through the corporate structure. However, it did not lead to their termination or demotion. They were permitted to remain at this level, in spite of (in fact, because of) their incompetence.

The conclusion was that non-growing companies were more likely to have incompetent employees at many levels of the organizational structure. This was not believed to be the case with growing companies, that could postpone the inevitable results of the Peter Principle by rapidly adding new positions.

Belief in the Peter Principle can underlie misgivings about a new leadership opportunity presented to you, especially if you are doing well in your current job. Why should you be willing to put yourself at risk? You, like all junior scientists, do not wish to fail, just as hardworking, corporate employees do not wish to be incompetent. However, when promotions are offered to these employees, the employees commonly accept them in good faith. The employee is being rewarded for the clear demonstration of their competent efforts, and the reward is offered by a management group that believes the employee will succeed in the new, higher position. Ultimately, the promotee chooses to believe that she will succeed as she has succeeded before, i.e., through the sustained application of her good practices, skills, and work habits.

It is this last comment that undermines the ability of the employee to successfully rise, and may interfere with your rise to a leadership position. Promotion requires not that you practice your old skills at a higher level, but that you instead learn new skills. Competence in your current job means that, while you have demonstrated the ability to perform well, even admirably, you also may have become tolerant of the your weaknesses. These weaknesses continually exert their influence, but over the months and years you have learned to work around them, essentially, to make room for them and be comfortable with them.

These weaknesses, while not doing any tangible harm in your current work activities, can cripple your efforts in the new job. The Peter Principle assumes that you are limited in your ability to overcome your weaknesses when you accept a new demanding position. Therefore, when you take on a new position of leadership, you must be willing to critically review your weaknesses, with the view to converting them to strengths. Relying on your natural skills is not sufficient to meet the new challenge; you must develop new ones.[*] You don't have to know how to do this. You must simply be willing to do it.

Begin by assessing yourself. While appraising and undoing your weaknesses, take some time to evaluate your strengths. The talents that you had in your former job are in all likelihood not enough for your new tasks, and you will need to develop new skills. This can be a delicate matter. You have earned your new position by demonstrating (and essentially relying on) your capable skills. To advance to a new position successfully, you will need to look at those skills critically with the goal of retooling them and developing new ones. In a sense, you must de-emphasize the talents that have permitted you to rise to this level, so that you can develop new ones.

You grow into leadership by developing new strengths, and leaving old weaknesses behind. Expose yourself to new concepts and ideas. The secret to defeating the Peter Principle is self transformation and growth. Being free from the fear of being damaged by failure, you can extend yourself into new areas, working with new energy and diligent effort to develop new strengths that are not "natural" for you. Spe-

---

[*] Discussed in Chapter 1, section 1.3.1.

cifically, this means that you should 1) acknowledge that you have within you the strength to learn the new skill (even though you may not know how), and 2) utilize that strength by applying the best of your knowledge, training, experience, and expertise to the exercise. If you have always been quiet and shy, take the opportunity to extend yourself into first limited and then expanded gregarity. If discipline has been a problem for you, take the time to gain self-control. If you are loquacious, then devote yourself to governing your tongue.

The key to defeating the Peter Principle's hold on you is your directed energy to shatter your own self-limitations in the face of promotion.

8.4 Leadership Traits

With your source of self-worth secure, and your recognition that you need to learn new skills acknowledged, we can now discuss some of the traits and characteristics of good leaders. Execution of these talents in the right combinations are what allow the team to make good progress. Experience provides the intuition and the sensitive feel of action in applying leadership skills in science.

The traits that are discussed in this section are not meant to be exhaustive, but merely demonstrative of the tangible abilities that the outside observer identifies in good leaders. As you work to develop these traits, try to avoid the temptation of focusing on one at a time, i.e. "Today I will try to be charitable, and tomorrow will be my 'resourcefulness' day". Instead, let the blend of these principles accrue and develop naturally.

Many days are so unpredictable and varied, making it difficult if not impossible for you to see what skills you will need to apply. Instead, develop an attitude that prepares you to demonstrate each of these leadership talents during your activities. As this attitude becomes easier for you, you will be able to wield these traits in very effective combinations.[*]

---

[*] You will see that several of these characteristics were covered in earlier chapters. In these situations, reference will be made to the earlier discussion.

8.4.1 Knowledge and Resourcefulness

Resourcefulness is the ability to use the material and personnel that you have in the most effective way to solve the problem that faces you. Resourcefulness requires that you do three things. First, know your problem. Second, know your resources. Third, be driven to solve your problem.

One of the most resourceful leaders in US history was Thomas Jonathan Jackson. After earning the nickname "Stonewall" for his leadership at a critical moment at the First Battle of Bull Run, he was given an important command for the Confederate Army in the Shenandoah valley in Northwestern Virginia. Facing a Union army much larger than his own, he had to choose his targets very carefully. When confronted with an opportunity to attack a city held by the "Federals" he would spend days carefully planning the attack.

Jackson's evaluations were thorough. Part of his appraisal required that he learn exactly where his adversary was and how many troops were present. Jackson would also try to learn how far away their nearest help was, in order to see if there was any possibility that they could be rescued once his attack began. Jackson would also devote tremendous effort to learning the geography and topography of the surrounding land. Anxious to learn all of the important details, he would sometimes enlist the aid of someone who lived in the region of interest. Once identified, this person would explain to Jackson in great clarity the paths of the available roads, the locations of rivers and where they could be crossed, and, the surrounding hills along with the best way to climb them. Jackson would also spend time learning about the strengths and weaknesses of his own men.[*]

Always trying to find the best way defeat his opponents, he would carefully work to formulate a strategy that

---

[*]Some might say that he learned their weaknesses too well. It was not uncommon for Jackson to place his own immediate subordinates under arrest for not operating at the standard he required.

would leave him the clear victor in the coming fight. After he formulated a plan, he would methodically put his resources (cavalry, cannon, and foot soldiers) into place. Sometimes Jackson's work was so carefully considered and executed that, when his Union adversaries learned where he was, and what he had done, they would simply abandon their emplacements, leaving the field to Jackson's men.

Knowing your problem specifically means that you must know all about your problem. Understand its genesis. Why is it an obstacle that blocks your way? Have others faced your problem? What solutions have they tried? Why did those attempts fail? If phone calls to authorities would be helpful, then make these important contacts. Do anything that you can to learn about your problem. Become the problem's expert.

Secondly, know all about your resources. Your resources are provided for you to solve the problem. However, they cannot be used effectively if you don't understand their strengths and their limitations. Become acquainted with them all. If you have computing resources, then understand of what these machines are and are not capable. Completely familiarize yourself with the instrumentation. Know what they do, how reliable they are, and how much they cost to use.

As essential as it is for you to learn about the material resources, it is even more critical to understand the personnel who are under your direction. Learn their strengths and weaknesses. Look beyond their job descriptions. Who are these people? Who among them is the writer? Who is the debater? Who has the technical skills? Give them relatively small and simple problems to address, allowing you to gain an importance sense for their ability to interact. In addition, take the additional step of helping them to overcome their weaknesses. Make the commitment not just to the project's success, but to your staff's development as well.[*] You may find that you do not have enough resources. If that is the case, do not hesitate to ask for more, with the full intent of applying these new resources to the problems at hand.

---

[*] This was discussed in detail in Chapter 3, section 3.8.2.

Finally, you must want to solve the problem. The desire to solve the problem is the source of the energy that will drive your repeated efforts to unravel the issue. Attempting to solve the problem means assembling and reassembling your resources in one intelligent combination after another as you try and retry to resolve the issue. Like finding the right combination to the lock of a treasure chest, your desire is the energy that fuels your search for the right solution. If you don't really want the prize, you will give up after a few half-hearted attempts.

8.4.2 Imagination

Difficult problems are commonly perceived as such because they defy the common approaches that work so well in the solution of simpler problems. The solution to a tough problem commonly require ingenious and innovative ideas. [*] It require imagination.

Commonly, imagination is perceived as a gift that is, in some mysterious fashion, genetically or otherwise conferred. Many people believe that "you either have imagination or your don't" This is generally not the case. Imaginative solutions are the result of the combination of information, intuition, and the drive to solve a problem. Knowledge leads to intuition, and intuition plus desire produces the insightful, creative solutions that commonly are considered to be the product of imagination.

Specifically, imagination is developed from repeated attempts to apply novel approaches to the problem at hand. In order to be productively imaginative, you must have solid knowledge of the problem, as discussed in the previous section. However, you must implement this knowledge in new ways. One such example of an approach might be to ask if the problem can be broken into smaller pieces? If these smaller pieces can each be solved then, perhaps, the final solution can be created from the assembly.

Yet another maneuver that might work in solving the problem is to attempt to discover an assumption that, if it were true, would make the problem easy to solve. Once you have identified the assumption, apply your resources to make the desired assumption a reality. Having accomplished this, the problem will be more easily solved. First solve

---

[*] This is colloquially expresses as "thinking outside of the box".

the problem anyway that you can, then solve it the best way that you can.

There is a mental flexibility and alacrity involved in trying these approaches. The primary energy source for this cerebral activity is your drive and commitment to identify a solution. Finally, the ability to think imaginatively is an important dividend of having a secure and separate source of self-worth. If you fear the blame of failure, you are not likely to take the risk of proposing an untested and imaginative solution. Cutting yourself loose from the fear of failure frees you to develop ingenious and innovative approaches to your team's complicated problem.

8.4.3 Keep short-term and long-term perspectives

In leadership you have to successfully manage both the "big picture" while staying in close contact with the daily activities that are essential for the continued operation of the project. This can be complicated because the management of these two issues can require contrary solutions. Specifically, the successful resolution of a short-term problem can lead to the unraveling and destruction of the long-term plan. This sometimes requires important redirections of goals and objectives, itself a complicated maneuver.

There is perhaps no more visible example of the complexity of this issue than observing the tasks of those who manage campaigns for the various candidates of the major parties for President of the United States. Gaining this high office requires that the candidate first win their party's nomination, then use that nomination as a springboard to the presidency. However, since the 1960's, winning his party's nomination means that the candidate must satisfy the needs of those who vote in the primary elections. If the candidate is running for the Democratic party nomination, he traditionally must satisfy primary voters who tend to be more liberal. If the candidate is running for the Republican nomination, then he typically will have to satisfy voters who are likely to be more conservative. However, once the nomination is gained, each candidate has to appeal to the vast majority of voters who tend to be in the middle. Here is the difficulty. By working too hard to achieve the short-term goal of their party's nomination, the candidate runs the risk of alienating the voters in the center whose support they will need in the general election. Additionally, the candidate's post-nomination "move to the center" can alienate the voters who supported the candidate in the primary elections. The management of the short term (party nomination) vs. the long-term (national election) goals is a delicate operation.

While the issues are somewhat less climactic in science, the need for both clear vision and a deft touch in steering the team is essential. Sometimes a step or two away from the long term goal is required to reach the end. Like a pilot who detours an airplane around a storm to reach the destination safely, the best path may be a circuitous one. In this matter, there is no substitute for a good view of the target.

8.4.4 Develop administrative skill and diligence

Administrative skill teaches you how to avoid wasting time. This might be considered an unusual statement, because many junior investigators believe that their involvement in administration *is* wasting time. However, the effective assembly of your resources to solve your problem requires that you understand where they are, what state they are in, and what their needs are. You may have developed a good plan of action to solve a scientific problem involving the creation of a database, only to learn that the programmer whose contribution to the project was key is scheduled to take vacation during a critical phase of the production. Simple but diligent attention to this type of issue early in the project's development would avoid this critical and unnecessary delay in your project's completion.

There is no getting away from administration. You either spend a little time up front dealing with it or spend critical time later in the project trying to catch up. Sedulous and prompt administrative attention can save the project a good deal of wasted time down the road. We have had much to say about administrative diligence in Chapters Three and Four.

These next two traits separate leaders from "managers"

8.4.5 Boldness and achievability

Boldness is the force that activates and energizes the imaginative idea. Rather than a wild hunch, boldness is based on shrewd reasoning and a calculated risk.

One of the differences between a good leader and a good manager is that the leader has a touch of the gambler in her. She is willing to take a risk that can produce a major advance for her team. However, taking a risk is not the same as engaging in a reckless enterprise. A good leader puts her leadership and her team at risk only after very thoughtful and detailed consideration, and a complete exploration of all of the ramifications. The most productive bold activity is based on the most detailed plans and considerations. The resultant actions are not based on immature, snap decisions, but are instead rooted in solid motivation and well considered plans.

In the Winter of 1776, the American Revolution had effectively ended as a victory for the British Empire. In the six months that followed the Declaration of Independence, Washington's army of 18,000 had been whittled down to 5,000 men. No longer an effective fighting force, greatly outnumbered by a well organized and competent British/Hessian army commanded by the confident General Howe, the American force managed to escape south to the Pennsylvania side of the Delaware River. Rather than pursue this ragtag group at the beginning of a cold winter, Howe let them go, believing that the bitter and frigid Northeastern weather would finish off the rest of the American "militia".

However, Washington, after retreating from the British for half a year, also realized that encamping his army for six months in despicably frozen conditions would finish it. Having a touch of the risk-taker in him, he decided to do the unexpected and attack. Recognizing that there were 900 Hessian soldiers encamped in Trenton for Christmas, Washington took half of his 5,000 men, and re-crossed the Delaware to attack these German soldiers on Christmas day. The American assault was completely unexpected and totally successful. Not only was the battle won with minimal casualties (two Americans froze to death on the ride across the freezing Delaware river), but his victory electrified the American cause. The countryside, heretofore wary of the revolutionaries, opened their homes and supplies to them, and volunteers flocked in join Washington's army.[*] The British, on the other hand, were more than embarrassed. They realized that the war would not end quickly, and would require the one thing that neither the Crown nor its subjects had in this matter — patience.

Washington's decision to attack an unsuspecting force was not a rash action, but a well considered, and carefully executed gamble. Bold ideas have to be planned with great care and meticulous attention to detail in order to accurately gauge the likelihood of their success. Washington had to know his adversary and their Christmas day habits. He had to understand the limits to which he could push his men. He also had to successfully discern whether the denizens of the surrounding countryside could be trusted not to warn the Hessians of the pre-dawn American advance. While Washington's imaginative idea was sparked by boldness, it was guided by the very best discipline, planning and judgment.

Without audacity, coupled with a sense of the achievable, a leader is simply a manager. While it is certainly appropriate for the young scientific leader to fear rashness, she must also fear irresolution.

8.4.6 Master, and Take Advantage of your Mastery

New science is fueled by new concepts and new technology. Each of these can offer important intellectual hurdles. However, each contains critical material that might be applied effectively by your team. In order to assess the potential of these important contributors, you must understand the new ideas and/or the new technological advances. Although this is difficult material, a good leader will insist on learning it.

---

[*] Many of the volunteers from Pennsylvania joined Washington's army because they were delighted at the prospect of invading their New Jersey neighbors!

More than this, a good team leader will not just learn the material; he will become skilled in the subject. The new technology offers a steep learning curve. The leader will acknowledge it, and successfully climb it. He will understand the topic in all of its subtleties, complications, and implications. He will comprehend them so that he can explain its salient features to his team, explicating it in such a way that his team members are able to absorb all that they need to in order to apply the material to their role on the team as well. This is not just learning the material — it is mastering it.

However, learning the information for the sake of learning it does little to advance your team's progress. Once the science is mastered, move rapidly to make new progress on your project based on what you have learned. Seize the opportunity that your mastery of the new material has earned.

What commonly happens is that, although a group or leader is able to understand the utilization of a new technology, they are unwilling to extend themselves to take the next step of application. They absorb the new material — then wait. Acting as though someone or some organization will seek them out after the leader and his group have learned the new material, they do not aggressively seek out the new opportunities that this knowledge has gained for them.

While you can take comfort in you mastery, do not languish in it – take advantage of it. If after mastering the material, your scientific team, through their learning and their own disciplined review of that learning has developed a new concept, then move rapidly to get this concept out into the mainstream of your field. Move aggressively to identify a venue that would give you the opportunity to discuss your idea. Look for and seize the opportunity to write manuscripts that allow you to disseminate your idea. While learning is important, it is not the only important thing. Developing ideas based on what you have learned is also important. Don't wait for the sake of waiting. Consider the following illustration.[*]

---

[*] Ackerman T., and Berger E. Deal brings rivals to the same table. Hospitals partnering but Cooley, DeBakey might not. Houston Chronicle. Friday April 23, 2004. Page 1.

In 1951, Dr. Michael DeBakey, preeminent cardio-vascular surgeon in Houston, Texas, offered Dr. Denton Cooley a position at Baylor College of Medicine. This offer permitted Dr. Cooley, who had just completed his training in Baltimore, to return to his home of Houston. Dr. Cooley's arrival ushered in a period of productive collaboration for these scientists. Year after year, the two surgeons worked together as they taught, conducted research, and developed new devices. However, after ten years, Dr. Cooley left to form the Texas Heart Institute. While remaining close, the two famous surgeons chose to no longer operate together.

In 1965, DeBakey participated in a federally funded project to develop an artificial heart. After many months of work, the project was near completion, and several physicians advocated that this first artificial heart was ready to be studied in people under the most tightly controlled circumstances. This next step would have been a first in human surgery, and the successful development of this device would have, in the eyes of some, been the event that would have earned Dr. DeBakey a candidacy for the Nobel Prize. However, DeBakey demurred, continuing to work on his device.

To international acclaim, the first artificial heart transplant took place in 1969. With great care, the artificial heart was implanted in a 47 year old man who was awaiting a heart transplant. The patient survived for 65 hours, dying after the artificial heart was itself replace by an organic heart from a donor. The research community reacted with thunderous applause at this tremendous surgical feat. However, the cardio-vascular surgeon who was responsible for, and who carried out the surgery was not Dr. DeBakey, but Dr. Cooley.

Dr. DeBakey accused Dr. Cooley of misconduct. Stating that the artificial heart Dr. Cooley had transplanted into the patient was identical to the one under development by Dr. DeBakey, Dr. DeBakey stated that Dr. Cooley had implanted the device without Dr. DeBakey's permission. The American College of Surgeons chose to censure Dr. Cooley, and after an argument with the trustees of the College of Medicine, Dr. Cooley resigned from the institution.

The inability to retain the initiative by one, and the unethical conduct by a second, further corroded a relationship that had been so productive for cardiovascular research.

Part of the reason for being quick to take advantage of your team's mastery of a topic is competitiveness, but there is a deeper motivation. Moving forward with the idea requires good clear-headed thinking about the application, deep thought that might not be so incisive in the absence of a public review of your work and ideas. Secondly, moving this ideas into the open spurs the ideas of others, while clearing them from you, allowing you to move onto newer important work.

Erring on the side of caution is an inadequate excuse for the lack of boldness and resolve in a leader.

8.4.7 Developing Other Leadership Traits

It is rumored that Napoleon Bonaparte, at the height of his reign over France in the early 19th century, was asked why the world did not have more good leaders. He replied that a good leader was required to have disparate and contradictory traits. During the rise to leadership, the candidate had to be single-minded. He had to be venal, merciless, dishonest, conniving, and malevolent in order to gain power. However, once the goal of leadership was attained, the requirements changed. The new leader, in order to be a good one, has to replace these unenviable traits with other, more enduring characteristics. Among these are were open-mindedness, generosity, inquisitiveness, honesty, and kindness. Since few people could make the transition, Napoleon reasoned, the world was bereft of good leadership.

If Napoleon said this (and he was certainly in a position to know), than perhaps a useful, modern day interpretation of his statement is that people have to grow into good leadership. Leadership requires self-transformation. It requires leaving old weaknesses behind while you develop new strengths. The ability to develop these traits is directly related to your desire to develop them. While you cannot in general just think yourself into a good character, you can develop the depth of desire to improve your character, and then let that desire drive you. As someone once said, "Its not the skill—it's the will".

What specifically does this drive compel you to do? Let it compel you to meet and speak with people who you believe have good character. Let it compel you to read about people of good character. Let it compel you to discuss these people with others who would be willing to listen to you. By these activities, you begin to embed yourself in the sense of standard, sensitivity, and judgment of those men and women of character, opening your own character up to be altered and shaped by the experience. The good character that develops leads to strength. This strength produces self control, and self-control produces both courage and endurance.

8.5 Source of the Best Ideas

As a leader, you have the power to command, a power that has been granted to you by a legitimate authority, be it a department chairperson, a dean, stockholders, or a legislature. However, the art of leadership is not the brusque exercise of this authority.

Abraham Lincoln said that the art of politics was the ability to get people who do not like you, and who want to do what they want to do, to in fact do what you want them to do. The closer the option of commanding by fiat is, the more delicate the art of leadership becomes, and the greater the need for discipline. Thus, the beginning of the art of leadership is learning not to use what is available to use. Do not lead by force of authority.

To develop this skill, you might consider how you would lead without any sanctioned authority. If you were a member of the team, and not a team leader, how would you convince others to follow your direction? By persuasion. The ability to persuade is one of the most effective traits of a good leader.

As the leader, you begin with the recognition that your team members are themselves intelligent adults who, like you, feel the need to understand the relevant information concerning a decision you must make. In the ensuing discussions, they would like to provide, and you would need to listen carefully to, their input and observations. However, as their leader, do more than merely listen. Listen with the attitude that your position can be altered and influenced by their observations and opinions. Let your team know that you are open to modifying your own point of view based on their observations and reasoned conclusions.

After your team members have each had the opportunity to provide their own opinions, challenge them with alternative ideas. Let them listen and respond to the criticism that others might bring against their perspective. Help them to think critically about their points of view, while keeping yourself open to accepting their modified position. Encourage you team to develop confidence in identifying useful observations, ideas and suggestions. Listening to this advice in the spirit of acceptance allows you to absorb the best of their ideas, for the good of you and the team.

There are two advantages to this approach. The first is that, after all, a team member can have a better solution than you do. One of the best ideas that a leader can have is that they, as leader, do not always have the best ideas. Commonly, the preeminent concepts are generated by the team members themselves.

Secondly, and perhaps most importantly, you transmit to your team the attitude that you are willing to adjust your point of view based on what they have to say. This is the central piece of persuasion. By being willing to adjust to their attitude, you can create in them a new willingness to adjust their position toward yours.

After having carefully listened and discussed with your team their own perspectives, provide your own position that has been modified by the conversations that your team has just completed. Point out to them exactly where your own point of view has been altered by those of your team. Show them where their points of view have been incorporated into your own. Combine tact, prestige, firmness, and character to appeal to the better natures of your wavering team members.

After having all points of view in hand, and completing your own deliberations, make the required decision, and follow this by explaining your rationale. This clear explanation is important even if (perhaps, especially if) it is not obligated. Your willingness to extend yourself to explain your answer demonstrates your concern for the point of view offered by the team members who may disagree with your decision. Even though you disagree with them, be willing to explain how you came to your decision.

Despite your best effort, you may have to make a decision in the absence of unanimous support among your team. In this circumstance, make the decision that you believe is in the best interest of your group, but make the decision in a way that keeps the team together rather than in a way that creates fissures. Begin by recognizing that those on your team who believe that you have not decided correctly will nevertheless have a very useful perspective, and ultimately may be proven right in the end. It is this group that will most likely be among the most vigilant for observing signs that your decision was incorrect as the group moves forward with implementing your decision. By staying in close contact with them and listening carefully to their observations, you can use their perspective as a useful early warning if your plan is not producing the result that you anticipated. Alternatively, if your decision was ultimately correct, by remaining observant, your critics in the group will be among the first to see it.

These are important points. However, even the best leaders are not always successful at it. One of the most critical and, to this day, most controversial breakdowns in leadership occurred in the Confederate command on July 2- July 4 in 1863 at Gettysburg.

At this time in the US Civil War, the South was at its military zenith. After repelling a Northern invasion of Virginia, the South won a stunning victory at Second Manassas, followed by a stalemate at Antietam Creek in Maryland. This was succeeded by stunning victories at both Fredericksburg and Chancellorsville. The war was taking far longer than most Northern leaders had believed possible, and a peace movement with serious political strength was growing in the North. General Lee, the commander of the Army of Northern Virginia, reasoned that a second invasion of the North, this time resulting in the capture of Philadelphia and perhaps Washington D.C., would compel the North to sue for peace, permitting the South its independence as a separate nation.

Again, events favored the South. Even without his cavalry to tell him where the main enemy forces were, Lee found lead elements of the Union Army in the small college town of Gettysburg and quickly chose to become the aggressor. His commanders, having served under him for many months, by and large knew what he wanted to accomplish, and they gave him a smashing victory on the first day of this three day battle. The Union army was rolled back into, through, and out of Gettysburg, up into its eastern hills. Here, the spent northern forces replenished their supplies, and new Union troops arrived from the north and east as news of the fierce fighting spread.

Lee began the second day of the battle intent on renewing the attack, hoping to destroy the remaining Northern army and finally ending the war. However, his trusted subordinate and second in command, James Longstreet, argued for a different strategy. Longstreet had heard the reports of the growing strength of the Union armies east of Gettysburg. Believing that the northern army was no longer weak and susceptible, but renewed and determined, he argued that the southern army should disengage, and move south toward Washington, away from their adversary. He contended that this move to the south would force the Union army to chase them, and finally to attack the southern army when Lee had found a good defensive position.

Lee disagreed, seeing no reason to leave a battle that he was winning. However, he failed to convince Longstreet who, in turn, was not persuaded that Lee's point of view was correct. Longstreet moved sluggishly to carry out Lee's commands for attack. General Lee conferred with Longstreet several times, stating that there was no alternative to standing and fighting where they were. The southern forces, Lee argued were cut off from their supplies while they remained in the north and would only grow weaker in Pennsylvania. The northern armies, on the other hand, fighting on their own soil, would only grow stronger. Best to fight while the South retained the upper hand, Lee argued. Furthermore, to retreat after a first day of victory would be perceived as a defeat by the fighting men in Lee's army, leading to their discouragement.

Lee argued again that the time to attack was sooner, and not later. However, Longstreet, sensing defeat and destruction by a superior military force, moved slowly to carry out Lee's orders, his lassitude produced by depression in the face of an imminent disaster. Further delay led to defeat for the South on day two of the battle, and the rout of the final Confederate attack (Pickett's Charge) on the third day.

There remains to this day debate between historians as to whether Lee or Longstreet was most at fault. However, there is no doubt that closer work and coordination among the Confederate high command could have led to a very different outcome. Both Lee and Longstreet had grown over the years in their ability to command. Nevertheless, the new demands of Gettysburg required that they grow some more. The fact that they could not extend themselves to do this is one reason why their campaign failed.

Finally, be ready to apologize to any of your team members. If it turns out that the individuals whose point of view you chose not to accept were right, be sure to acknowledge that to them. Learn how to apologize from strength, and not from weakness. To apologize from strength means that, although you were wrong, that in no way diminishes your worth or value since these are independent of your achievements and mistakes. Your apology can be earnest, sincere, simple and deep, with no motivation other than to be certain that the fact that you were wrong is understood by others. Alternatively, apologizing from weakness occurs when your self-significance is linked to how correct your decisions are. Such apologies can become complicated because the requirement of acknowledging that you were wrong becomes entangled in your need to help to regain your lost value through the act of apologizing. In this case, the apology is converted from the simple sincere admission that you were wrong to an attempt to soothe the pain of self-diminishment that occurs as a consequence of linking your value to your performance[*].

---

[*] Discussed earlier in this chapter.

8.6 Learning to Lose

"A trial attorney is not a good trial attorney until he has lost a case".

A lawyer's adage

Your cannot be the best leader until you have dealt with and absorbed defeat. In science, defeat comes in many guises. A major grant may not have been funded. A manuscript on which you are first author has received nothing but a steady stream of rejections from the peer-reviewed literature. Another research team may reach a goal that you had hoped your team would reach first. Your fund raising effort may have fallen far short of its goal. An interview by the media may have become a public relations disaster. These types of setbacks lead to loss of stature, loss of a promotion, loss of prestige, perhaps ultimately, the loss of your job.

There is perhaps no better time for the team leader to set an example than in the face of failure. As the leader, all eyes will be on you to determine how your team will conduct itself in its moment of crisis. Thus, how you choose to carry yourself in this critical time is central to the reaction of your team.

In the face of failure, there are really only two types of behavior in which you can engage as team leader; character destruction or character construction. Your choice is based on your source of self-worth. The performance-significance point of view i.e., the perspective that permits your sense of self-value to float up or down based on your performance will fail you here. By linking your own sense of value to the success or failure of your operation, a spectacular failure will dictate that you are of less worth due to the inadequate performance of your team. Demanding superior judgment from yourself in a time of crisis can be a near impossible expectation when you have permitted your sense of self-worth to be diminished, and your character to be reduced, by the team-failure over which you have presided. While you may not be emotionally paralyzed by the loss of self-worth, its loss complicates your ability to perform in a new and complex environment. Reduced self-worth can produce in you an awkward and unbalanced approach to the new and complicated environment of failure. This deep loss that you feel can be quickly transmitted to your team.

Defeat hurts. However, there is a difference between the initial painful reaction to a loss, and the creation of long-term personal damage. Defeat can and will break your heart. You must not let it break your spirit.

By patiently building up a sense of self-worth that is independent of your activities and performance, you may rely on that undiminished sense of value to power your actions during this time of crisis. You are able to retain your judgment, your standard, your intellectual prowess and your ability to apprise a situation during these threatening days. With no fear of loss of self-value, you are not threatened in an important way, and face no lasting damage from the defeat. This fundamental understanding of the tightly limited impact that defeat has on you personally permits you to be confident and reassured. Your confidence is easily sensed by your team members, and by outsiders as well. With this spirit of assuredness, your team is free to apply the best of its talents to learning the major lessons from its defeat.

Becoming a good leader involves the ability to accept and absorb the right lessons from defeat. Specifically, these right lessons are only those lessons that lead to the growth of your character and the development of the character of your team. This automatically relegates blame and condemnation to conduct unworthy of a fine team leader. As the leader, you should first take responsibility for the defeat, and then focus the attention of your team on rectifying the defect that lead to the defeat. Don't fix the blame—fix the problem. As a leader, times of defeat should be among your best times. During this difficult period for your team, their confidence should be built up, and not destroyed. Your team will rely on you for this.

Being a leader makes you the "point-person" for criticisms directed at your team. Sometimes, this effort leads to calls from others, (and occasionally, from within your team itself) that you be replaced. As was the case for facing other crises of leadership, your sense of security is the key for confronting challenges to your authority. Look at these engagements as an opportunity for your character to grow and strengthen, rather than as a confrontation in which you will be damaged. Remaining secure in your own sense of value allows you to deal with threats to your authority on an even footing. This "self-ownership" ensures that no core damage will be done to you, regardless of the outcome of the investigation. Being immune from damage, you come of the investigation. Being immune from damage, you are free to state your position clearly, directly, and, most importantly, in a non-threatening way. This level of security allows you to defend your decisions, not as someone who is besieged, but as a confident scientist you has learned from her mistakes and is ready for future challenges. As before, it sometimes pays to remember that what can be taken from you, in the end, may not be worth having.

If someone threatens your authority, recognize that threatening your authority is not threatening you. All of your activities should have as a consequence the growth of your own character or the development of the character of your team.

8.7 Final Comments on Leadership

Locked in the heart of every competent junior scientist is the spirit of a leader. You will have to work hard to first find, and then develop these skills, but as a junior investigator, your first task is to acknowledge with your own approval that you can become a scientific leader.

The key to successfully leadership is security and a solid sense of self-valuation independent of your outward experiences. With this core in place, you are protected from the personal damage that comes from the demands of leadership. Moreover, you are free to develop and use the best of your intuition, knowledge, training, experience and expertise without the fear of damage to you. You are free to give the best to your team because you fear no damage from the consequences of your best considered actions. You can avoid the unfortunate habit pattern of being at your best when you are liked. Additionally, you cannot take care of those for whom you are responsible if you are preoccupied with your own sensitivities. If you can win this fight for your own self-worth, than many more victories await you.

Becoming a leader is a gradual, stepwise process. You gain experience, making the small, predictable and unavoidable mistakes of someone growing. Start with some small and limited opportunities for leadership. Seize the opportunity to chair a subcommittee or a grant review session. This allows you to make mistakes from experience without paying too great a price for them. You are going to make some mistakes; be sure to learn the right character-constructing lesson from them.

Build your research team carefully. If your leadership is fair-minded, diligent, and capable, then the search for competent colleagues to join your research effort will not be in vain. Once you have chosen and built your team, resist the desire to do all of the team's work in person. This leads to overexcited, zealous and ultimately exhausting and counterproductive efforts on your part. Don't over-direct. A good team, like a good instrument, requires not a strike but simply a touch to make it vibrate

Trust competence, encourage initiative, and do not impede ability by needless direction. You have assembled your group based on their experiences. Give them the opportunity to use and develop their expertise. Just as you will make mistakes as a leader, so they will make mistakes as members of your team. Know the qualities and limitations of your subordinates. Challenge and encourage them to grow. Dominate a scene with your ideas without being deliberately conspicuous.

Also, as leader, when it is time to decide, make a decision. Having prepared thoughtfully and carefully about the project and the issue, make the decision that must be made. While one enemy is rashness, a second and equally dangerous adversary for a leader is irresolution. Many scientists who disappoint their own expectations do so because at the controversial moment, they will not accept responsibility for an immediate decision that they are called upon to make.

Finally, remember, that everyone is a subordinate and a superior. Don't be a generous and kindly leader, but a difficult and touchy group member.

References

1. Peter L.J., and Hall, R (1969). The Peter Principle: Why things always go wrong. William Morrow & Company, Inc. New York.

Chapter 9
Nova Progenies

At this new dawn of the information age, what is dawning on our culture is not just the availability of information, but that information devoid of insight is unhelpful. It therefore comes as no surprise that society, in its attempts to integrate this new data, prizes not just information, but information that is coupled with intuition and wisdom. We are progressing from "What?" to asking "What does it mean?" The contributions of science, commonly offered on a plate of increasingly technical and sophisticated experiments, are promising, tinged with controversy, and at times foreboding. Therefore, society will need the counsel of creative, insightful, disciplined and mature scientists to guide it. These are most likely to be capable researchers who both contribute to scientific progress and understand the implications of that progress. They must diligently work in science, but must also possess solid principles and good judgment. They must be educatable and of sound ethic. These are men and women who are both scientifically productive and of good character. It is my hope that this is the category of scientist to which you aspire.

The foundation for character growth begins with a solid, unshakable sense of your high value. There is only one person, and, throughout the existence of mankind, there has been only one person, with the unique combination of abilities, strengths, knowledge, curiosity, diligence, and intuition that you have. The instillation of these capabilities and insights within you first imbues, and then empowers you with value separate and apart from external circumstances. External threats do not occur because you are valueless, but quite the contrary, because you have value. Avoid falling into the traps of 1) believing that your value is determined by how you feel at any given time, and 2) believing that your value is controlled by your performance. Generate within yourself a sense of worth that can neither be added to, nor subtracted from. Don't be productive to generate self-value. Be productive because you possess value.

If you can come to see that the reality of your elevated and constant value is greater than the reality of your day-to-day failures, then you can understand that no real damage can be inflicted on you if you fail in your diligent work efforts. This realization permits you to apply yourself with your full energy to your tasks, making bold efforts to learn, to teach, to grow, to think, to calculate, to postulate, to develop, and to mature. Scientific failures are temporary and its defeats are transient, while your high value retains its permanence. A solid sense of self-value permits you to be open to accepting the responsibility for leadership by protecting you from the damage produced by blame. Finally, it allows you to be secure enough to give the best of yourself to others, the hallmark of charitable prosperity.

As a junior scientist, first critically evaluate your strengths and weaknesses[*] with the view of building up your ability to deal with issues that have been a chronic problem for you. Work on and strive for

---

[*] If you really cannot think of any weaknesses, ask your spouse or significant other for their perspective on the matter. They may have identified a few that might be helpful for you to know.

self-transformation, converting your weaknesses into new positive energy. An affirmative sense of self-value permits you to stretch yourself to do what you don't feel like doing, in order to become what you want to become.

As a junior scientist, your environment is, and in all likelihood will continue to be, tumultuous. Many of your days will be unpredictable. You will have to balance stability with adaptability, imagination with discipline, strength with compassion, intellectual exertions with restoration, professional priorities with personal ones. It is just as important to equilibrate these aspects of your life as it is to be productive. Put another way, you must be productive in science, while simultaneously developing the balancing and coping skills in order to prosper in a chaotic environment. Investing all of your effort in productivity to the exclusion of character growth will fail you. Professional maturity requires that you develop both diligence and the ability to sensitively assess priorities calmly and unhurriedly during the daily cacophony of your job.

Do not ignore administration as you develop. The fact of the matter is that you will spend an important component of your time doing administrative work. This time can be spent in two ways. You can spend it consumed by and attitude of resentment and frustration that will ultimately stunt the development of your project. Alternatively, you can be governed by a spirit an attitude of time-generosity. As a diligent worker, you will find the time you need, once you have the attitude that you need. Don't just generate unhelpful experience; develop discerning expertise.

As a junior investigator you only need your education and a solid, stable sense of self-worth to be a full participant in collaborative projects. With your sense of self-value that is separate and apart from your performance, you are free to participate and engage in the project, using all of your talents and abilities to support the group effort. Don't shrink from, but instead, actively seek out opportunities to help other coworkers in the project. Be prepared to receive the unanticipated email or phone call that provides an opportunity for you to engage your talents and capabilities for the good of the project. When you make a mistake, apologize clearly and easily. Be willing to extend yourself, and even put yourself at risk, to provide support for a colleague. The product from these efforts is a well-balanced, focused, and knowledgeable investigator who recognizes the importance of the project, and communicates effectively with all of the team members. Moreover, you will also have the important combination of vigilance coupled with the willing attitude that permits you to shoulder not just your share of the work effort, but to help with the burdens of others as well.

Also, remember that it is up to you to inject some of the fun, satisfaction, and stimulation that pulled you into your science into your days. To that good end, insert a "productivity hour" into your day so that you might work quietly on a scientific matter of your choosing.

As a junior investigator, begin to deal at once with any presentation anxiety or stage fright that you have. If there is an "enemy" to be faced in giving a presentation, then that enemy is not the audience, but the fear of failure. If you are fearful, then confront that fear well before you get behind the podium. A strong sense of self-value that is independent of your performance permits you to shine bright illumination on the dark shadow that is cast by fear, revealing that no lasting damage occurs to you if the presentation does not go as you hoped.

Choose to actively and affirmatively embed an ethic in your career. Ethics are more of an approach to life than a mere collection of rules. Your ethical behavior is the living expression of your core principles that govern your relationships with others. Just as you have self-worth on which you rely, your sense of the worth of others regardless of their opinions and actions governs your ethical treatment of them.

Take the opportunity to recognize that ethical researchers are not paragons. Ethical people make honest mistakes. However, what characterizes the ethical scientist is her response to those mistake. When she recognizes that she missed an opportunity for ethical conduct, she apologizes, make appropriate restitution, and, having learned the right lesion from her error, she moves on. Ethical behavior is not perfect behavior. It is behavior that calibrates and self-corrects.

The skills that you develop as a junior scientist can naturally evolve into the foundation of good leadership. Begin to think of yourself as someone with good leadership potential who only needs experience and tempering. Again, the key to successfully leadership is security and a solid sense of self-valuation independent of your outward experiences.

Finally, you don't know what opportunities and dangers the coming day will bring. The small number of days that required me to make important, and career altering decisions began like every other day, providing no perceptible warning to me that I would be involved in an event or operation that would change my career. Be watchful for the unanticipated event that can alter your perspective and adjust your career for the better.

Finally...good luck. We are relying on you as a member of a *nova progenies*, a new generation of scientists.

Author's Background

Dr. Lemuel A. Moyé, M.D., Ph.D. is a physician and a biostatistician at the University of Texas School of Public Health. He earned his medical degree at Indiana University Medical School in 1978 and completed a Ph.D. in Community Health Sciences with concentration in Biostatistics in 1987. He is a licensed physician in Texas and has actively practiced general medicine from 1979 to 1992. He is a diplomat of the National Board of Medical Examiners and is currently a Professor of Biostatistics at the University of Texas School of Public Health in Houston where he holds a full time faculty position.

Dr. Moyé has carried out cardiovascular research for seventeen years and continues to be involved in the design, execution and analysis of clinical trials. He has participated in the mentoring of junior scientists for many years. He has served in several clinical trials sponsored by both the U.S. government and private industry. In addition, Dr. Moyé have served as statistician/epidemiologist for six years on both the Cardiovascular and Renal Drug Advisory Committee to the Food and Drug Administration and the Pharmacy Sciences Advisory Committee to the FDA. He has served as an *ad hoc* member on other FDA advisory committees as well. He has served on several Data, Safety, and Monitoring Boards that oversee the conduct of clinical trials, and taken part on many reviews of grants that have been submitted by fellow scientists for federal funding.

Dr. Moyé has published over one hundred manuscripts in peer-reviewed literature that discuss the design, execution and analysis of clinical research. He is sole author of the book *Statistical Reasoning in Medicine-The Intuitive P value Primer* that appeared in 2000 and sole author of the textbook *Multiple Analysis in Clinical Trials: Fundamentals for Investigators* that appeared in the summer 2003, both published by Springer. He has also co-authored two texts in mathematics.

Index

A

abuse. *See* ethics
academia
    academic freedom, 221
    advising students, 223
    and productivity, 223
    defination of promotion, 231
    defininng productivity, 223
    definition of tenure, 232
    developing a work lifestyle, 234
    ghost authored manuscripts, 239

organizing your days, 233
plans for publication, 237
productivity and community service, 229
productivity and grants, 228
productivity and publications, 225
productivity and research, 224
salary vs. freedom, 222
self-rsstriction of your committments, 234
skills of a teacher, 235
sole authored manuscripts and writing, 239
teaching and producitivy, 223

283

ISBN 1412033888-8